Villi the Clown

Villi the Clown

WILLIAM CAMPBELL

FABER AND FABER
London and Boston

*First published in 1981
by Faber and Faber Limited
3 Queen Square London WC1N 3AU
Filmset in Great Britain by
Latimer Trend & Company Ltd, Plymouth
Printed by
Redwood Burn Limited, Trowbridge*

British Library Cataloguing in Publication Data

Villi the clown.
1. Campbell, William
2. Clowns—Correspondence, reminiscences, etc.
I. Title
791.3'3'0924   GV1811.C
ISBN 0–571–11794–5

Contents

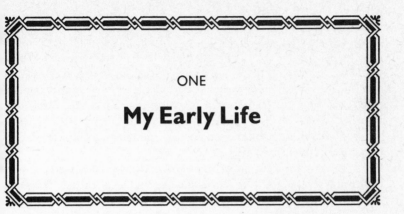

ONE

My Early Life

I was born in Paisley, Scotland, in 1910. My father, James Carlin, a true Scotsman, was a riveter at the Renfrew Shipyards. This gave me the right later on, when I was living in Russia and filling in thousands of forms, to reply to the question 'What is your class extraction?' with the answer 'Working class'. I do not remember my father. In 1914 when I was four years old he marched off to the war to end all wars, and gave his life for this noble lost cause, leaving behind a widow with five children.

My mother was Irish. Sarah O'Donnell was her maiden name and it is difficult to be more Irish than that. Although she was disillusioned by mankind in general and, as a widow, by the British Government in particular, she was not the kind of woman to weep on anyone's shoulder. Dauntlessly, she concentrated on spreading terror among the civil servants of the Social Security Office who had found a loophole in the law which reduced her already pitiful war widow's pension.

Even when Mother had achieved her increased allowance it was never enough to fill five hungry mouths. She had to take part-time jobs, and as the eldest I was left to hold the fort. I am afraid I was rather despotic. I remember the first dinner I ever cooked, because I forgot to salt the potatoes. Few dishes are nastier than unsalted potatoes, but my three young brothers and one sister ate them without a murmur. I had learned from my mother how to rule with an iron hand.

My first confrontation with the merciless laws of capitalism came at the age of nine. For sixpence a week I sold myself to a local newsagent as a delivery boy. All went well, and my relations with my bilious boss were amicable enough, until the day when I inserted a paper into the wrong letter-box. My boss, who happened to be suffering from a severe attack of indigestion at the time, gave me a stiff reprimand and a clout on the ear. It was the first time I had made a mistake, and my sense of justice was offended. I had no means of expressing my indignation, so I gathered the pile of papers and silently left the shop. On reaching the first drain round the corner, I pushed each paper down into the depths of Paisley's sewerage system. With the satisfaction of having had my revenge, I stalked off, head held high.

Among many odd jobs, my mother played the piano every Saturday evening at the dances held by the local British Socialist Party. To leave five vigorous children at home all alone was asking for trouble. She had no option but to take us with her to the dance. The sight of the five of us, ages ranging from two to eight, sitting demurely behind the piano (we were not naturally demure of course, but Mother had a heavy hand), dressed as well as Mother's purse could afford, cleaned and scrubbed to a shine, was evidently a touching sight. We were treated to more ice-cream and lemonade in one evening than I now have in a year.

It was at the BSP gatherings in 1918 that my mother met an up-and-coming socialist called John Ross Campbell who had just returned from the war. He had lost both feet and gained several medals for bravery. He also sustained an exceptionally strong desire to overthrow the capitalist system. He fell in love with our mother, and despite the terrifying prospect of having to help bring up five little monsters, he proposed marriage and was accepted. In the first few years this was a common-law marriage for the simple reason that an official marriage would have meant that my mother would lose the war pension she had won with such difficulty. With all due respect to the invalid Campbell, he would have found it extremely difficult to provide for such a big family. When my sister, Millie, was born in 1922 the marriage was officially registered and the conventions satisfied. Although we had different fathers, I call Millie and Jean, who was born two years later, my sisters since we were all brought up in one big family. As the eldest, I was responsible for the greater part of their upbringing. We all became Campbells, and after a certain amount of persuasion from my mother we stopped calling our new father Johnny. He became Father, a title which was even retained by his grandchildren. I call him Father and am proud to do so. At the age of fourteen, John Campbell had been known as the 'schoolboy orator'. He was a self-educated man who became a brilliant economist, a no less brilliant journalist—he was the first ever editor of a communist newspaper published in Great Britain—and a recognized authority on the poetry of Robert Burns. His place in British history is assured by the famous 'Campbell Case'.

In 1924 he was arrested for an article in the communist paper *Worker's Weekly*, in which he allegedly 'incited the Armed Forces to mutiny'. Father defended himself and demanded that the Prime Minister of the first Labour Government, Ramsay MacDonald, should stand trial with him for the offence. He pointed out that at a mass meeting in Dublin in 1912 Ramsay MacDonald had exhorted: 'Soldiers, sailors and airmen! Do not shoot the workers, turn your guns the other way!' The Attorney General had no alternative but to drop the case and set Campbell free. As a result the Tory opposition proposed a vote of No Confidence and the minority Labour Government fell, having been in office for only nine months.

All his life, Johnny Campbell was dedicated to the British Communist Party, of which he was a founder member. He was a good stepfather, and although none of the family became communists, his influence on our education was profound. He died in 1969, and despite all his talents, left the sum of £1,500 in his will, which proves how unprofitable it is to be a professional communist in Britain. Father's faith in international communism was somewhat dented towards the end of his life when the Kremlin 'excommunicated' him for two articles he wrote condemning the Soviet invasion of Czechoslovakia. The only leader of the Communist International still alive, Campbell was not invited to Moscow for the fiftieth anniversary of that now defunct organization. Much worse, the Soviet Embassy did not send him its usual Christmas gift—a bottle of vodka and a tin of caviare!

Paisley was a quiet, respectable mill town. One can imagine the horror of the Town Fathers when Paisley was declared to be a 'cesspool and breeding ground of communism'. The reason for this astounding statement was that three of the twelve members of the Communist Party who in 1926 were arrested and tried for 'inciting the people to overthrow the ruling government'—Bill Gallagher, Arthur McManus and Johnny Campbell—came from Paisley. This trio were the only communists in the town, but the Town Council, fearing an uprising, toyed with a proposal that during the trial the troops should be called out and a curfew observed. The idea was rejected after a number of the more sober-minded councillors pointed out the ludicrousness of comparing Paisley with revolutionary Petrograd. The waters of the great Neva River certainly played an important role in the 1917 Revolution, when the guns of the battleship *Aurora* boomed out the signal to start the uprising; Paisley's single waterway, the River Cart, on the other hand, was hardly wide enough to hold a rowing-boat.

The street where we lived ended on the banks of the Cart, which trickled through Paisley and meandered sleepily into the fields beyond. The town was like the river and the river was like the town and, as an example of the bustling activity of both, I recall an incident which has stuck in my mind since my childhood.

A crowd had gathered on the bridge across the Cart next to the Town Hall. They were watching, with intense concentration, the approach of a dead dog, floating in the slow-moving current. The corpse took nearly an hour to reach the bridge from the point at which it had first appeared, some fifty yards away. When it disappeared beneath the bridge, the crowd crossed the road unhurriedly and stood at the opposite parapet, waiting for it to appear again. Someone announced that the dog had belonged to Mrs MacPherson; others maintained emphatically that it was Mrs MacDougal's. Two camps formed, each vigorously defending its point of view. The argument was settled when a passing postman declared that the dog belonged to neither of these ladies, and that he had never seen it before. No one disputed this statement. Who better than a postman to know which dog belongs to whom? Then the crowd dispersed in silence.

The first school I attended was Roman Catholic. Later I was transferred to a 'Protestant' school, the name given to the State school on the grounds that it was not Catholic. Then I was taken back to the Catholic school, subsequently to the Protestant and so on, to and fro. The reason for all this was the religious differences between my grandparents on either side. Grandfather O'Donnell was equally popular among both Scots and Irish for his gift as a story-teller, and the ability to get a good tune out of any fiddle. He was a jolly man who could hold his drink, a peaceful and law-abiding citizen, a rare quality in an Irishman. Grandmother O'Donnell was a large, handsome woman, and in contrast to her husband, aggressive and quick-tempered. Both were Roman Cath-

horse and cart. It didn't take long to load the vehicle with our worldly possessions, and my two brothers, Jerry and Bert, and I perched on top of a feather bed. Uncle Joe sat next to the driver, holding four-year-old Alma on his knees. Taking the rhythm from the horse's hooves, Uncle Joe rendered the soldiers' version of 'Mademoiselle from Armentières'. We all joined in, and when he sang the more lurid verses, Jock frowned and told him to 'hisht in front of the bairns'.

As we entered Glasgow and passed over Broomilaw Bridge we were held up by a large group of Irish settlers who had just arrived on the ship *Pride of Ireland*. 'Totty howkers' or 'potato pickers' they were called by Glaswegians, and as we children chanted this derogatory name a thin, fair-haired girl scored a bull's-eye on my nose with a handful of mud. She was Sally Ann O'Reilly, who later became my first love. When the dust had settled her father, Patrick O'Reilly, and Uncle Joe got together for a pint with the result that the O'Reilly family came to live in the house on Stobcross Street in the Anderston district where we had our flat.

Stobcross Street divided Anderston into two parts. The lower part sloped down to the River Clyde where warehouses and small factories jostled with pubs, dance-halls, gambling dens and brothels. All the tenement houses were in the upper part and they must have been some of the worst slums in Europe. The streets were littered with empty cans and broken bottles. We were all shocked into silence as our cavalcade drove up to our new home, which was badly in need of repair. Our parents established themselves in one room, with my little brother Archie. All the rest of us slept in the other room in a huge bunk built into a recess. The kitchen consisted of a small gas-ring in the corner. The only source of water was a small wash-basin, with the lavatory next to it. This served all the tenants on our floor.

The O'Reillys slept in our place that first night. The only other free space was the basement where the water was knee-deep. When the time to go to bed came, somebody asked Uncle Joe where he would lie. 'Who, me? I wouldn't stay in this place for all the gold in the world,' he cried. And he began to tell us about the weird sights he had seen down in the bowels of the house, about the strange people there: a man with no legs or arms propped up on a chair on the landing, an ugly dwarf with a squeaky voice. Later we met and became great friends with these and the other people in the slums, and a nicer lot it would be hard to find. In general, the slum folks were not anything like as bad as they were made out to be. They were certainly rough and ready, but wonderfully kind-hearted, and even after a noisy quarrel they would share their last potato. It was a motley crowd—shipyard-workers, sailors, prostitutes and their pimps, thieves and drunkards.

Within six months we had become children of the street. I remember on one occasion two of my brothers came home crying from a Sunday School party. The street bully, Danny Turnbull, had stolen their Sunday School oranges. So down I went in search of Danny, and met him in Oak Street round the corner. Oak Street runs down a slope and I made a tactical mistake in taking up my stand below Danny, who was half a head bigger than me anyway. He gave me a good walloping and walked off. My tears were more in anger at my stupidity than sorrow for myself. Father listened to my tale of woe and, taking me by the scruff of the neck, told me to go out and bash Danny's head in or he would give me a hiding himself. Of the two evils I chose Danny, and although I didn't bash his head in, I did come home with two half-eaten oranges and a big black eye. 'The survival of the fittest' was Father's motto.

Father was highly respected among the slum people. Although they had not the faintest idea what he was talking about, they understood his sincere desire to ease the lot of the poor. I used to sit quietly in the corner of the room when he held his 'Marxist circles'. I watched the knitted brows and perplexed looks in the eyes of his students and wondered if they had the slightest inkling of Karl Marx's message. Now and again Father would hold an exam to ascertain how much they had learned. To the question 'What is a capitalist?' Mickey Dundas, a little hunchback ship-welder, replied: 'A capitalist is a bastard of the first water!'

I do not think the inauguration of the first branch of the Young Communist League in Glasgow will go down in the history of the British revolution, nor indeed will my own election to the post of secretary. Of the seven founder members, six had not yet reached their teens. Mother had by this time become a keen communist and it was on her initiative that an enthusiastic seventeen-year-old youth, Davy Ferguson, was commissioned to organize the revolutionary youth of Anderston. Davy thought he had a profound knowledge of politics, and to demonstrate his superiority he smoked a pipe. Our inaugural meeting was held in a cellar beneath a bookshop owned by a communist sympathizer. The younger members of the Young Communist League soon began a game of hide and seek among the piles of books and boxes, and it was with difficulty that Davy managed to call us to order. His opening speech was full of expressions like the 'proletariat' and the 'bright horizon of communism'.

Davy proposed my candidature as secretary and I was elected unopposed. When he proposed that Sally Ann should head the girls' section, she dissolved into fits of laughter. 'How can I head a girls' section,' she spluttered, 'when I am the only girl here?' A protracted procedural wrangle developed, in which neither would budge an inch. Davy began to bang the table with a stick, which reminded everyone of school. Then the adventurous mood of the gathering evaporated and we all began to play noisy games. The bookseller, in spite of his communist leanings, decided that he had had enough of future Bolsheviks and threw us all out into the street. It was an ignominious end to our attempts to overthrow capitalism.

I began to appreciate the benefit of a good Scottish education at the Finnieston Elementary School. It was a relief to be able to settle down in one school, and to get used to the same teachers. A feature of Scottish education was the strap, a traditional instrument of punishment which, for all its painfulness, taught us to behave ourselves. Besides, we found nothing wrong with the strap. The technique of catching it on your fingers, by a tiny jerk backwards, instead of on the palm, was easy to acquire. To be confined to school after class to write hundreds of lines was a much worse punishment. Strangely enough, my mother became a strong opponent of officially sanctioned strapping, although she herself kept a strap hanging on the wall. She enthusiastically supported a proposal of the Women's Committee of the Party to campaign against physical chastisement in schools and commissioned me, much against my will, to organize my schoolmates.

Morning assembly at Finnieston Elementary School was commanded by the caretaker, an ex-Army sergeant. All the classes were lined up in strict ranks and at nine o'clock the Headmaster emerged, with the teachers trailing behind. After a short pep talk we were marched into our classrooms. Urged on by Mother, I agitated about fifty lads (who treated it as a joke) into starting a protest demonstration. The plan was that we would refuse to join the ranks but wait outside the school gates until the teachers appeared, then march in and present our demands to the Headmaster. Placards were written with appropriate slogans: 'Hands Off Our Hands!' and 'Down With The Strap' and 'Up With Our Pants!'

The great day came, and we gathered outside the gates at about eight-thirty. The ex-sergeant took absolutely no notice of us as he organized the rest of the boys. The cat-calls and shouting died away as the teachers appeared on the quadrangle and stood to attention, waiting for the Headmaster to talk. The moment had come and I, the leader, strode in defiantly. I stopped in front of the Head and piped something about the strap being a tool of World Imperialism. Before I could dodge away, the Head grabbed me firmly by the ear. I twisted round to call upon my comrades-in-arms to rescue me, but to my horror I found I was all alone. At the sight of the Head the rest of the mutineers had deserted their leader. 'Cowards! Traitors!' I shrieked as I was dragged away to my execution. Never again did I organize a protest demonstration.

To keep me off the streets after school, my mother dispatched me to help Father in the *Glasgow Worker* offices on North Frederick Street. The editorial staff was not an extensive one. There was Father, who wrote everything, and Jimmy Logan who administered the business side. I typed envelopes, made the tea, ran errands and was even allowed to write items for the Children's Corner, my first venture into journalism.

Father was entirely dedicated to the paper; a budding worker-poet wrote this verse about him.

> There's wee Johnny Campbell,
> In his North Frederick Street den,
> He hasn't had a shave,
> Since Christ knows when.

To work as the editor-in-chief of a communist paper was not a remunerative job, and if it had not been for his disablement pension and my mother's pension we would have been in a bad way. My stepfather's dedication was astonishing. Once a week he would spend all night in one of the main bookstores where he dressed the windows for nothing in order to gain access to the books he needed for his research.

However much people might disagree with the cause, my stepfather was certainly a martyr to it, as was Bill Gallagher, one of only three communists to become a Member of Parliament. Bill was a good-hearted, kind man despite his belligerence. Lloyd George wrote of him: 'When Gallagher enters my office, it is only strong will-power that prevents me from climbing out of the window.'

Nevertheless, Bill was one of the most popular men in Parliament and much respected for his integrity.

It was from the top-storey window of the one-room editorial office of the *Glasgow Worker* looking down on to St George Square, that I witnessed the giant demonstration of frustrated, jobless workers on 31 January 1919, so-called Black Friday. It seemed the revolt on the Clyde had come. Gallagher was the main speaker. The police attacked in the middle of his speech. The next thing I saw was Bill being dragged along the ground with the blood pouring from a wound in his head. 'Moscow's Bolshevik Agent Incites Workers to Revolt', shrieked the headlines. Bill was not a Moscow agent, nor did the workers want to rise in revolt. When the citizens of Paisley walked behind his coffin on a sunny day in September 1965, they were paying homage to one of their best sons.

The Glasgow Party Centre decided to transfer the paper to London in 1924 with J. R. Campbell as the editor. I was fourteen and in my last year at the Kent Road High School. I was always miserable at this school. The boys were of a different class, with better-off parents, and I was shunned because I couldn't dress well and was the son of a dangerous Bolshevik. So I left for London in mid-term and shared a bed-sitter with Father until a flat was found for the rest of the family. By this time I was fed up with learning and keen to earn my own living. Before leaving Glasgow I bought a bowler hat and a coat with a velvet collar which, I believed, would create a smart image to impress potential employers.

I caused quite a small sensation on the eve of my departure when I appeared in front of my pals on Stobcross Street dressed in my new outfit. Everyone, including the girls, had to try on my bowler hat. There were no emotional scenes when I said goodbye: in those days Glaswegians were emigrating by the thousand in search of a better future. Among these were our friends the O'Reillys who had now left for Australia.

In London, Father found us a flat above a row of shops in Palmers Green. For the first month we all had to sleep on the floor. Mother had sent our furniture by rail and it had got lost on the way. The three-bedroomed flat seemed like a palace to us, and it took us a long time to get used to having our own bathroom and lavatory. A newly-wed young couple lived next door. We became good friends and it was the husband who taught me to play the ukulele, which stood me in good stead when I went to live in Russia.

London, for me, is the loneliest city in the world. During the eight years I lived there in the twenties I never made any real friends. I must have had about half a dozen jobs but could not settle down in any of them. I started as an apprentice in a printing house but was sacked for hitting a man who said insulting things about my stepfather after the 'Campbell Case'. After studying at night school, I became a clerk, but the itch of dissatisfaction made me change jobs in the City as often as I changed my socks. Even when I did make friends with young folks at work, it was impossible to keep it up as they usually lived miles from my home.

I did, however, achieve a long-standing ambition when I bought a lightweight cycle. Touring was very popular in those days and I had often envied groups of cyclists riding past, joking and laughing. I joined the Clarion Cycling Club which had some connections with mild socialist circles. It was here that I met new people and found there were other ideas about how to achieve equality for all. I hadn't taken to the London communists, a different breed to the simple, unsophisticated comrades in Glasgow. It was pleasant to talk to people who didn't ram their dogma down your throat as the communists did. With the Clarion Club I toured all over the English countryside and my weekends became a pleasure to look forward to. The mild political arguments of my fellow cyclists usually took place in the tranquil atmosphere of some picturesque village pub after a simple but satisfying lunch and a pint of brown and bitter. It was then that I took my first faltering steps towards show business with my ukulele. With another man, who played the saxophone, I became a welcome guest at social gatherings, with a song and dance performance in which youthful exuberance made up for lack of professional technique.

The only occasion on which I took part in a sizeable political demonstration was out of purely personal loyalty. In 1926 my stepfather was arrested, along with eleven other members of the Executive Committee of the Communist Party, for 'plotting to overthrow the existing government by means of armed rebellion'. Their trial, like the affair of the 'Zinoviev Letter', which brought the Conservatives to power, was a frame-up. Industrial unrest had taken a dangerous turn and the Conservative Government was under the impression that the Communist Party was responsible for all this, and that the Party threatened to become a mass movement of workers. Their fears were entirely unfounded.

Three of the accused—Harry Pollitt, Bill Gallagher and my stepfather—defended themselves. This gave them a unique opportunity to outline the aims and policies of the Communist Party. All three were sentenced to terms of imprisonment, but a judicial blunder made the general public sympathize with the convicted men. Before sentencing each prisoner individually, the judge declared: 'If you renounce your communist convictions you will be set free, otherwise you go to prison.' When my stepfather calmly but loudly answered, 'No!' I shouted, 'Good for you, Father!' I was escorted from the court room by a policeman.

Public sympathy was such that the Party decided to organize demonstrations every Sunday evening, with marches to Brixton Prison where the men were incarcerated. Speeches were made outside the walls and revolutionary songs sung, even though most of us didn't know either the words or the music. Then came the big moment. The gathering was to shout some slogan like, 'We are with you, comrades! Long live the world revolution!' Then we were told to be silent so we could hear the answering call. Dead silence would reign and then someone would break the hush by shouting, 'I can hear them, they are answering us!' Then everybody would cheer and sing some more songs. We had a good laugh afterwards when Father told us that they never even heard the call. He and his comrades had all been moved to a secluded wing of the prison and threatened with solitary confinement. Father told a press conference that during his year in prison he had learned German. When Harry Pollitt was asked the same question, he answered: 'I learned to fart the Party anthem, The Internationale!'

The 1930s began with unemployment figures never known before in British history. The catastrophic Wall Street crash was beginning to have repercussions all over the world, creating havoc in the already weak British economy. Millions were searching for jobs that didn't exist. London's streets were crowded with small choirs of Welsh miners, singing beautifully as only the Welsh can, trying to earn a few shillings to keep themselves and their families from starvation. I was no longer bored by my book-keeping job, only frightened that I might lose it and join the ranks of the jobless. In 1931, when my firm closed down, my fears came true. At the beginning I was rather perky and was sure I could quickly find work, but the more I wrote and telephoned the more I found myself at a dead end. There were no jobs. Eventually I gave up. Then, by chance, I met my cycling saxophone-playing friend. He was also out of work and suggested we polish up the songs we'd hammered out on those weekend outings. He knew a variety artiste currently 'resting' who was prepared to rehearse with us, make the act look professional, and 'sell' us to the pubs and workers' clubs where he had contacts. There was nothing very artistic about those performances in halls where the smoke and the smell of beer hung like a London fog, but through them I began to develop that vital instinct of feeling for and responding to your audience.

As a temporary measure, these performances provided me with some money and gave me a feeling of independence, but soon I realized I had to do something to get out of the rut. An aunt in America wrote suggesting I should go out and stay with her, but I was at the age when the domination of my parents added to my frustration. The idea of escaping from a powerful mother into the hands of a no less powerful aunt seemed to be exchanging the frying-pan for the fire.

Throughout the Depression, the Soviet Union was proclaimed by communists and left-wing members of the Labour Party as the answer to the workers' problems. My mother insisted that my future lay with the young Soviet state. My stepfather, curiously enough, was very much against the idea. He had just returned from Moscow where he had been for a few months in his capacity as a leading official of the Communist International. As a man of an extremely practical mind, he told us that life was terribly hard there and declared I would not stick it. I, being young and thin-skinned, misconstrued his meaning and took it as a personal slight. So when my mother announced that she had arranged for me a free passage to Leningrad on the passenger ship *Kooperatsy*, the only vessel making the crossing from Leningrad to London, I agreed to go, prompted mainly by the desire to get away, to be free, to stand on my own feet, and, of course, to prove to my stepfather that he was wrong about me. How many times, especially in that first year, did I realize how right he had been. It was only youthful stubbornness that prevented me from returning home to London.

And so I was seen off at Hays Wharf by the whole family but one. My favourite brother Jerry could not bring himself to be there. When the family returned home afterwards they found him in an armchair, hiding behind an upside-down newspaper. As the ship moved away down the Thames and I gazed at the tearstained faces of the ones I loved so much, only then did I realize that I was possibly leaving my homeland for ever.

TWO

Comrade Campbell

The first morning on board, I woke up with all the buoyancy of youth. I had lost the heavy heart I had gone to bed with the night before and was all ready to see what this new world had to offer. I quickly made friends with the few other passengers, especially a young twenty-six-year-old fellow called Misha returning to his home city, Leningrad, for a holiday. Misha worked in the Soviet Trade Mission in London. Another happy friendship I struck up was with Edna (Eddie) Sinelnikova about whom I shall write later.

About a day before we were due to arrive in Leningrad, the ship became stuck in heavy ice floes and could not move. The captain had to call for help. All the passengers gathered on the top deck early in the morning, and a cheer went up when the ice-breaker *Ermak* appeared on the horizon. It seemed to me to be a good omen as we followed her along the broken path, watching her as she smashed the ice. I felt I was battling my way to a new life.

The next morning we passed into the quieter Gulf of Finland. The morning was a beautiful one with that crisp air of a spring day in Russia. As we passed Kronstadt Fort on 6 May 1932, the Customs officials came alongside and boarded the ship. Even their stony faces showed surprise when they came to examine my luggage. It consisted of one suitcase, a racing cycle and a ukulele. My foreign currency declaration was brief. I had exactly one pound sterling.

I had heard all about the Russians' fanatical love of their Motherland and of how exiles, returning from abroad, would fall to their knees and kiss their native soil. When the ship docked at the Troitsky Bridge, my fellow passengers flocked down the gangway to be kissed and hugged with typically Russian fervour by relatives and friends. I was so engrossed by this happy scene that, as I stepped down the gangway, with my cycle in one hand and my case in the other, I failed to see the last step, tripped, and kissed the soil of Mother Russia as no Russian had ever done, causing hilarity amongst the bystanders. Misha, my friend from the voyage, picked me up, brushed me down and loaded my luggage on to a four-wheeled, horse-drawn carriage called a *drojhky*. He had invited me to stay with him until I could find a place of my own.

A ride in a *drojhky* is something you never forget. Perched precariously on a mound of luggage, I felt like a sailor at the top of a mast during a gale. There was very little motor transport in those days, and therefore no traffic regulations. Our driver drove his horse at a gallop, as if competing in a race, whooping and cracking his whip, zig-zagging between the crowds of jay-walkers and other carriages, leaving a wake of curses and four-letter words. One old lady displayed unbelievable agility. I cried out as she disappeared beneath our horse's head, but to my bewilderment and admiration she leapt up, skirts flying, and in one jump reached the pavement safely.

Our route took us through the centre of Leningrad, and as we entered the Nevsky Prospekt, by the Winter Palace, I marvelled at this great, wide avenue that seemed to stretch for miles. It was lined with exquisite but dilapidated buildings, and its line was broken at intervals by hump-backed bridges over the canals. I began to see that Leningrad deserved its title of the Venice of the North. We cantered past the magnificent Kazansky Cathedral towards the far end of the Nevsky Prospekt through the October Station Square and into some side streets. With another whoop from our driver we dived under an archway into the courtyard of Misha's tenement house.

It was here that I first met what could be called a typical Russian family. In fact there were three families, living in a four-roomed flat (two grandparents and two daughters, Maria and Nina, together with their husbands and two children). The flat had once belonged to the *dedushka*, the Russian name for grandfather. With the Revolution had come a Government regulation called *uplotnenie* under which a family living in a flat was forced to squeeze itself into one room, giving up the others to the needy. Misha's family were comparatively lucky to have saved their dining-room.

Dedushka had worked all his life as a waiter at the once fashionable Europa Hotel. He was no admirer of the new Soviet system. I remember him showing me a picture of himself taken before the Revolution. It showed a stout, benevolent-looking man.

Dedushka was now about half the size and his neck, withered and scrawny as a turkey's, hung loosely over his hard celluloid collar. It was difficult to conceive that he was the same person.

In the absence of my interpreter, Misha, the old man considered that he was best fitted to talk with me. As a waiter, he had served many foreigners and had picked up a smattering of French and German. The trouble was that his knowledge was confined to waiters' expressions, and our conversations seemed to revolve around whether I wanted my eggs boiled or fried. 'Wollen sie herring?' was one of his favourite phrases, as it gave him the chance, despite the displeasure of Grandma, to treat the two of us to a couple of glasses of vodka and, as he proposed, a piece of raw herring.

With Misha and Nina, a good-looking, plumpish girl, we discussed my future and what I ought to go in for. Misha declared that the future lay in aviation, as everyone in Russia was air-minded. There were few cars on the streets but they all wanted to fly! I agreed, saying that I would like to enter an aviation college. Misha hurriedly explained that I would have to learn Russian first.

'So why not go to work at the aviation factory, pick up the language and then go to college?' he suggested. 'As a foreign worker you can get much better ration cards for the closed store, Insnab.' It all seemed perfectly logical, and so I agreed.

The next day Misha and I went to the International Department of the City Party Committee, housed in the famous Smolny Institute from which Lenin had directed the Revolution in 1917. I was met by the department head, a Hungarian, a very pleasant man. He seemed very glad to meet me and congratulated me on my wanting to work at the aviation factory. He explained that the First Five Year Plan was nearing completion and must be fulfilled. Russia, the First Workers' and Peasants' State, was in dire need of specialists and qualified workers. I refrained from telling him that they would not find much of a specialist in me: I had once bought a second-hand Citroën for twenty pounds which, with my brother Jerry, I had taken to pieces and reassembled. I did not want to spoil my chances of getting the coveted Insnab ration book.

Armed with the department head's official recommendation in my pocket, I almost danced out and made my way across the Neva River to the factory at Novaya Derevnia. Here I was met no less enthusiastically by the management and the Party Secretary, who were particularly delighted to hear that I didn't need a room. With the help of Misha, I filled in the necessary forms. The questions are the same to this day, with one exception: 'Did you serve in the counter-revolutionary White Army?'

On my first day in the factory I woke up brimming with enthusiasm, eager to roll up my sleeves and help fulfil the Five Year Plan. I was up at six, did fifteen minutes of exercises, washed and dressed. When it came to breakfast I had my first confrontation with reality. I had no idea how to light the primus stove—the only means, in those days, of boiling water or cooking. No matter where you went or who you visited, the smell of paraffin would hit you as soon as a door opened; and the hissing of primus stoves could be heard continuously from early morning until late at night. Even my first visit to the Winter Palace was spoiled by the smell of paraffin. I had a ridiculous vision of some forgotten Tsar, complete in royal robes and crown, frying eggs and bacon on a spluttering primus stove somewhere in the Palace cellars. The idea made me giggle and I received a disapproving look from the guide, who was dilating on the despotism of the former Tsarist autocracy.

After breakfasting on a lukewarm glass of water and a hunk of black bread, I started off for the factory. The number of the tram I had to take was 31 and it is branded on my mind to this day. The tram consisted of a front car with trailers behind, each one as overcrowded as the next. Inside, the passengers were squashed so tight that they could not even raise an arm. This fact was often turned to advantage. When the conductor roared, 'Come on, you lot, pay your fares!' the usual answer was, 'I would if I could but I can't get my hand into my pocket!' Among the first Russian jokes I understood was this one, which came from this source:

'Where did you get that terrible hair-cut?'

'In a tram.'

'How come?'

'A woman behind me chattered so much, she clipped all the hair off the back of my head with her teeth!'

But the people inside the tram were the lucky ones. The other travellers either hung on to the rails at the entrance or, if the windows were open, clung perilously to the sides. They would hop off at each stop to give their aching arms a rest, and I marvelled at the way they carried on lively conversations with friends inside. Many a young fellow would risk losing his life under the wheels as he chatted up a girl in a red headscarf. It was a dangerous acrobatic feat to write down a phone number while hanging on to a fast-moving tram by one arm.

On that first morning I stood in complete bewilderment. To get on the tram seemed totally impossible. Obviously, a combination of experience, brute force and dexterity was required. I was appalled by the prospect of either arriving late to work on my first day, or, as seemed likely, not at all.

'You're going to be late, Comrade C'm*bell*!' came a voice from behind me. (I spell my name as it was pronounced with the stress on the *bell*. No matter how I strove to have my name pronounced properly I never succeeded. C'm*bell* it remained.) The voice belonged to a complete stranger, who turned out to be one of my fellow workers at the aviation factory. He seemed to know all about me. I explained my predicament to him, in the few, halting Russian words I knew.

'Never mind,' he said. And he came out with a slogan which I soon learned was a stock one. 'There are no obstacles a communist cannot overcome!' Although I did not fully understand him, I got the gist of what he was saying and disloyally wondered how even a communist was going to storm this particular fortress. I must say, though, that he lived up to his slogan and got me on that tram. He used a trick which, in those days, was guaranteed to work like magic. 'Make way for a foreign worker,' he shouted.

And the impossible was achieved. I found myself squeezed up against the massive bosom of a woman whose photograph I saw later on the factory Honours Board as an *udarnitsa*, an 'outstanding shock worker'. As I am a little chap and she was an Amazon type, her breasts wobbled in my face, making it difficult for me to answer her many questions. My Party Committee friend came to the rescue again. 'Comrade C'mbell has come from England to contribute his expert knowledge in fulfilling the Five Year Plan,' he announced.

The whole tram was overjoyed at this outrageous statement. I caught the word 'expert' (it is the same in Russian as in English) and was suddenly terrified that I would be exposed as an impostor. Little did I know that my meagre knowledge of cars really did put me in the category of specialist. Most of the factory workers had only recently seen a steam engine, to say nothing of the planes they were supposed to be making. My fellow workers virtually carried me off the tram, and all along the half-mile walk to the factory they gazed at me in silent curiosity, which made me feel a fool. I was glad when we reached the factory gates.

I was taken to a small building that stood apart from the other three enormous shops. It looked insignificant, dwarfed by the factory buildings, but I soon discovered that it housed the brains and power of the whole complex, the Managing Director and his two Deputies. One of the Deputies was the Red Director, appointed by the City Party Committee, and his sole function was to watch the other two. It was a function that greatly intrigued me. It was strange to see someone sitting alone in a room all day doing nothing, when everyone else was in a state of feverish activity. In those days, Red Directors were appointed in all the factories, and mostly were former sailors from the Revolutionary Navy. The theory was that sailors were supposed to know all about machinery though, in fact, with the odd exception, they were simple peasants whose only contact with machinery had been washing out the engine room of warships. However, the sailors had seen the most active service during the Revolution and Civil War, and so they had the unenviable task of exterminating any opposition to the Party in the factories. Naturally, many of them joined the Cheka, as the KGB was called in those days. The original name Cheka, the Russian acronym for Extraordinary Commission, was changed several times over the years, first into GPU (State Political Administration) and then to NKVD (People's Commissariat for Internal Affairs). When People's Commissariats were abolished to become Ministries, the latter became MVD in Soviet jargon. The Secret Police was subordinate to the MVD but its importance became such that it was separated and became the MGB (Ministry of State Security). After Stalin's death and the execution of Beria, the Ministry was reduced to a Committee and became the KGB. In all cases throughout this book I shall call it the KGB. This name is more familiar and the Organs, as the Russians call it, has never changed. Call me a pot, they say, only don't put me in a stove.

I was equally astonished by the power of the Party Secretary whom I also met on my first day at the factory. No director was able to take a major decision without the participation of the Party Secretary, who often had the final say. In many factories this led to chaos because the majority of Party Secretaries were appointed for purely political reasons and knew nothing at all about industry. Sergei was a rare exception. He had been a worker, and later a Shop Foreman in the aviation factory before being elected Party Secretary. A big, heavily-built man, he looked like the archetypal hero of Soviet myth with an open, honest face and deep-set, clever eyes. He was a fine man, jovial, considerate and able enough, despite the lack of education which he was continually trying to improve. Once, when I fell ill, I stayed at his place and he nursed me like a brother. We would talk into the small hours and I had to answer innumerable questions about life in Britain. 'Only tell me the real truth,' he would say. 'No propaganda, please.'

After an initial conference, during which I was surprised to see that the Trade Union Chairman was the least important officer in the factory, it was decided to start me off working in the fitting shop, so that I could get used to the factory and find out for myself what I was best suited for. I put on the dark blue boiler-suit with which I had been issued and, clutching my factory pass, I was led off to my new job. The pass was the most important part of my equipment. In those days there were widespread fears about sabotage and subversion. I was told terrible tales of whole factories being blown up by enemies of the people who had managed to infiltrate the buildings with the aid of lost passes. I had a dreadful panic one morning when I came to work and could not find my pass. After frantically searching all my pockets I explained my predicament to the gate-keeper and suggested I should go home for the pass. To my amazement he laughed, and pushing me through the turnstile, said, 'No need for that. Get into work or you'll be late. An hour and a half's work for the Five Year Plan is much more important than a pass. Off you go!'

I was introduced to the Shop Foreman or 'master' as he was called, a young man in his early thirties. His name was Rodionov and I never learned his first name. His features were dark and he didn't look like a Russian. In fact, he was a Tartar, a descendant of the nation that once invaded Russia in the thirteenth century under the command of Genghis Khan. Now, the Tartars are confined to a small, autonomous republic on the banks of the Volga. He was always rushing about looking worried, and he was laconic in the extreme. One had to have a perfect command of the language, or rather of the vernacular, to understand the monosyllables he would utter as he rushed past. Even when my Russian improved, I had to have an interpreter to decode 'Kronshtein', which meant 'Go over to filing 10 mm brackets.'

My interpreter was Rita. She was our forewoman or 'brigadier'. Like all the one hundred girls in the shop, Rita wore a shapeless grey work-coat and the inevitable red scarf tied round her head. A slight, rather plain girl, she had lovely eyes, sometimes green, sometimes brown and, when she was angry, which was not often, black. She took me under her wing and patiently showed me the work I had to do. After lunch together in the canteen, she and I would often sit on the banks of the river, a tributary of the Neva, just outside the factory gates.

Rodionov seemed to be on cool terms with Rita. He would from time to time have long talks with other foremen, but with her he was at his most laconic. One day, I happened to be walking in the big park on the Islands nearby when whom should I see but Rita and Rodionov strolling arm in arm happily laughing together. I was so surprised and embarrassed that I darted up a side alley. The next day I was talking with one of my mates and mentioned the incident. 'What's funny about that? Rodionov's her husband!' And so it was. They were deeply in love with one another, though this became apparent only outside the factory. Rodionov's sombre, pock-marked face would light up at the sight of Rita, making him look positively handsome.

Although she was only a couple of years older than me, Rita adopted a maternal attitude that I sometimes found a little irksome, though, looking back, she was wonderfully kind in leading me through the labyrinths of this strange new life. With her help, I stopped idealizing the new Russia, and began to discern the good from the bad in this socialist society.

Whatever the propagandists say, Soviet society was, and is, just another way of running a country. A bureaucratic Party hierarchy rules everything, and the people have no choice but to adapt themselves to it and make the best of a bad job. Bureaucracy creates shortages of food and clothes, and often causes the incompetent distribution of what little there is. Bikinis are to be found in abundance beyond the Polar Circle, skis and skates gather dust on the shelves of shops in tropical Armenia. I had an early experience of the absurdities that abound in Soviet life. In the thirties there were very few trained engineers in Soviet factories, and they tended to be non-communists. Their superior education set them apart from the workers, who addressed them as *baryn*, meaning 'master', which could be construed either as a term of respect or irreverence depending on the intonation. But the older workers continued to raise their caps to the *baryn*, as was the custom before the Revolution.

One day, a meeting of the workers in my shop was called by the Komsomol or Young Communist League with the purpose of putting a stop to this cap-lifting. On 'trial' were a number of the older workers, among whom was a wily individual called Khromoi, or 'The Limper'. He was of a type to be found in any factory, in any part of the world, always asking awkward questions, antagonizing the management and always ready with a glib answer himself.

The meeting was presided over by a newcomer, the Komsomol Secretary. Even I, with my scanty knowledge of Russian, understood that his tone and manner were inappropriate for such an audience. His name was Kirichenko and he was a Ukrainian. Kirichenko was not a worker. He had long, oily hair, a sallow face and wore spectacles. All this made the workers suspect, quite wrongly, that he was an intellectual. He had been imposed on them by the City Komsomol Committee and had never worked in a factory before. Although there was some logic in what he had to say, it was his dogmatic approach which put the workers' backs up.

'You are no longer the slaves of the bosses and their hirelings. By raising your caps you are contradicting the whole essence of socialist society and lowering your own dignity.'

Khromoi interrupted.

'Wait a minute. Whose cap is it, yours or mine?'

'Comrade, you are confusing the issue. It makes no difference whose cap it is. The point is, you must stop raising it to the managers and engineers!'

But Khromoi was not to be side-tracked.

'Young man, when I fought in the Civil War . . .' This was met with smothered spluttering from the audience, who knew perfectly well that Khromoi's famous limp was not the result of a war-wound, as he claimed, but from tripping over a step while drunk. 'As I was saying when I was rudely interrupted by these fine comrades, when I fought in the Civil War, I thought we were fighting to free ourselves. Is that correct?'

'That is quite correct and we have won our freedom.'

The innocent Secretary did not realize that he was in for a real leg-pulling, the like of which you can only find among factory workers. (How many novices have spent hours searching for left-handed spanners?)

Khromoi continued, 'How is it that we've got freedom when a little squirt like you can tell me who I can lift my cap to and who not?'

The Secretary broke in indignantly, 'There's no need to be insulting.'

Khromoi's face took on an apologetic expression. 'I'm sorry, *comrade.*' There was an uncalled-for stress on the last word, comrade.

'Tell me, *comrade*, has the Party put a ban on raising caps?'

'No, it hasn't. It's a purely personal affair. It's a question of how and to whom you raise it.'

Khromoi was fawning on him now. 'You must excuse us ignoramuses. We never went to college like you did. You just explain to us how and who we should raise our caps to.'

At that moment another elderly worker joined in. Highly respected for a number of outstanding qualities, he was a good worker, had fought in the Civil War, sported a fine bushy beard and drank a large glass of vodka every morning before coming to work.

'When I raise my cap,' he said, continuing the leg-pull, 'I am showing my respect for the man I'm raising it to. Should I or should I not raise my cap to Mikhail Ivanovich, our Chief Engineer? I worked with him before the Revolution and we workers liked him. He was very considerate and when he could he shielded us from the boss. Right? Right! We always raised our caps to him, not because we were slaves as you put it so aptly, but because we respected him. If we stop now, he'll think he has offended us and will get worried. Maybe he'll not sleep at nights. Right? Right!'

The last statement appeared to move the workers profoundly. The Komsomol Secretary looked completely bewildered. To add to his misery, the Party Secretary Sergei had come in quietly and was obviously enjoying himself. He had been a worker here and recognized a leg-pull. Kirichenko decided to assert his authority.

'Now then, I won't have this meeting turned into a debating society. You are being asked to stop this servile pre-Revolutionary manner of raising your caps to your superiors.'

He looked towards Sergei for support, but the latter's bland face showed nothing. Khromoi noticed this, as did the others, and with unconcealed relish went into the attack.

'You just used the word "superior". How can we have superiors if we are all equal in the eyes of the Revolution? There are no superiors or inferiors now, we did away with that when we stormed the Winter Palace.'

A voice from the back was heard saying, 'Khromoi, you were in bed, cuddled up to your wife's backside, when we stormed the Winter Palace!'

When the laughter had subsided, Khromoi waved a finger towards the back row. 'I was speaking figuratively . . .'

One of the young workers gasped, 'Fi—gur—at—ive—ly . . . What does that mean?'

Khromoi struck a pose like a professor delivering a lecture. 'To think of what ignoramuses I have to work with . . .'

'Never mind all that. You tell us what that word means.'

It was obvious that Khromoi was only playing for time. At last he took a deep breath and said, 'Well, it's like this. Say you had played for our factory team when we won the City Cup by that one goal in the final, scored by our young Petya here. By the way, Petya, good for you. What a goal! What a goal! Tell us how you did it.'

Petya seemed embarrassed by the spotlight suddenly turned on him and was inarticulate for a minute. However, egged on by the others, he went on to describe his glorious goal. When he had finished, Khromoi continued, 'As I was saying, Petya here, God bless him, scored that goal but we all say *we* scored it.'

The voice at the back was not to be stifled. 'We all know you support the Dynamo, and anyone who supports that policemen's team doesn't know anything about football. Up with good old Zenith!'

This started off a heated argument on the merits of the two rival Leningrad teams. All the attempts of the Komsomol Secretary to bring the workers back to the subject under discussion were in vain. Taking advantage of a moment when two of the men were facing up to one another in what promised to be a fight, he quietly slipped away. The moment he had gone, the two combatants lowered their fists and, along with everybody present, began to roar with laughter.

I heard later that the Managing Director and the other top executives were pleasantly surprised by the increasing number of men who raised their caps to them. As for Kirichenko he was soon transferred, and, inevitably, was promoted to a higher post on the City Komsomol Committee.

The summer of 1932 was at its height when the factory's Trade Union organized an excursion to the countryside. We were all issued with a special coupon. This gave us the right to buy a packet of food containing two cheese sandwiches, five spoonfuls of sugar and a loaf of white bread. It was a sufficient guarantee of a good turnout.

It was a pleasure to see my workmates outside the factory. Gone were the drab grey work-coats. The girls looked lovely in summer frocks, some of which had obviously been bought by their grannies before the Revolution. The men looked smart as well. Their white open-necked shirts, white trousers and shoes reminded me irresistibly of a cricket team.

We made the journey by rail. This was no easy matter since the trains were always packed on Sundays, mainly with people going to work on their allotments. Then as now this was an important source of vegetables. By sheer force of numbers our party captured a whole coach to itself and, to the sound of laughter and song, we were off. Russians are very musical and their tastes tend towards the plaintive, a fact which, it is claimed, is due to the exploitation they suffered in the old days of the Tsar. Even in the new Workers' Paradise they still seemed to prefer mournful ballads. I well remember the beautiful song which celebrates the life and adventures of Stenka Razin. The Party did not object to this particular song. It considered Razin to be some kind of a revolutionary. From what I could understand of his doings it seemed that he was a bandit who had a hundred and one methods of getting rid of his enemies. Chopping heads, hands and legs off was nothing compared to some of the other executions he would order. His fellow mutineers were very upset, according to the ballad, when he captured a Persian princess and fell in love with her. In the end he agreed to get rid of her and ordered the unfortunate girl to be pushed overboard 'into the swirling waters of Mother Volga'.

Eventually, it was my turn to sing, and I accompanied myself on my ukulele. My repertoire consisted almost entirely of negro spirituals—picked up from a book: 'Poor Old Joe', 'Way Down Upon the Swanee River' and so on. Later on, as a professional, I included them in my act, and when the censors complained that they sounded 'jazzy' I explained solemnly that they were the songs of the slaves crying to be freed from their chains. This never failed to do the trick, and my repertoire book was always stamped.

The scene of the outing was a country meadow. It lay beside the banks of a little winding river, with woods beyond, a piece of typically Russian countryside, lovely but severe. Everybody contributed to a huge picnic lunch. Rodionov had a big bag, made of an old but very clean padded jacket, and out of it, like a conjurer, he produced a large pot. He undid the rope that held the lid in place, and inside there was a potful of *grechnevoi kasha*, buckwheat porridge, a favourite dish of the Russians. It was delicious. The rest of the feast consisted of soggy pickled cucumbers, pickled mushrooms, *pirojhki* (patties with cabbage), boiled potatoes, beetroot and onions. It all proved the fertility of the workers' allotments and the hard work they put into their little plots of land.

A wise man once said that after a good dinner anyone could love his relatives. The menu that day might not have appealed to a gourmand, and certainly these simple, unsophisticated folk were not my relatives; but I loved them. After lunch a lorry was transformed into a makeshift stage, and an amateur concert began. The many performers who sang and danced may have lacked finesse but they made up for it with peasant vigour and enthusiasm. I sang at the end of the impromptu show. It was strange to find myself standing on a lorry surrounded by hundreds of people lying on the grass. I sang, naturally, in a language nobody knew, but, if I may be excused some immodesty, you could have heard a pin drop. When I had exhausted my not very extensive repertoire there were shouts of 'Bis' and 'Encore', so I sang the soulful ballad 'Who's Sorry Now?' without my ukulele. My Russian audience could not of course understand that eternal question, but their reaction was boisterous, especially to the lines 'Right to the end, just like a friend, I tried to warn you somehow'—perhaps because I put a theatrical sob into my voice. It was my first success and I got carried away.

A little popularity is the cheapest thing in the world to buy. How many times in my early years on the stage did I suffer disappointment, frustration and loss of faith in myself as a result of empty compliments. In his advice to young actors, the great Stanislavsky warned against believing the praise of admirers. Listen to them, he said, but learn to sort out the gems from the rubbish.

But here I was surrounded by a crowd of people, clapping me on the back, telling me what a wonderful artiste I was, and how I ought to be on the stage. I stood there in a world of bliss. I forgot Rita, Rodionov and the rest of my mates as I was dragged from one group of fans to another. Soon other attractions appeared and my admirers began to disperse in search of new entertainment. Finally, only three men were left and I clung to them. They told me how after listening to me they found life worth living, that all other Soviet artistes were lousy and that the Soviet system was lousy, too. One of them, Victor, a prematurely balding youth, declared that Russian girls were lousy, too. His dream was to go to bed with a French girl. He asked me if I had ever slept with a French girl. I was on the point of telling some fisherman's story of lurid exploits during an Easter excursion to Paris, when Stepan, who seemed to be quite a pleasant fellow, produced the inevitable bottle of vodka. I had never drunk vodka in my life before and I half-heartedly refused the glass Victor poured out for me. Russians never take no for an answer, especially where vodka is concerned. A whole arsenal of persuasion was used to make me drink that glass. No one, they said, could call himself a man unless he emptied a glass of vodka or two now and again. It was good for the stomach, they claimed. And so on. To appease them I took a sip. This didn't satisfy them. That was not the way to drink vodka. 'Throw your head back and pour it down your throat.' Then Victor said, 'What can you expect from him? He's an Englishman!' And so, defending the good name of the British nation, I duly threw my head back and poured the vodka down my throat. A sort of Big Bertha exploded in my gullet. I fell back on the grass, gasping for breath, and the remaining contents of the glass splashed down my shirt. Victor made matters worse by making me follow it up with a pickled cucumber.

I recovered my breath eventually but, for the first time in my life, I began to feel the effects of tipsiness. By this time Victor and the third man, Ivan, had started a violent quarrel which ended in a fight. Stepan had to separate them. Another glass of vodka appeared in my hand. I drank a little of it and was violently sick. I must have lost consciousness for a few minutes because when I came to, Stepan had disappeared and the other two were quarrelling again. At that moment I heard the welcome sound of Rita's voice. She was wild. 'I told you, I told you! All I have to do is to lose sight of him for a minute and he's in trouble. You stupid boy! You stupid . . . Oh, what's the use? What have these swines done to you?'

I must have been a dreadful sight. Rita began to wipe my shirt clean. Someone brought a jug of water and she wiped my face. This was all accompanied by a torrent of abuse aimed at Victor and Ivan, who replied, with interest. I tried to get to my feet to protect Rita. I could have spared myself the effort. She was perfectly capable of dealing with them herself. Then Rodionov came running up, and in a second, Victor and Ivan were flat out on the grass, nursing their jaws.

'And now,' said Rita to me, 'you know the difference between good Russians and bad Russians.'

'When are you going to have a revolution in England and be free like us?'

I was frequently bemused by this question during my first few years in Russia. Whenever I went to the smoking room at the factory, I was asked about the English Revolution while my questioners admired my boots. These were a pair of army officer's boots I had bought for thirty shillings in a surplus store. The workers would shake their heads in wonder. 'What marvellous workmanship! That's leather for you! You can't beat English boots, can you?' They told me I shouldn't wear such marvellous boots every day, but keep them for Sundays. And then the inevitable question would come again: 'When are you going to have a revolution in England?'

I could only marvel at their simplicity and their faith in the Revolution. They were living on meagre rations, pulling in their belts, and working hard and enthusiastically. If an unemployed man in Britain had been offered the thin soup, grisly boiled fish and grey mashed potatoes that was the staple fare in the canteen he would have chucked it down the nearest drain. The attempts of the management and engineers to look smart and decently dressed in their threadbare but meticulously cleaned and pressed suits were courageous but unavailing. (I discovered the reason for the carefully sewn slit on the right side of the breast of most men's jackets. The suits had been 'refaced', that is to say, turned inside out and re-tailored. Naturally, the breast pocket changed over from left to right.) Of course I could not tell them so. They were so engrossed in creating the splendid life of equal opportunity and plenty for all, that they hardly noticed their poverty. I wore my boots as little as possible.

I worked so hard in the daytime that I had no chance to be bored, but the evenings were purgatory. I continued to live in Misha's flat, but he had gone back to London and Nina, his wife, had very few nights off from the cinema where she worked as a projectionist. Nina could always get me free tickets to the cinema, but I did not often go as my Russian was still very faulty. I remember one film in particular which rather dampened my enthusiasm for Soviet cinema. The film was called *Sniper* and was about the dauntless Red Army bravely resisting foreign invaders, mainly British, in the early twenties. In one scene a large number of women appeared in long skirts, red tunics and white belts. This was the first time I had heard of women in the British Army actually taking part in battle. I had always assumed that they restricted their activities to nursing, typing, driving generals and so on. To the delighted whoops of the

Russian audience, the Red Army soon routed these mysterious females who fled, dropping their guns as they ran. They had a difficult time taming their long skirts and some resorted to pulling them up above their knees. I thought that this was all rather curious. There was nothing very valiant about the Red Army defeating a bunch of women. I made the point to Nina afterwards and she laughed uproariously.

'What? Didn't you recognize them?'

'Of course not. Who were they?'

'That was a Scottish brigade!'

Nina was my only companion for a while after Misha's departure. Whenever she could, she took me to the Hermitage, and to other museums and picture galleries. Through the cinema she got me complimentary tickets to the opera and ballet. She also took upon herself the task of improving my Russian, for which I am eternally grateful. Russian is a beautiful language, and to read Pushkin, Tolstoy and Chekhov in the original makes the difficulty of learning it well worthwhile. But my early ignorance led to some comic situations.

Whenever Nina saw anything she thought might interest me she called me over by saying, 'Eedee syuda' which means, 'Come here'. One evening we were going to the ballet and Nina was dressing in the next room. I was reading a book and heard her call out. I just caught the word 'syuda'. I jumped up, went into her room, and then stood spellbound. She was standing with her back to me, completely naked as if she had stepped down from Da Vinci's picture in the Hermitage. While I admired the lines of her well-built body, I wondered why she had called me. Was this an old Russian custom? Or was Nina a member of some free love sect? Sensing my presence, she yelled at me to get out—which I did. When she appeared fully dressed, I was scolded roundly. I tried to appease her.

'But you yourself told me "eedee syuda".'

'I didn't. I said "nelzya syuda".'

'What does "nelzya" mean?'

'It means *don't* come here!'

But in spite of Nina, who looked after me like a big sister, I was lonely, and to be lonely in Leningrad or Moscow was as grim then as it is now. Dance-halls hardly exist, there are no pubs and very few restaurants. There are cafés, but you have to stand for hours in a queue waiting for someone to leave. Shortly after the death of

Stalin, when there was a short-lived relaxation of this strict life, many youth-cafés serving dry wine and coffee were opened. Groups of amateurs appeared to play pop music, and poets recited their own verses. It seemed that a new era of free thought and expression had come. This all appeared quite innocent until the authorities began to realize that the seeds of dissidence were being sown and that they were beginning to sprout. Yevgeny Yevtushenko became the leading light of the angry young men, with his extravagant outbursts and confrontations with the leaders, especially his verbal altercation with Khrushchev. Youth blamed the older generation for allowing the Stalinist repressions and when Yevtushenko declared in one of his poems, 'We shall see to it that this will never happen again,' it became a clarion call. Twenty years have passed and the ominous signs of the Stalin Personality Cult have appeared again. That generation of youth along with Yevtushenko is in middle age now, with greying hair and poor memories.

In those early, lonely days my evenings were spent walking aimlessly up and down the Nevsky Prospekt, the venue for all and sundry. As is so often the case in socialist countries, the crowds were dressed in standard clothes. At that time the men wore open-necked white shirts and dark trousers. The girls, who could not afford or were unable to procure the fashionable dresses of the time, wore white blouses and dark skirts to their knees. The more fortunate ones wore dresses produced by the local factory. They were made of a kind of knitted artificial silk and stretched baggily right down to their heels. A belt in the middle made them look like 'a bed at a flitting', as my mother used to describe it. The shame of it was that most Russian girls had magnificent figures. The moment they put on these bell-tents it was difficult to believe they were the same girls. Although the people are better dressed today, in a utilitarian way, any woman wanting to appear fashionable has a formidable task. She has to have a contact in a Commission Shop where foreign clothes can be bought under the counter, or better still a friend in one of the big dance ensembles or circus companies travelling abroad. A well-known Russian actress once complained to me that as long as she continued to live under socialism, she would never discover whether or not she had taste in clothes.

From time to time I went to concerts and was astounded to learn of the official taboo on Tchaikovsky, who was accused of pandering to the tastes of the aristocracy. One of Glinka's beautiful songs, 'Somnenie', meaning 'Doubts', was prohibited by the censors on the grounds that the great Soviet people had no doubts! As for Bach, the Anti-Religious Society was dead against him. No less ridiculous was the screen of silence around the names of such great envoys of Russian culture as Anna Pavlova, Fedor Chaliapin and Igor Stravinsky, who were considered to be traitors of the Motherland merely because they had no desire to live in a restricted society.

When Chaliapin died the only mention of it in the Soviet media was a two-line report. This was followed the next day with an outrageous article by a Bolshoi Opera Theatre singer, Pirogov, who declared: 'Chaliapin has left nothing to posterity.' Pirogov was, metaphorically speaking, sent to Coventry by the entire musical world, and would have given anything to recant from an article that had obviously been dictated by some official in the Party's Central Committee.

My interest in music continued to grow and one day, I saw a notice of a lecture on classical music to be delivered by a well-known authority, so I hastened to get a couple of tickets. The evening provided yet another example of the enormous gap between revolutionary theory and the Russian character. The first half of the lecture was extremely interesting. The lecturer evidently had deep knowledge of Russian classical music, and he told us many of the stories behind this or that symphony. His illustrations on the piano were excellent. He talked at great length about an opera called *Ivan Susanin* by Glinka which proved, I thought, how little I knew about the composer's works. Only when he sat down to play some pieces from the opera was I able to recognize *A Life For The Tsar*, which I knew fairly well. The second part of the lecture was devoted to modern music. The lecturer had chosen works by Soviet and foreign composers who were dedicated to the Revolution. The music was difficult to follow and there didn't seem to be much melody to it. The lecturer then turned to Western music which he described as decadent rubbish. To allow us to judge for ourselves he played some pieces which seemed to prove his point. But then he announced he would play a piece that was a perfect example of the eroticism, the debauchery and rottenness of Western art, and which would undoubtedly contribute to the downfall of capitalism. He sat down at the piano and began to play the well-known tango 'Jealousy'. For the first time that evening the audience sat up and took notice. The lecturer felt the interest he had aroused, and played with increasing passion. Completely carried away, he thumped the piano with great flourishes of his hands, and reached the climax with a resounding chord. The audience went mad. I have never heard such an ovation. They stamped and clapped and cried 'Bravo' and 'Bis'. The lecturer seemed stunned. As an artist, his whole being thrilled to the raptures of the audience, but as he rose to bow, he seemed to realize the enormity of what he had done—and dashed off the stage. Presumably he wanted to avoid being accused of deliberately spreading Western infection. The organizer of the evening and the Party Secretary tried in vain to stop the ovation, but the more they shouted for quiet the more thunderous were the cries for an encore. The audience dispersed only when the lights in the hall were extinguished. The lecturer was never invited again.

Although I knew of the existence of the Foreign Specialists Club I was not eager to join it. I wanted to become a part of Russian life and get to know Russian people, not Germans or Americans. But one summer evening, bored with my solitary walks up and down the Nevsky, I turned off and went along the embankment enclosing the Fontanka Canal to the Club. It was housed in a splendid old palace which had been restored to its former grandeur to please the foreigners. The magnificent marble staircase was covered in a thick red carpet, and from the high ceilings cut-glass chandeliers glistened brilliantly. There was a notice announcing the first lesson of a Russian language course to begin that evening. I decided to join and get a proper foundation to my knowledge of the language. It was a rather motley gathering, consisting mostly of Germans. A lady announced that she was the teacher. She was obviously a remnant of what was called the *byvshy* class, the former well-to-do and aristocrats. I could see that she had ransacked her wardrobe in order to appear more or less decently dressed. The result appeared very old-fashioned, a blouse with a frilled collar, but she wore it with grace, elegance and a kind of defiant dignity that commanded respect.

There were only two English-speaking pupils in the class, myself and a young girl about eighteen or nineteen years old. She was the first person I noticed when I entered the room. She was lovely. Her blonde hair was tied tightly into a bun which made her look older than her years and more severe. Her dress was distinctively foreign and did credit to her figure. Her name was Helen, and she was a factory worker. She introduced herself to me after the lesson was over.

To this day I cannot describe the relationship that existed between us. There was nothing sexual about it. It was a friendship between two very lonely young people, in a beautiful but amazingly dull city. We clung to one another and were afraid that any crude gesture or thought would create a barrier which might spoil our relationship. The innocence of the relationship was mostly to Helen's credit. She was extremely naive about sexual matters. I was more sophisticated. During my years in London, in communist circles where free love was practised as a protest against the capitalist regime, I'd had my experiences with female comrades and knew what it was to climb down drain-pipes when the comrade-husbands arrived home unexpectedly. Communist husbands were all for free love so long as it did not include their wives.

But Helen was shy, demure and trusting. When she held my hand as we strolled in the park, or gave me an affectionate hug, she reminded me of one of my little sisters. It has to be said that Helen's attitude to sex was purely personal and was typical of neither Soviet youth nor young foreigners. The Revolution had destroyed the patriarchal rituals so religiously practised up to 1917, such as asking parents for permission to marry, weddings in church, bridal veils and so on. Registry offices still existed, but many lived as man and wife without registering, as that was considered to be *otryzhka starovo rezhima*, meaning 'a belch of the old regime'. Even if a young couple did register their marriage, they could just as easily go back the next day and get a divorce. Thus marriage as an institution fell into disuse for many years until the authorities discovered that the rate of population growth had fallen drastically. The older generation looked on these violations of the conventions with extreme disgust and horror. Whenever they could, they tried to return wayward youth to the old paths of a much stricter morality so typical of the Russians. This was proved to me not long after I met Helen.

Many evenings, when we were late in town, I would see Helen home, a forty-minute tram ride. I lived in the city centre, and if I missed the last tram back I had to walk. This was hard, as I had to be up at six in the morning. Helen knew this and often insisted I should go home and not accompany her. I always refused. One night, we left a party in the small hours, to find that the last tram had gone. This meant that I would have to walk Helen home and then come all the way back myself. We both had the same thought in our minds, but I was the first to broach the delicate subject.

'You know, Helen, if you're not afraid, we could sleep the night at my place.'

From the way she opened her eyes wide I couldn't tell whether she was shocked or pleased.

'Afraid? Of what?' she replied, just like that, without the slightest trace of affectation.

'Well, I mean to say . . . you know . . .' The more I blundered on the worse it sounded. 'I will sleep on the floor, of course!'

'The only thing I'm afraid of is that you won't sleep well. Your bed is too narrow for both of us.'

Helen had been to the flat before, and they all knew her, but I was apprehensive about how they would take to the idea of her sleeping in my room. The door was opened by old Dedushka, in his coarse linen underwear. He was still half-asleep and seemed not to hear my explanations about the last tram having gone, how Helen would sleep in my room and how I would sleep on the floor. I ushered Helen into my room and gave her a pair of my pyjamas. The old man called me into the corridor as if I was his own grandson, and taking me by the arm, led me into the dining-room. He showed me a pillow and blanket lying on the divan and muttered something in French or German. I gathered that Granny would not be pleased if I slept with Helen, even on the floor. Then giving me a knowing man-to-man look of commiseration, he waddled off to bed. I went to tell Helen of this turn of affairs, to find her fast asleep. Thus all the rules of propriety were observed.

Helen's mother, a Polish American, was one of those enthusiasts for the First Workers' and Peasants' State, and much to the detriment of her family, had applied for Soviet citizenship, which was granted immediately. As a result she had poor ration cards and a small room with no furniture. If she had retained her American passport she would have been given the much better Insnab ration cards for foreign workers and a more comfortable place to live in for herself and her three children. Although I criticized her then, I made the same stupid mistake of applying for Soviet citizenship seven years later. I ought to have known better.

I had the bright idea of taking Helen to Party Headquarters in the Smolny Institute to see whether I could win over the Hungarian Chief of the International Department. I could not understand why Helen and her family were not entitled to foreigners' rations. After all, they were Americans. We arranged to meet in October Station Square one morning. When I saw Helen crossing the open space, I could not help admiring her. She had put on an American frock which made her stand out vividly among the badly dressed crowd.

But despite the brilliant sunshine she looked pale, and when I suggested we walk to the Smolny as it was such a lovely morning, she said she preferred to go by tram as she was not feeling well. I could have kicked myself for not realizing that quite probably she had had no breakfast that day. Then there was the anxiety of the forthcoming interview which she wanted to be over as quickly as possible. She kept on repeating that nothing would come of it, as they had applied many times and had been refused foreigners' rations.

'You are a foreigner just the same as I am. So why shouldn't you get the same treatment?' I protested.

'We are Soviet citizens. It was a terrible mistake of Mother's. We could have done the same work and remained American citizens and been respected more for it.'

This seemed to me to be ridiculous.

'But by becoming Soviet citizens you ought to be respected *more*, because it is such a splendid gesture.'

'There is nothing splendid about it. We are worse off in everything. Even at the plant where Mother works as an interpreter for an American engineer she is not allowed to take her meals in the canteen with him. They have a separate hall for the foreigners and management.'

This was true. They had the same system at my plant. My idea of socialism was equality for all and I couldn't reconcile myself to this contradiction. So I had my meals in the common hall with my mates. They of course thought I was an idiot: the food was disgusting and I had great difficulty in keeping to my convictions. Then one day I went to dinner, suffering from stomach pains, and saw fish eyes floating in the watery soup. I gave in.

I tried to ignore these inconsistencies. Helen on the other hand was not impressed by my egalitarian principles.

'I don't believe in all these poppycock Utopian ideas about equality. People are people and there will always be those who want to be better off than others, and communism can't change human nature,' she said. We were sitting on a bench in the gardens of the Smolny. The Hungarian Chief had been called away to a meeting and, as usual, everybody had to wait. I tried to reason with her.

'The State is young yet, and the people are illiterate. Give the new regime time and things will change. Then it'll be easier to put their ideals into practice.'

Helen was not to be put off. She was irritable, a state I rarely saw her in.

'I don't care what you say. When a little child gets a bad habit it must be stopped at the beginning; later on it becomes harder to get rid of it. This business of differentiating between people at such an early stage will grow and create a privileged class some day.'

When I became a Soviet citizen a few years later I realized how right she was. The privileged class has grown since and it exists today in the professional Party and State officialdom, whose members enjoy all the benefits of society so long as they adhere strictly to the Party line. Should they do anything to break the law they will get an admonitory finger waved at them and be moved up to a higher position. Years after I went to live in the Soviet Union, there was a perfect example of this. The President of the Moscow City Council, the City's Mayor in the 1960s, was caught redhanded in a gigantic bribes scandal. He had been handing out free State flats. In a raid on his house, over a million roubles were found behind the radiators. Not a word appeared in the media, but the underground communication system among the Muscovites operated admirably as usual, and we all knew everything down to the smallest detail. The affair was hushed up and the millionaire Mayor was quietly moved to another high post as First Secretary of some provincial Party Committee. After a few years he re-appeared in Moscow—as a Deputy Minister!

At last, our Hungarian bureaucrat arrived back at his desk, and after waiting in the queue, we finally entered his office. I was eloquent about the dire state of affairs in Helen's family. He listened attentively and with sympathy, and declared that something had to be done about it. He reached for his note-book, wrote Helen's name and asked for her passport. When she handed him her Soviet internal passport he didn't even bother to take it from her.

'What? Are you a Soviet citizen?' he exclaimed loudly.

Helen explained how her American passport had been taken away from her.

'We can do nothing for you!' He slapped his note-book shut as if we had been trying to make a fool of him. I intervened.

'But she is American and a foreigner just as I am. Why should she have to suffer for the mistake her mother made?'

That was a statement I should not have made.

'So you consider her mother made a mistake by becoming a Soviet citizen, do you?' His tone was aggressive.

'No, I don't. It is you who consider she made a mistake and have left her and her family in such straitened conditions.'

'All our people are living in such conditions.'

I had no answer to that. I changed my tactics and soon our talk became more amicable. He did take Helen's name down and promised to help, a promise which he in fact kept. Helen's mother was given the engineer's ration cards and a pass to the canteen. The plant helped with some furniture. As we left his office, the Chief called me back.

'That's a very nice girl of yours. Is she your sweetheart?'

I was surprised at this unexpected question and hurriedly replied, 'Why, no! She's my friend and I wanted to help her. Why do you ask?'

'I wanted to suggest you should marry her. As your wife she could be included in your Insnab cards. Think about it. I can help.'

Helen was indignant when I told her what he said.

'I wouldn't dream of it! What would you think of me if I were to marry you for your ration cards? Anyway, we have nowhere to live.'

I pretended to be offended.

'What a way to put it, you'd think I wasn't good enough to marry you.'

We had returned to the bench in the Smolny Gardens and there were quite a number of people around. Kissing and hugging in public in those days was strictly taboo, but Helen seized my face and kissed me heartily. Then she began to reproach me.

'How could you say such a thing! I don't know much about love, I mean the sort of love that makes you want to marry. I have a special feeling for you which I have never felt for anyone in my life, possibly because I've never been so grateful for such a friendship as yours.' She looked at me. 'Tell me, is that love?'

With the presumptuousness of the young, I wagged my head sagaciously and gave her a laconic, and as it seemed to me, a complete answer.

'No, it isn't.'

'Then what is?'

'I don't know.'

'Do you love me?'

'Yes!'

'How?'

'I don't know. Do you love me?'

'Yes. And I don't know why either.'

After this profound discussion, we rose hastily, fearing that we might spoil a splendid friendship. Many, many years later I could have answered Helen. I had discovered that if you can tell explicitly why you love someone it means you don't love them at all.

THREE

Hard Times

One day in the autumn there came a change in my life at the plant when Sergei called me to his office.

'A new worker has arrived from America,' he told me, 'he's a qualified tradesman and worked at the Lockheed Aviation Plant. The trouble is he doesn't speak Russian and we can't afford to keep a special interpreter for him. So I want you to go to work in the assembly shop with him. You're beginning to speak Russian quite well, so you can help us out and at the same time you'll be earning more money.'

I met the American the next day. He was Italian by birth and had only lived in the States for a few years. His name was Petranio. He turned up in a white boiler-suit with the name 'Lockheed' stitched on its back. He seemed extremely proud of this, and since the Russian workers and I wore dark blue boiler-suits, with no names on their backs, he stuck out like a sore thumb. Apart from knowing his job and possessing this boiler-suit, he had nothing much more to boast of. He was of a very low intellect and spoke English like all the Italian comedians I have ever seen in films. He was vindictive, vicious and vain. He was of medium height, thin and wiry, with a tight-lipped mouth. From all this, you may gather I didn't like Petranio, and the feeling was entirely mutual.

The aircraft produced by the plant were for training purposes and were about one rung up the evolutionary ladder from the Wright Brothers' prototype. The wings, fuselage and body were all made of plywood, covered with a specially treated canvas. All this was put together in the carpentry shop and was then moved along to us in the assembly shop where we fitted on the engines, the chassis and the steering wires. Everything was extremely primitive. The shock-absorbers were made of thick elastic cords wound on by a young peasant who could neither read nor write but had biceps like a weightlifter. The tools, too, were as primitive as the methods. This gave Petranio an advantage. He had brought a large kit of modern tools from America.

It was Petranio's tools that caused the trouble. He and I were in a work-team of ten men. Our fellow workers could not keep up with the pace we set thanks to Petranio's speedier and easier tools. The carpenters couldn't make the bodies and fuselages in sufficient quantity to keep up with us, and the men who came after us in the production line had neither the strength (they were all under-fed), the ability, nor the tools to cope with what we passed on to them. On top of this, Petranio was constantly complaining to the management that he wasn't earning enough. I was the target for much of his irritation as I tried to explain the Russian workers' side of the story to him. He didn't want to know. The unfortunate part of it was that the management and the Party were on his side.

It was now that I learned the truth behind the propaganda that Soviet workers and farmers have an equal say in running the factory or farm. Disraeli said, 'My idea of an agreeable person is a person who agrees with me,' and that sums up exactly the position of the Soviet working class in running the economy. So long as they agree with the Party line, they have a say; if they don't then they have no say. Even the trade unions are in the same position. There is a popular Russian joke that illustrates the situation vividly.

A Western correspondent declared that he did not believe in the Soviet workers' absolute adherence to the Party line. So he was allowed to address the workers in a factory. Speaking into a microphone, he declared that the Party had increased working hours. There was no response from the audience. 'Your wages are to be cut by half!' he said. Still no response. 'No holidays for the next ten years!' Nothing. In desperation he cried out, 'You are all to be hanged tomorrow at dawn!' To his delight a worker turned from his lathe and raised his hand. 'Do you protest?' the correspondent asked hopefully. 'Oh, no,' was the reply, 'we want to know if you have enough rope for all of us or do we have to bring our own?'

Petranio and I were awarded the title of *udarnik* (outstanding worker), and our photos were printed in the factory newspaper. The call was issued to follow our example, which made me rather proud of myself, until I discovered that we had aroused a great deal of hostility among our mates. The management and the Party decided

to increase productivity by at least 50 per cent, a physical impossibility. Our Foreman approached us and asked us not to agree
to the increase. We were on piecework, and he explained that if we
fulfilled the 50 per cent target for the next month, the management
would cut the rate paid for the job. That would mean working
harder for the same wages. I could not believe the Party would allow
this, and went to see the Party Secretary, Sergei. But he had gone to
Moscow on a course, so there was no one with whom to discuss the
matter.

Petranio was all for signing the document, and with some
misgivings, I signed it too. We fulfilled our quota for that month.
To Petranio's satisfaction our rates were not touched and we had a
bigger pay packet. Petranio now decided to raise output to 100 per
cent, which we did, but with difficulty. Our photographs appeared
on the Honours Board again, and then the management did exactly
what our Foreman had prophesied. They cut the rates and our pay
was reduced at a stroke to the old level. Petranio raised hell, but his
protestations were met with blank poker faces. Meanwhile, our
fellow workers ostracized us completely.

When Sergei returned from Moscow I spoke to him, but he just
shrugged his shoulders. He said there was nothing he could do
about it. Then he suggested a way out.

'If you could persuade Petranio to let our designers copy his
tools, we could produce them ourselves. Then the Russian workers
could increase their own productivity.'

'But what's the use if the norms are increased to keep wages
down?' I protested.

'That's our problem and we'll take care of that part of the
business. Your job as our comrade is to get those tools copied.'

Petranio wouldn't hear of it and locked his tools away even from
me. I approached Sergei with the proposal that Petranio be given
some kind of payment which might possibly get us out of the
deadlock. Sergei agreed that it was a good idea and promised to
speak to the Head Book-keeper. Petranio demanded twenty-five
roubles for each tool, and as he had about a hundred, the total
amounted to 2,500 roubles, the equivalent of a year's wages. I
pointed this out to Sergei.

'Never mind,' he said, 'don't put him off. The main thing is to get
the designs.'

Within a week the new tools began to appear, poorer in quality,
but definitely superior to the old primitive ones. Everybody was

pleased, except Petranio. Although the plant management had agreed to pay him his 2,500 roubles, a higher central organization vetoed the idea on the grounds that there was no legal statute that allowed payment for copying tools. Bureaucracy had done its work.

Petranio went berserk but there was nothing he could do. So he decided to take it out on me, as the initiator of the whole idea. He had only been at the factory a few months but was already extremely unpopular. Things came to boiling-point one day when we were working under a chassis and I asked him to pass me a screw-driver. With a bad-tempered snort he threw the tool at me and the sharp point struck me just under the eye. A little higher and I would have looked like Horatio Nelson for the rest of my life. In a second I was on my feet and laying into Petranio.

At school in Glasgow, our physical instructor had been a boxing enthusiast, and most of his lessons were devoted to that sport. At first, Petranio and I slammed at one another like a couple of Irish navvies, until I realized that my only chance of winning the fight was to use my boxing training. He was taller than me, so I concentrated on his body. His wild swings were easy to avoid and I began to backstep and retaliate with body blows. Petranio became enraged. This was just what I wanted. It is fatal to lose your temper in boxing. I got my chance when he swung a right hander at me. I side-stepped and caught him in the solar plexus. He doubled up like a pen-knife.

All work had been suspended during the fight, the workers standing at a respectable distance, watching silently, making no attempt to interfere. Instinctively, I felt that they were on my side and when I got in the final blow, I heard a murmur of 'Molodets', which means 'Good for you'. Petranio got to his feet and stumbled off to the lavatories. I was left standing alone in the middle of a circle, my face covered with blood from the wound below my eye. The workers looked at me, and only when I sat down wearily on a box did they disperse.

The news spread fast that the two foreigners in the assembly shop had been fighting, and the first to arrive on the scene was Rita. No sooner did she see me sitting there, wiping the blood from my face, than she began to scold me. Despite my protestations she dragged me off to the factory clinic where the doctors cleaned my face—the wound could hardly be seen. Medical supplies were very poor and there was no sticking plaster, so they wound about a mile of bandage round my head, making me look like the victim of a multiple car crash. I tore the bandage off as soon as I left the surgery—everyone would have thought that it was I who had lost the fight, which was the last thing I wanted.

Rita was waiting for me when I got back and I came in for another scolding: I ought to be ashamed of myself for fighting like a street urchin. The whole plant had heard about the disgusting brawl. All I wanted to know was whether they all knew who won.

'Of course they all know. Just the same, you had no right to settle the argument by fighting.' I pointed to the wound under my eye. 'That was no argument. I could have lost an eye.'

At that moment Sergei appeared, looking very belligerent. 'I want to see you, Comrade C'mbell!'

I didn't like the tone of 'comrade', and felt I was in for trouble. I was. Sergei attacked me the minute we entered his office.

'What kind of a young communist are you, teaching our youth to beat each other up? It is against our ideals and principles.'

'I don't know much about your ideals,' I said, 'but nobody's going to poke my eye out and get away with it. An eye for an eye and a tooth for a tooth.'

'Don't you start quoting the Bible to me,' the Party Secretary cried. 'What with fighting and trying to spread religious teaching, you're going to get me into trouble. I know Petranio is a bloody nuisance but we need him. What kind of a Five Year Plan can we fulfil if you two keep on fighting?'

'The Plan doesn't depend on us two. Anyway, there won't be any more scrapping. Petranio has had his fill and he'll leave me alone in future. I had to fight to get that.'

After I had promised there would be no more trouble, Sergei and I went to the canteen for dinner. We had just sat down when the plant's Sports Secretary came over to us.

'Listen, Bill, they tell me you put on a fine exhibition of boxing today. The whole plant's talking about it. Where did you learn to box? We'd like to start a boxing club. Could you help, maybe show the lads the basics?'

'I don't know whether I can,' I replied. 'The Party is against boxing. You'll have to ask permission from Sergei here. He has just made me promise not to fight again.'

Sergei laughed loudly at this and wagged his finger at me.

'Just look at this fellow! He's only been in our country about six months and he's already as cunning as a Tambov peasant. There's a difference between boxing and fighting. I'm all for boxing.'

So among my many other activities I now had to teach boxing. I didn't mind doing this. I had decided from the very beginning to throw in my lot with the Russians whom I admired for their fortitude under the hard life with all its privations. I wanted to help and not to be thought of as *chuzhoi*, 'a stranger'. I began to feel I was becoming *svoi*, 'one of our own', and I liked it. As a result I came into contact with some of the better-known Soviet athletes of the time. Unlike today, Soviet achievements in sport were mediocre in those days and there was not a single athlete of European, let alone world, class in the country. The first Soviet world champions appeared fifteen years later, after the war, when Mihail Botvinnik won the world chess title in 1948 and Maria Isakova became World Speed-skating Champion in the same year.

The backwardness of Soviet sport can be judged by the appearance in 1933 in the Soviet Union of the world middleweight boxing champion, Marcel Thil of France. He was forty-two at the time. The organizers made the mistake they are still apt to make now, by advertising the contests as a chance for Soviet boxers to show that they can hold their own with the world's best. The first bout was held in the Moscow State Circus. The first two rounds were enough to demonstrate the gigantic difference in class between the Russian and the Frenchman. Imagine the audience's surprise when Thil stopped boxing and began to give the Soviet lad a lesson in technique, which the latter, to his credit, took in good spirit. The remaining matches were held in the Central Park and were called exhibition bouts.

Many years later, when I added the title 'sports-writer' to my many professions, I had a behind-the-scenes view of the intrigues and scandals in Soviet sport. These are always strictly hidden from the public. Not a word was published, for instance, when the lovely Inga Artamonova, Absolute World Speed-skating Champion for a number of years, was stabbed to death by her husband, Voronin, also a speed-skating champion. She was a lesbian and was 'married' to another female athlete. Artamonova concealed her 'marriage' for fear of losing the splendid flat which she and Voronin had been given. When Voronin discovered her secret, he begged her to give up her other 'husband', but in vain. When he found them together in bed, he seized a kitchen knife and attacked both of them. Inga died immediately. Voronin was tried in some village court, to avoid publicity, and was sentenced to eight years. Inga's lover did not appear in court. It was a well-known fact that this woman was a hermaphrodite, but the Sports Committee kept it quiet. If the truth had leaked out, her world sporting records would have been annulled.

I knew quite a few Soviet women athletes, with international titles and records, who were active lesbians or hermaphrodites, but the authorities strictly forbade any mention of this and countered any move to exclude them from competition sport. It was only in the 1960s, when the Committee of the European Games insisted on a complete examination of all female participants by a medical panel, that a number of famous Olympic champions were discreetly withdrawn by the Soviet Sports Committee.

Although I am a racing cyclist, most of my sporting activities in the plant were confined to football and boxing. Only once did I enter a road race, but that was enough. In a fit of weakness, I agreed to take part in a 100 kilometre road race. My machine, a 'Selbach', was the only lightweight racing cycle in the field. All the other riders were mounted on heavy bicycles like bedsteads on wheels. The manufacture of cycles was limited to a few small workshops where they were made by hand. The Sports Committee did buy a few dozen racing cycles of foreign make, but these were given only to champions and were ridden only on the track.

The word 'road' in Russia then and, for that matter, now, has to be qualified for Western readers, for Russian roads bear little resemblance to those of the industrialized world.

We started off in town where even though the streets were paved with cobbles the road surface was not so bad. The real test came when we left the city and emerged on to what is still called the Moscow Highway. An eighteenth-century revolutionary writer called Radischev, who was later exiled to Siberia, wrote a book entitled *A Journey from Petersburg to Moscow* which became a Russian classic. Radischev used the account of a coach journey from city to city to describe the terrible lot of the serfs he encountered along the way. The only apparent changes 200 years later as I picked my way along part of the same road were that Petersburg had been renamed Leningrad, and the serfs were now called *kolkhozniki*, collective farmers.

The Moscow Highway was a dusty country track winding its way over open plains and up and down hills. As I rattled along on my lightweight cycle I felt as if I had a pneumatic drill in my hands instead of handlebars. When I halted to repair the inevitable puncture, the rest of the field, who were riding Russian-built bicycles, much better suited for this safari, clattered past me. Soon I was alone, except for an elderly peasant sitting by the roadside. He was a burly man with an unkempt beard. Beside him lay a bundle of chopped wood and an ugly-looking hatchet. He watched me as I changed my tubular tyre, and soon began to make comments which I barely understood. But I gathered that he thought I was an idiot and didn't know how to change a tyre. All Russians consider it their duty to interfere in anything and everything, however profound their ignorance. However, I was in far too much of a hurry to take any notice of him. But soon he began to get angry and tried to pull the wheel out of my hands. I pushed him away and told him to mind his own business. The tyre was exceptionally tight and I was having difficulty rolling it on to the wheel. To my horror the burly peasant picked up his hatchet.

I wasn't quite sure whether he wanted to ease the tyre on with it or hack me to pieces but I didn't wait to find out. I picked up the cycle, the wheel, the tyre and the pump and cantered off down the dusty track. At a safe distance, I finished the change and pedalled off. When I met the rest of the field on their way back, I gave up the race and joined them. As we passed the peasant trudging along, he dropped his bundle and waved his axe at me, shouting insults. My fellow riders roared with laughter, which added to my discomfiture and lowered my prestige as the 'foreigner on the foreign cycle'. About ten miles from town I got another puncture and as I had no spares, had to walk all the way back to town with the bike on my shoulders. After that I gave up road-racing in Russia.

Gradually I was getting a clear idea of my new country. I discovered that one of the prime characteristics of the Russians is their fanatical love of children. In Russia everything is for the children. Party propaganda continually declares that every care must be lavished on the 'future generation'. When the 'future generation' grows to become the 'present generation', Party propaganda loses all interest.

When oranges appear for sale in Moscow—an infrequent event— long queues form whatever the season. Mothers or grandparents will suffer an interminable vigil for the sake of their children, ready to buy as many oranges as possible, since they consider them to be the most beneficial fruit of all. No adult will ever eat an orange himself if he has a family. And every member of the long queue will ask the shop assistant, in a wheedling voice, to put the best oranges on the scales as they are 'for the children'.

The economics and corruption in the orange trade is a study in itself, and since it is still thriving in the Soviet Union, worth a brief digression. Oranges are usually sold on makeshift stalls or tables on the streets, rarely in proper shops. They are packed in standard boxes weighing twenty-five kilos, and the price is one rouble forty kopeks per kilo, or forty-nine pence per pound. Of this the porter has to have his share, which ranges from five to ten roubles. The stallholder always has a 'protector' or 'pimp' standing nearby, ready to deal with over-vehement customers, who throw the spoiled oranges off the scales and demand good ones. The stallholders are allowed 14 per cent off the bulk for spoiled goods. They will naturally try to foist the rotten fruit on to the customer so that they can pocket the 14 per cent.

Their best customers are provincial black-marketeers. In the provinces oranges never appear in the shops. The stallholders are 'strictly forbidden' to sell the oranges to these black-marketeers, but a couple of winks to the salesgirl and her pimp picks up a whole box of oranges and carries it round the corner where the transaction takes place. The black marketeer pays fifty roubles per box instead of thirty-five and in turn sells the oranges at six or seven roubles a kilo, raking in a profit of a hundred roubles, the official monthly wage of the salesgirl he bought them from. She, by such illegal transactions and under-weighing, can put aside as much as 300 roubles in a day. By the time she has given the shop manager and his deputy their shares as well as the 'pimp' and the porters, she can reckon on making a hundred roubles, her month's wages. Everybody is satisfied, even the customers who are overjoyed, despite the fraud, to have got oranges for their 'future generation'.

In my first couple of years in Russia, until 1934, I became accustomed to the shortages of all food, not only oranges. Although apples could be bought on the *kolkhoz*, or peasant markets, the price was ridiculously inflated. The campaign of terror, which I witnessed, to force the peasants to join collective farms had only just started, and very few of them were willing volunteers. Although they had received their land free, the peasants were not as enthusiastic about the Five Year Plan as the workers, and rightly so. Theirs was back-breaking manual work around the clock. There were almost no tractors, and the Five Year Plan made no provision even for the most basic implements. Worse, their grain and livestock were constantly being 'confiscated' by what were called the *prod otryad*, looting raids on barns and homes to extort 'surpluses'. It seemed there would never be an end to the shortages while this continued. In fact, these *prod otryads* often took the whole harvest, including sowing-seed.

Conditions in the cities were in many ways even more appalling than in the countryside. I found that one of the most tragic and terrifying aspects of city life was the vast number of the *bezprizorni*, homeless children, who had lost their parents in the World War or in the Civil War. The Government was simply unable to cater for these millions of ragged, filthy, desperately starving children who roamed the streets in gangs, robbing and killing. In Leningrad when the River Neva melted in the spring, hundreds of dead bodies floated up from under the broken ice, bearing the hallmarks of the *bezprizorni*, stab-wounds or marks of strangulation. Prostitution was also rife, and ten- to twelve-year-olds sold their bodies on the streets. If any Government policy was really genuine, it was the plan to help these children. But of all the organizations commissioned to perform the task, the choice of the Cheka (or KGB as it is now known), was the most unfortunate. The Cheka was headed by the most ruthless of the Party leaders, Felix Dzerzhinsky, and the mass of the people, especially the *bezprizorni*, hated it. When captured, they fought like tigers, using every trick in the book to free themselves. Many a militiaman lost his life or received terrible wounds from the knives that these children wielded with such dexterity.

Helen and I were strolling in a side street off the Nevsky Prospekt one evening when we saw a crowd standing at the railings of a churchyard. We could hear shouts of indignation and anger, so we crossed the street to find out what was going on. We squeezed our way through the crush and on reaching the railings saw that two or three *bezprizorni* had been collared by the militia. Although they seemed to have surrendered, the militiamen were still beating them up. One of them had a boy face down on the ground and was twisting his arm behind his back. The boy was screaming with pain as the man kept pulling him off the ground by his arm. Everybody around was shouting at him to stop torturing the boy, but they did nothing to interfere. This was understandable with an organization like the Cheka.

Partly from genuine anger and partly so as to show off to Helen, I hopped over the railings, rushed up to the militiaman, and tried to drag him off. I didn't help the boy much; in fact the more I pulled at the militiaman, the harder he twisted the boy's arm. Then suddenly he released the boy and struck me on the chest. I stumbled and fell. To my horror, I saw that the boy had a knife in his hand and was getting ready to jump on me. I had enough sense to roll over as he lunged. In fact, as he dived, he dropped the knife, which I grabbed. Instead, the boy started biting and scratching, but the militiaman hauled him off and I was able to get to my feet, the knife still in my hand. Reinforcements arrived and the next I knew I was being marched off to the militia station, along with the *bezprizorni*.

I could see Helen tearfully trying to convince the captain I was not with the *bezprizorni* and that I had only been trying to help the militia. I shouted to her to contact David Blaize, the Chairman of the Leningrad Trade Union Council, whom I knew very well. Things looked bad. I was being accused of interfering with the militia in the course of their duty, and of trying to knife one of them. I pretended I knew no Russian. I could see that the militia captain was perplexed. He was sensible enough to hold me in his office, while the boys were confined to cells. The hours passed, it began to get dark, and there was no sign of Helen or of David Blaize. Nobody took any notice of me. I was beginning to realize what a fool I had been. Just after midnight, Blaize arrived with Helen trailing behind him. Blaize soon cleared things up and once he had given the unfortunate militia captain a piece of his mind, we all marched triumphantly out of the station. I tried to insist that the militiaman should be punished for undue cruelty to the boy, but Blaize advised me to forget it, and to consider myself lucky to have got off so lightly. 'And keep clear of the *bezprizorni*, if you don't want to go to a communist heaven.' When I got over the shock later, I realized the significance of his warning. After that I always avoided the *bezprizorni*.

One day, at the height of winter, I was on my way to visit some friends in the Hotel Astoria in the square opposite the magnificent St Isaac's Cathedral. On Gertzen Street, I saw a number of militiamen struggling with the *bezprizorni*. Two boys and a girl were lying dead on the cobbles. At first I thought they had been killed during the fight, but it appeared that they had all climbed into an underground communications tunnel in search of warmth. There was a gas leak down there, and only one of them had managed to clamber out and call for help. At first, the passers-by took no notice of him; on the contrary, they steered well clear of him.

Eventually someone did have the sense to telephone for the militia. A whole unit appeared on the scene, and at the risk of their lives dragged the children out of the tunnel. Three of them were dead, and the others were in a bad state, but even in a semi-conscious condition they tried to fight off the militia. The *bezprizorni* were prepared to die rather than go to the Orphan Homes where they would be disciplined, washed, fed and educated to be good communist citizens. Of the two evils, they preferred their terrible freedom.

As that first Russian winter began to make itself felt, I realized that I was in trouble. During the preparations for a hurried departure from London, I hadn't given proper thought to the severity of the Russian winter, and now I found that my English overcoat and cap were by no means sufficient protection from the cold blasts and frosts of Leningrad. Even worse, I had not known that it was essential to procure firewood in the summer. Now I had no wood to burn in the stove in my room. These stoves, called Dutch stoves, were built into the wall and kept the air pleasantly dry and warm. It was a pleasure to come in and out of the frost and warm your back against it. Old Dedushka lit my stove once a week, not so much out of consideration for my comfort as to ward off the damp, which might otherwise spread all over the flat. Our relationship was changing. Nina had gone with her little daughter to London where Misha was still working in the Soviet Trade Mission. No longer was there any supper left for me. The old arrangement whereby I handed over my Insnab food and clothes cards, paying fifty roubles a month for my board, was losing its worth as the food problem had become worse and the rations for foreign workers had been curtailed. So I became more dependent upon the plant canteen. My digestion began to give way under the strain of poor-quality food, badly cooked. It got so bad that the doctors decided to put me in hospital to be 'analysed' as they put it. This episode made me realize how much further Russia's development had to go, at least in medicine.

I arrived in the morning and entered a small building near the gates. I had a tooth-brush, tooth-paste, slippers and a pair of pyjamas. The registration clerk took my doctor's certificate and told me to wait. I said I was feeling unwell and would she please speed things up, but my plea fell on deaf ears. I sat down and began idly to read the notices recommending the advantages of cleaning one's teeth, washing hands before meals, and feet before going to bed. I nearly fell off my chair when I read 'Corpses are issued from four to six o'clock!'

Eventually my name was called, and a nurse took me into another room and told me to undress. I was led to the bathroom where three old men were waiting for a fourth to finish his bath. From the look of them, they had reached a condition where they could easily have been 'issued between four and six' without bothering the doctors or staff. The nurse gave me a small bottle of paraffin and told me to rub it on my head and rinse it off under a tap. I tried to protest, but it was pointless. In the next room I was issued with the most amazing linen outfit I had ever seen in my life: a pair of coarse linen underpants with strings at the bottom to tie round the ankles, a smock of the same material, a pair of well-worn slippers and a dressing-gown of indefinite colour and vintage, patched and covered with dozens of stamped markings. I looked like a badly wrapped parcel.

By this time almost all my resistance was gone. But when the nurse opened the door and pointed to the main building a hundred yards away I protested. The snow was knee-deep, and the temperature around fifteen degrees below zero. Finally, in an effort to get rid of me, they lent me the janitor's sheepskin coat, felt boots and fur hat, all of which smelt as if they had come out of the Ark with Noah. But this was nothing compared to the smell in the wards. There were thirty patients in a room that could have held six conveniently. The only possible entry for fresh air was through a small window called a *fortochka*. It was supposed to be opened twice a day for fifteen minutes, but no sooner did the nurse open it and go off on some other business than some patient would leap on to a chair to close it.

Worse than the stench was the din. Russians always tend to be noisy but are even more so in places where silence is particularly desirable. Doctors shouted down the corridors, nurses answered them in kind, patients bellowed to one another across the ward. Someone was reading the newspaper out loud, at the top of his voice. This was common practice at the time as most of the peasants were illiterate. In a word, pandemonium.

I could not but marvel at the way in which the doctors managed to work under such circumstances. There was a chronic lack of drugs, medicines, instruments and experienced staff; many of the doctors and nurses looked so frail from undernourishment as to need treatment themselves. I got on very well with the staff, one of whom could speak English. In the quiet of the evening they would invite me into their Common Room where they asked me to tell them about life in Britain, about literature and the arts, and once more to try to answer the eternal question: 'When is there going to be a revolution in Britain?'

After a time, I got used to the noise and artless sociability of these simple people. Most of all I enjoyed listening to the tales told by the patients, peasants mainly. They spoke of the drudgery under the Tsars, but they would add with a sigh that the drive for collectivization was like changing 'a sixpence for a tanner'.

'Under the Tsar it was terrible, but a loaf of bread cost four kopeks. Now it costs sixty!'

The upheaval of the Revolution had brought internal conflict to the Russian family. Fathers fought against sons, brothers against brothers, and all in the name of the Motherland. One man, who looked at least seventy but assured me he was only forty, told us of his neighbour, a peasant who had worked hard all his life, had never drunk or smoked, and had managed to build a good house and secure a better life. He was a good father and his family had grown up to work on the land. His brother was called up and served in the Navy. He returned one day leading a *prod otryad*. The ex-sailor succeeded in confiscating all his brother's grain, having re-membered all the hiding-places. In a fit of fury at the betrayal, the peasant seized a shot-gun and first shot his brother and then himself. The tragedy was that the brother did not die, but recovered to be hailed as a hero, while the peasant's family was banished to Siberia and his land confiscated. These stories reminded me that there are always two sides to a coin. Although I sympathized with the peasants who had been caught up in this maelstrom, I felt more for the workers whom I knew better. It seemed unfair that they should suffer semi-starvation while food was stored away in peasants' barns.

Helen visited me a number of times in hospital. She was not feeling well herself: not only was malnutrition having its effect, but also the doctors had found something wrong with her lungs and advised a complete change of climate and an improved diet with plenty of meat and fresh vegetables.

'I must go back to the States,' she said, 'I don't know how, but I must. I have some relatives left there and I'm sure they'll help me until I get on to my feet. I must leave this country. I feel I'm sentencing myself to death.'

I did my best to console her. 'Wait until I get out and we'll look for some way out. I'll write home. Maybe things have changed there and we could go together. If they won't let you out, we could get married.' We left it at that.

I came out of hospital at the end of January 1933, when the winter was at its coldest. I made my way to the Hotel Astoria, where a friend of mine, Maurice, an American engineer, was living. He insisted that I stay with him in the hotel. He was leaving for the States in a couple of days as he had ended his contract. Maurice was only twenty-eight and had graduated in America as a road-building engineer. 'I came to help,' he told me, 'but feel like a parasite. I was taught to build roads with machinery and I found they hadn't got any here. I don't know how to command hundreds of men working with picks and shovels. I'm giving up and going home.' I saw him off at the Baltic Station, and as the train started to move, he stood on the steps and said, 'I'll probably never see you again. My advice to you is to get out of here as soon as you can. This is a cemetery. We were not made for such hardships. Get out before they carry you out. Goodbye!'

As I walked back to the Astoria, I made up my mind to go home. I could spend the night in Maurice's room. It had been paid for until the next day. Maurice had left some food behind, together with an electric kettle, so I made myself a pot of tea and dined on a hunk of bread and a tin of meat and rice. I could hear the sound of voices coming from the corridor, which only added to my feeling of loneliness. I hadn't been in Russia a year but already I wanted to go home. My stubborn determination to prove my father wrong had disappeared. I just wanted to be back with my family, to eat a good steak and kidney pudding and forget the frosts. I didn't regret I had come. I had known a fine, brave people who had been kind to me but, as Maurice said, we were not made for such hardships. I reckoned the Soviets would have to build communism without my help. To cheer myself, I picked up my ukulele and began to sing a few songs from my not very extensive repertoire. I was halfway through a sad love song I'd learned when I heard a knock at the door. When I opened it, my whole life changed.

FOUR

Villi, the Red Star

I opened the door to see three young men dressed in identical quiet grey suits. One of them, a stout chap, asked me if I spoke German. I answered, 'Nein'. After this asinine reply, I hastened to inform them, in Russian, that I was English. The portly man, whose name I learned was Leonid Dietrichs, and who was the son of a rich pre-Revolutionary piano manufacturer, continued in English.

'We were passing and heard your gramophone playing. We are musicians from the restaurant downstairs. Do you mind if we listen to your records?'

I shrugged my shoulders in the continental manner I had acquired, and told them I had no gramophone. Dietrichs' face expressed bewilderment. 'But we heard someone singing in English and we thought . . .'

'Oh, that was me singing,' I said, softening to their interest. 'But come in.'

After that I didn't need much coaxing to sing to them. I have always loved singing. When we lived in Anderston I used to sing while I washed the dishes by the kitchen window. I sang soulful ditties such as 'Who's Sorry Now?' or 'I'm Only a Bird in a Golden Cage', putting plenty of sob in my voice, something my mother abhorred. She was, after all, a good pianist and had excellent musical taste.

After a while my visitors excused themselves, saying that their break was over, but they asked permission to return later with their leader. I was surprised when I saw him. Ury Landsberg looked more like a slovenly dressed scientist than the leader of a jazz orchestra. In fact he was a brilliant biologist, though his true love was jazz. After listening to me, he asked if I would like to go down and sing in the hotel with the orchestra there and then. I was amazed that they thought I was anywhere near good enough and I objected, saying I had no other clothes with me except the ones I had on, baggy flannels, an army khaki shirt and a pullover.

'That's all right,' Landsberg said in his excellent English, 'the band sits between two marble columns and you can stand behind one of them and nobody will see you.'

I agreed with some misgivings, and so we went off to the musicians' room to choose from their repertoire some numbers that I knew. I took my place behind the column, and waited for a nod from Landsberg to start the first song I had ever sung on a professional stage. The song was 'Just One More Chance'.

The people dancing were obviously curious about who was singing and where the voice was coming from. If I had set out to attract maximum interest, I could not have staged it better. Afterwards I was introduced to the band in the musicians' room. Landsberg was exuberant. When he learned that I could perform a sort of tap dance, in fact what is called in Glasgow 'the clog wallop', his joy knew no bounds.

'You have been sent from heaven!'

I told him this was an exaggeration.

'No, no. You must understand. We all want to get out of this restaurant and on to the stage, but we had no one to be the star!'

This all seemed mad to me. I had come from heaven and I was a star! I knew exactly what the reaction of our Party Secretary would be. But after supper I began to see things in a different light. If, as Sydney Smith suggests, heaven is eating *pâté de foie gras* to the sound of trumpets, then that evening, heaven for me was rissoles and chips to the sound of compliments. It was agreed that I should sing three times a week, on Saturday evening, on Sunday in the afternoon at what was called 'Five o'clock Tea', and later in the evening. This arrangement lasted for a month, and although I enjoyed it I was exhausted working at the plant by day and singing at night. So one day I approached Sergei to ask permission to leave. At first he took it badly. Under no circumstances would he agree to free me. I told him that the Astoria management and its Red Director were very pleased with me. I was attracting more foreigners, who were paying the *valuta*, or foreign currency, which was so badly needed to buy tractors and machines. I had become quite a demagogue and knew all the jargon. Sergei looked at me with new interest.

'Foreign currency, you say? Are you sure they're spending more because of your singing?'

Tongue in cheek, I said that this was the general opinion.

'Well, that's a different thing. It makes no difference where the money comes from so long as it helps to fulfil the Five Year Plan ahead of time. All right, you can go.' It was an example of just how highly prized foreign currency was in those days, as the following joke, popular at the time, also demonstrates.

The Government decides to open a State Brothel for the benefit of sex-mad foreigners. A house is renovated for the purpose, and a couple of dozen girls selected from the hundreds of Young Communist volunteers who had responded to the call of the Party. The Madam is appointed by the Central Committee and in a pep talk she informs the girls they must comply with the client's every whim, no matter how bizarre. A few days after the opening the Madam is horrified to hear the voice of one of the girls shouting, 'No, no! Not that! Please not that!'

Madam calls the quivering girl into the corridor and angrily scolds her, reminding her of her duty to the Party and communism to excel in all Labour Achievements. The girl interrupted her, 'You don't understand, Comrade Madam. He wanted to pay me in Soviet currency!'

I spent my first week at the Astoria filling in forms, listening to lectures from the Red Director and the Party Secretary. There was a mysterious man with no title, who occupied an office that bore no visible signs of activity, who was, of course, the representative of the KGB. As he was learning English he struck up a kind of friendship with me. This did not prevent him from attacking me with extreme ferocity at a Trade Union meeting when I asserted that Party propaganda was wrong to paint Soviet life in such glowing colours, and that the people abroad would respect and appreciate the Russians more for their courage in facing and overcoming their hardships. This was blasphemy. I was told that no crimes were ever committed in a communist society, that there was no privation, no floods, air-crashes, prostitution or professional sport, and definitely no homosexuals or lesbians. The whole of society was imbued with one great and sacred idea: to build communism.

I became a member of the staff of the Hotel Astoria with a salary of 750 roubles a month, which was about three times what I had been earning in the factory. Although I had lost my foreign workers' ration book I was much better off. The meals in the staff canteen were excellent.

Rehearsals began and I suddenly realized this was what I had wanted to do all my life. In the atmosphere of creativity, quarrels, argument and reconciliations, I was happier (and richer) than I had ever been before. Better still, out of this apparent chaos, a pretty good show was emerging.

I was now staying with our violinist, Gustav Uzing, Leningrad-born but of German extraction. His father was a music teacher and willingly undertook the task of teaching me the intricate techniques of breath control. After a few lessons I began to wonder where I ever got the idea that I could sing.

Helen, naturally, knew of my good fortune and listened patiently to my rapturous accounts of rehearsals, of the new people I was meeting and how, at last, I had found my true vocation. I was so taken up with my own affairs, so high on my own cloud, that I failed to notice the troubled look in Helen's eyes. We were sitting at supper in the Europa Restaurant and I had been telling her enthusiastically how the band was about to start its concert engagement in the foyer of the October Cinema on the Nevsky Prospekt. She still looked drawn and tired, but I was too excited to notice.

'This is going to be great for me. A well-known director saw us and said we could easily compete with Utesov's Jazz Revue.' There is a Russian saying, 'If modesty were a sin, I could get into heaven easily.' But at last when I paused for breath, Helen managed to slip a word in.

'Does this mean that you intend to stay in Russia for ever?'

This had the effect of a cold shower on me. I replied falteringly, 'Well, no. I'll get experience here, and I'd like to stay on for a few years, but when I feel sure of myself, I'll probably return to England or go to America. Why? What's troubling you, Helen?'

'Well, I wish you luck. When you do become a star and come to the States, I hope you'll look me up; that is, if you remember me.'

It took a moment for her meaning to penetrate. I had been so wrapped up in my own happiness, I had forgotten that nothing had changed for Helen. I had done nothing to share my good fortune with her and I was furious with myself for such selfishness.

'Look you up? But you and I are going to be . . . well, I want to say . . . you can't go away and leave me. We are going to get married, aren't we?'

Helen looked at me in astonishment. 'Well, I must say I've heard of all sorts of funny ways of proposing to a girl, but this takes the cake! Shouldn't you have begun by telling me how much you love me and how you can't live without me. That is, if you really do!'

'But I do! You know I do. And you love me too . . . it's obvious, isn't it?'

Helen laughed softly. She seemed to be pleased. 'I must be rather dense. It didn't seem to be so obvious to me. I've told you before that I don't know much about love, but if I have ever loved anyone it is you. But I won't marry you and stay in this country. I hate everything here, the system, the life, the boredom of the endless propaganda. And suppose you don't become a star, what then? We'll live like my mother. Have children, live in one room, do nothing but go to work, cook and wash the linen. There'll be no joy for us. No, thank you. I want to go home to the States and I shall do so at the first opportunity.'

No matter how I tried to convince her she was wrong, she was adamant. I told her that I was a self-satisfied fool who had proposed to her like a country yokel.

'It makes no difference, dear. Even if you had proposed as you should have, I would not have accepted. I just don't want to live here.'

And that was that.

When we said goodnight, Helen put her arms round me and kissed me warmly. 'There! You see, I do love you. Don't look so heartbroken. Everything will be all right and in a few years you'll become a star and come to the States. You'll look me up, won't you? Promise? Goodbye my dear, and thanks for a beautiful friendship. I'll never forget you, never.'

About a week later, I entered the foyer of the Astoria to see Helen coming out of the Intourist Booking Agency accompanied by a tall, pleasant-looking man of about forty. I was struck dumb when she introduced him. 'This is my husband,' she said. 'We are leaving for the States the day after tomorrow.'

I was so confused that I didn't ask her how it had all happened so suddenly. What about her mother, her family?

'They are staying on here. No, don't come to see me off. We'll say goodbye now. Maybe we'll meet some day. Thanks for all your kindness and your friendship. Goodbye.'

And she was gone. I was on the verge of tears. I could not believe that she had been deceiving me, yet even if they had been married only yesterday, he must have been courting her for quite a while. I had to wait for forty years to learn the truth.

I had lost a good friend and was both sorry and hurt. But I had no intention of drowning myself in the Neva River. The band was due to open in a few days at the October Cinema and my destiny depended on how I went down with the Russian public.

In all the theatres, cinemas and workers' clubs in Russia there is always a large foyer. It has always been the fashion for the audience to arrive early to promenade up and down the foyer in their best dresses. Often there is a buffet, with rare titbits like caviare, salami sandwiches and oranges which are snapped up and dropped into string bags. These bags are called *avoskas*, an evocative name that reflects the life of shortages and queues. It comes from the word *avos* which means a thing you come across by chance. Foyers are also used for half-hour concerts and propaganda lectures before the performance begins.

My feelings, when I saw my name in big letters on the billboards for the first time may be imagined.

Beginning 15th of March
DAILY
Half hour of jolly light music
THE ASTORIA KIDS
starring
The English artiste
VILLI KARLIN

'Jolly light music' was the Soviet euphemism for jazz. Villi Karlin was my stage name in Russia.

The novelty had created quite a commotion on the Nevsky, and when I arrived an hour before the first performance, I saw a long queue waiting to buy tickets for the last house. All the other performances were already sold out. The manager was rubbing his hands, for the film being shown after our act was an old and poor one. Normally it would have been shown to a half-empty hall. As a matter of fact, many people went home when our show was over, without bothering to see the film.

And so the moment came. The orchestra played the introduction to the slow waltz 'Always', I climbed the rickety stairs behind the

platform and appeared in front of a Russian audience for the
first time.

The foyer was packed with people in heavy winter coats and fur
hats, as it is still very cold in Russia in March. I sang my ballad and
received a certain amount of applause. It sounded more like respect
for a visiting Briton than enthusiasm for the singer or the song.
Later, I realized they were so tightly packed together that a
thunderous ovation was a physical impossibility. At the time, I
wanted to go away and hide myself in some dark corner. But I had to
go on, and when I sang my next number I got a better reception.
Utesov had been plugging Jack Hylton's signature tune 'Goodnight, Goodnight, I'll See You in the Morning', so the tune was a
familiar one. I wound up the show with a number I had devised
myself. To the tune of 'Charlie is my Darling', I appeared in a
bowler hat and tiny moustache, wielding a cane. As the audience
knew and loved Charlie Chaplin, I went down well. To insistent
shouts of 'Bis' I sang a gypsy song in Russian. My finale was 'Some
of These Days' accompanied by a dance that was a mixture of the
'clog wallop' and a soft shoe shuffle. More by luck than good
judgement I finished at the same time as the band. The applause
was tremendous. We were in! We held the film show up for fifteen
minutes but nobody was worried about that.

I am not even going to attempt to explain the reason for our
popularity and success. The twelve-man band consisted mostly of
accomplished classical musicians, refugees from the Kirov Opera
and Ballet Theatre or the Leningrad Symphony Orchestra. They
played in the restaurant simply for the food and the little parcels
they managed to take home to their families. Showbiz brought
bigger money than they would have got playing *Swan Lake* or
Beethoven. There were two jazz enthusiasts who would sit up all
night, trying to tune in to the BBC to hear the famous Savoy Hotel
bands, but otherwise my colleagues played exactly what was written
on the music sheets, with no improvisation, and no jazz rhythm.
Not one of them could dance, and when I suggested teaching them
to foxtrot and tango you might have thought I had proposed
teaching them to play the mouth-organ or the bag-pipes. Did I
realize who they were? Did I know I was talking to the first violin of
the Symphony Orchestra or the first trombone of the Kirov House?
It didn't help when I reminded them they were jazz musicians now.
As for comic numbers, only the drummer helped me out. The first
trumpet didn't speak to me for a long time after I asked him to put

on a red nose for a number. 'I am not a circus clown!' he proclaimed with offended dignity.

I became very popular, but from a professional point of view, my success was entirely undeserved. I was simply a novelty. I gave little thought to the treatment of the songs I sang and my dances were chaotic. What saved me was a natural gift for the stage and an immunity to stage-fright. However, I did have sense enough to realize that I had to learn, and so enrolled for a year at the Leningrad Conservatoire. Later I had two years' study at the drama studio headed by People's Artiste of the Republic, Mikhail Tarkhanov of the Moscow Art Theatre. And then there was the experience of working with my wife, Elena, whose perfect discipline and knowledge gained as a ballerina in the Bolshoi Ballet School influenced me greatly. All this helped to turn me into a good professional. But that was in the future.

In the meantime, I continued to suffer from that terrible disease, a swollen head. I was recognized and pointed at. Groups of admirers would wait for me and accompany me wherever I went. I was the lion of the season, and the gilded youth of Leningrad tumbled over one another to invite me to parties. I was always being told that I was the finest artiste in Russia, much better than Leonid Utesov. The dreadful thing was that I actually believed it. How I suffered when I heard that the true professionals, critics and artistes, called me an upstart. 'Great talent,' I would announce, 'can never be suppressed.'

In the midst of all this I was overjoyed when I got a telegram from the young woman, Eddie, whom I had met on the ship coming out from England. The telegram announced that she was coming to Leningrad for a short stay. After we had parted at the port we kept up a regular correspondence and many were the times her wise letters had hoisted me out of my low spirits.

Eddie, who was English, had met a young Russian physicist, Kyril, when she was a student at Cambridge. He had come to England with three other scientists, including P. Kapitsa, to study under Professor Rutherford. Eddie and Kyril fell in love, and after their marriage she returned with him to Kharkov in the Ukraine, where he was appointed Principal of the Ukrainian Institute of Physics. Kapitsa refused to return to Russia when he was offered a laboratory at Cambridge. The big scandal came in 1939 when, as Professor Kapitsa, he came to Moscow to attend some scientific conference and on orders from Stalin was seized by the KGB and

forbidden to leave the country. He was, however, given a laboratory
in which to continue his work and became one of the world's most
eminent physicists. During the post-war Stalin purges he was
arrested, but suffered lightly: he was 'exiled' to the Kazan
University.

I was delighted to find that Eddie was just as fine a person as her
letters had suggested. I had only known her those few days aboard
the ship. She was five years older than me, handsome, in a masculine
way, with a well-built figure and an excellent sense of humour. She
was clever and extremely well-read.

Eddie had come to Leningrad partly to visit her husband's
relatives, and partly to renew our acquaintance. She stayed at
Kyril's sister Marina's flat, in a scientists' township on the outskirts
of the city. I found Marina and her husband, Gosha, to be really
charming people, especially Gosha who was also a young physicist.
He was tall and thin and had beautiful eyes which were so piercingly
blue that I could never forget them. They both spoke excellent
English and we all got on splendidly. They were the kind of people
you feel you have known all your life. I kept up my friendship with
them even after Eddie had returned home. Curiously enough, I
never knew Gosha's proper name. It was only after his death, at an
early age, that the many photographs in the press of the stout,
bearded Academician Igor Kurchatov, the man who created the
Russian atomic bomb, revealed that this was none other than my
Gosha! Whenever I passed by the Kurchatov Institute named in his
honour, in the picturesque woods on the northern edge of Moscow,
I always remembered Gosha with his beautiful eyes, his gentle voice
and infectious laughter.

Eddie left for home after a fortnight's stay and before leaving, she
made me promise to come to Kharkov for my holidays in the
summer. I had been told we would get a holiday in July when our
engagement at the cinema ended and the slack season at the Astoria
began.

I still kept up my friendship with my former factory mates. Rita
and Rodionov were my most ardent admirers and often came to the
cinema. Rita still played the role of a fussy hen, warning me not to
get a swollen head, and it has to be said that these good friends had a
steadying influence upon me.

I was amazed one evening when I was greeted by a more than
usually tumultuous ovation. The plant Trade Union had organized
a *cult pokhod*, a cultural excursion, and had bought all the seats for

the performance. Needless to say, the show went down tremendously and I was moved to tears when one of my old mates jumped
on to the stage and raised my hand on high shouting, 'He's our lad—
from the assembly shop!' To be popular with the public is one
thing, but to be recognized as 'one of our own' by the rough-and-
ready working class is an honour above all orders and medals.
When, at the factory, I won the title of *udarnik* (outstanding
worker), the Party Committee recommended me as a candidate for
membership. This meant a year's trial at the end of which, if I
proved to be a worthy exponent of Marxism, I could apply for full
membership. I did not last out the year in the factory and that was
about the nearest I ever came to being a Party member. My
affiliation to the communist movement never came from any great
personal conviction, but because of my parents. If they had not been
communists I would never have had anything to do with the
movement.

However, I was in the unenviable position of being the only
communist, even if only a candidate, in the orchestra, and this
brought me nothing but trouble. For instance, when we lost one of
our violinists, in utterly farcical conditions, I was the one who was
hauled over the coals by the authorities.

The violinist was a tall, thin man with an eternally funereal
expression on his face. As a boy he had been a *wunderkind*, a child
prodigy. Excessive praise had made everything too easy, and he
never learned to work hard. He had graduated from the Leningrad
Conservatoire as a violinist, but he never became a concert
musician. A wise man once said: 'The only place where success
comes before work is in the dictionary.' The violinist suffered
consistent nagging from his wife and would periodically go on
drinking bouts lasting for days. He would often come to work
drunk, but his colleagues usually covered up for him.

One day, the Soviet President, Mikhail Kalinin, arrived in
Leningrad for a short stay. After his tour of the factories, he was
expected to arrive at the Astoria in the evening. I watched the red-
carpet preparations with interest. I had never seen a live President
before. The top brass of the hotel, the Managing Director with his
eternal shadow, the Red Director, the Party Secretary and all the
others, lined up by the swing doors at the main entrance. The
grandfather clock in the foyer struck ten, the sound of a car braking
was heard outside, the doors began to swing round, everyone in the
foyer stopped talking and froze. The huge, bearded doorman

stepped forward, and through the rotating door staggered our violinist, drunk as a lord. He tripped over the edge of the red carpet and measured his length on the floor in front of the astounded management. To add to their discomfiture, they were told that President Kalinin had already arrived, through a side-door, and was impatiently asking for his supper. The violinist, of course, got the sack, while I was summoned by the Party Secretary and reprimanded for collaborating in covering up for a drunkard.

Soon after this there was another incident. We had only just finished the first number of the evening when an elderly, white-haired man in a well-pressed dinner jacket appeared in the restaurant. He looked around with an unmistakably commanding eye. Our first trumpeter leaped to his feet and began to play the traditional *toush*, the fanfare accorded to celebrities. The orchestra joined in, and some of the diners got to their feet and applauded, looking with reverence at the old man. I hadn't the faintest idea who he was but I didn't want to seem impolite, so I joined in.

I was on the carpet again the next day in the Party Secretary's office. It appeared that the old man was the brother of the notorious Admiral Wrangel, who had led one of the counter-Revolutionary armies against the Soviet regime, and had been responsible for many a heinous crime against the people. This brother had pledged allegiance to the new State and worked as *maître d'hôtel* at the Astoria. A few months previously he had been arrested by the KGB and had only just been freed. The Secretary declared that the playing of the *toush* and the applause were an act of provocation which I should have stopped and not condoned by applauding myself. I managed to convince him I knew nothing about the Wrangels. In fact, the old man thoroughly deserved a fanfare. He was a splendid *maître d'hôtel* and spoke six languages. Once he recited Byron's *Childe Harold*, in perfect English, for my benefit, a feat very few English people could perform, myself included.

The holidays came at last, and true to my promise to Eddie, I packed my case and bought a railway ticket to Kharkov. The train went through Moscow, but as it only stopped for an hour, I could do no more than look over the big station square and return to the restaurant to have a meal. It was a good thing that I did. It took the train twenty-six hours instead of the scheduled seventeen to get to Kharkov. It seemed to stop at every telegraph pole and covered the 450-mile route at an average speed of twenty miles per hour.

I was lucky to have booked a berth in the sleeping car and was fairly comfortable. The majority of the passengers travelled in what are called the 'hard' coaches with only seating facilities. Many were the times on my performing tours that I had to travel in these coaches and it certainly did not make a journey a pleasant one. When we passed over the border into the Ukraine, the bread-basket of the Soviet Union, I was confronted with the horrifying results of Stalin's collective farming campaign.

Collective farming, like many aspects of doctrinaire communism, has proved a complete failure in practice. Before the Revolution, the downtrodden peasants produced enough grain to make Tsarist Russia one of the biggest exporters in the world. Today, the Soviet collective farmers, despite modern mechanization, cannot produce enough to feed their own population. The collective farm policy was dictated first by the need to bring the individualistic peasant under the control of the Party and secondly, to merge the small peasant holdings into giant farms which in theory were easier to cultivate. The theory failed to take into account the basic facts of human nature.

A peasant gets satisfaction when he looks at his own holding and sees the results of his daily work. He gets none from looking at a giant collective farm, stretching beyond the horizon. Worse, the industrious farm-worker is no better off than his idle or drunken neighbour. The result is that the enterprising peasant spends most of his time on his *uchastok*, his private allotment, travelling to the city markets to sell his produce. These allotments were originally introduced to enable the peasant to grow vegetables for his own needs, and to keep cattle and poultry. Now, statistics show that these individual plots, whose size is minuscule compared with the giant state farms, are able to supply almost a third of the population's food requirements. The peasants sell their produce at much higher prices than in the state-controlled shops. When Soviet propaganda declares that there is no inflation, it does not take into consideration the exorbitant prices in the markets.

When, in the 1920s and '30s, Stalin ordered the peasants to unite into collective farms, he met with stubborn resistance. Propagandists from the city were beaten up and murdered. The peasants refused to till the land, so Stalin ordered the confiscation of their grain reserves. They would obey or starve. Our train was met at every stop by crowds of peasant women and children, with outstretched hands, and cries of 'Daite kusok khleba!' ('Spare a piece of bread!'). It was terrible to see the emaciated faces and distended bellies of the young girls and the naked, rickety children. Many lay on the ground, unable to stand. The men stood at a distance, sullen, angry and defiant. As we passed the fields, I saw the dead bodies of men, women and children, lying where they had fallen. It was my first experience of an almost unimaginable tragedy, and I was utterly shocked.

I arrived in Kharkov nine hours late. Naturally Eddie had gone home, so I had to find my own way. My foreign clothes and faulty Russian provoked the usual questions from the good-hearted Ukrainians. Where did I come from? How much did a suit like that cost? When are you going to have a revolution? I was passed from one tram conductor to another, with the explicit instructions that I was an *anglichanin* fleeing from capitalism and searching for the Ukrainian Institute of Physics on Tchaikovsky Street.

I eventually found the street, more like a cul-de-sac, and openly walked into the Institute's grounds. Nobody asked me who I was, nor did I see any guards: the place was still of little interest to the Kremlin.

The Institute received very meagre supplies for research. I remember helping in an all-out search of the city's dustbins and rubbish heaps for old tin cans during my stay there. My experience as a fitter was invaluable in converting the cans into the metal sheets needed for some experiment.

Eddie apologized profusely for not having met me at the station and introduced me to Kyril. He was just over medium height and extremely thin and pale from long hours in dark laboratories. He had lost all his teeth during some nuclear experiment and suffered from TB. He was the very image of a man entirely dedicated to science, and could speak of little else. He realized that this could be boring to a layman, so he listened more than he talked. He was a brilliant physicist. With no co-operation from Western scientists and poor facilities he had already accomplished the same feat of splitting the atom with which his teacher, Professor Rutherford, had astounded the world.

After Leningrad, I found Kharkov to be a typically provincial town and the half-million population, in comparison, looked easy-going and unhurried. The main street, Sumskoi Ulitsa, could hardly be compared with the Nevsky Prospekt with its jostling crowds. The only claim to large-scale industry was the giant tractor plant, but its presence was not much felt as it had been built on the southern outskirts of the city. The people were pleasant and polite and one seldom heard the bad-tempered quarrelling in the trams or shops that often exploded in Leningrad. The shops were emptier and the population depended mostly on the peasant markets for their food and vegetables, a 'tradition' kept, probably to a lesser extent, to this day in all Soviet cities. The signs over the shops and in the streets were bilingual, in Russian and Ukrainian, and although the citizens were mostly Ukrainian, they preferred to speak Russian. Whenever Ukrainian was heard, you could be sure it was peasants from the countryside who were speaking. The only waterway was a tiny river that trickled through the centre of the town. The only place to go swimming in the sweltering heat was a tiny lake about five miles away. Eddie and I made the walk along the dusty track and found it worthwhile nonetheless.

During that month, I got to know many scientists and students who were destined to become eminent in their various disciplines. In later years, I made no attempt to renew my acquaintance, as friendship with a former foreigner might have brought great harm to them. There was a young man, about the same age as myself, whom I was sorry to lose sight of. He was the epitome of the absent-minded professor. Eddie had taken him under her wing and looked after him like a mother. He was David Landau, already a professor at twenty-eight and later to become world-famous as one of the most brilliant mathematicians of the century.

Landau was a genius in his profession, and when I knew him his absent-mindedness was a standing joke. His whole life was wrapped up in mathematics and physics; he even spent his spare time in solving mathematical riddles. When I told him I was a performer in a jazz orchestra he looked at me as if I was a Martian. Later, he came to me with a perplexed expression. He had looked up the word jazz in the dictionary and failed to find it. I explained as best as I could. I am sure he remained completely in the dark, but was too polite to say so.

About a dozen of the top men in the physics hierarchy arrived for a conference and Eddie invited them to dinner. I was delighted to see Gosha again, and very honoured when I was introduced to the 'Father of Soviet Russian Physics', Academician Joffe, a venerable, white-haired man whose name was well-known even to me. Dr Joffe spoke good English, as did all those present at the table, and plied me with questions about life in Britain and the results of the economic crisis of the early thirties in the West. Throughout the meal I was struck by the politeness of these fascinating men, all of whom spoke in English in deference to my presence. As far as I was concerned they could have spoken in Mandarin Chinese, as the talk was mainly on scientific subjects, including nuclear physics, of which I was completely ignorant. I mention this incident to emphasize how freely these leading physicists could talk on the subject in the presence of a foreigner, something that was completely forbidden later.

Twenty years later in 1952 I once again visited the Ukrainian Institute, hoping to re-establish contact with Eddie and Kyril, whom I had not seen since before the war. I had just bought my first car, a mini Moskvich, and my wife and I had decided to go on a tour of the Crimea and the Caucasus, passing through Kharkov. The city had been occupied by the Germans and half-destroyed. We arrived late in the afternoon to find the place looking like a gigantic construction site. It was dark before I found Tchaikovsky Street. Confronted by a fifteen-foot brick wall and a large iron gate, I thought I had taken the wrong turning, but no, this really was Tchaikovsky Street. I noticed a small window in the wall and knocked on it. Immediately, big arc-lights blazed out over the gate, the window banged open, and the harsh voice of a security officer barked at me, 'What do you want?'

I explained in a very hesitant and faltering voice, 'You see, it's like this. We are on our way down south in a car, from Moscow. I had friends who used to live here in the Institute and I spent my holidays with them once before the war and I haven't heard of them since, so I thought I'd look them up . . . if you'd be so good as to tell me . . .'

'Name?'

'Whose? Mine?'

'Your friends'.'

'Oh, my friends', of course. Sinelnikov. Professor Sinel . . .'

'First name and patronymic?'

Suddenly, I could not for the life of me remember Kyril's patronymic. I stood there, gulping.

'Kyril . . . Kyril . . .'

'Well? Kyril what?'

This was terrible. The hard face of the security officer registered growing suspicion and disbelief. With a gasp, I cried, 'Kyril Dmitrich!'

'Wait!'

I was running with a cold sweat, cursing myself for coming

anywhere near the gate. The man was obviously ringing up the central KGB office and taking a long time about it. At last the window opened again—'No such person living here'—and was banged shut.

A year later I found that this was a lie. I learned, through a scientist friend, that the Sinelnikovs had returned to Kharkov after the war, that Kyril was now an Academician and still Principal of the renovated Institute and that they lived in the same flat. How I hated all that intimidating officialdom.

FIVE

'Jolly Fellows'

When I arrived back in Leningrad after my holiday in Kharkov, I felt ready to tackle anything, but I found a surprise waiting. The orchestra was to go to Moscow, to play in the Hotel Metropole. The musicians were not so pleased. It meant losing the cinema engagement and the extra money, but as it was only for a month or so, we agreed.

To my surprise, the capital was small compared with Leningrad's majestic buildings and palaces, wide streets and avenues. No wonder the citizens of Leningrad look down on Moscow as a peasant village, and have never forgiven the Government for moving the capital.

Life in Moscow seemed to centre on the Hotel Metropole which looked on to the Theatrical Square, with the Bolshoi Opera and Ballet House at one end. The rearing stallions on the roof seemed about to leap down on the milling crowds heading their way to the large department store officially called Mostorg but remembered among old Muscovites by the names of the two Scotsmen who owned it before the Revolution, Muir and Merilees. To the left of the Bolshoi stands the Maly Theatre, the Academy of Russian Drama, where most of the greatest actors and actresses have walked the stage. The grandfather of them all was Mikhail Schepkin who had once actually been a serf on the estate of some landowner, an intellectual who had his own theatre. His immense talent was so obvious that a patron bought him his freedom and he came to the theatre which is now called by the nickname 'Schepkin House'.

The Metropole was an old-fashioned hotel, a great square building where the restaurant occupied the whole inner courtyard. This was covered by a giant glass roof. In the centre was the dance-floor, with a fountain in a circular pool. How many times did I see some inebriate dancer pick himself and sometimes his girl-friend out of the pool after an over-extravagant movement! The platform for the orchestra was a large one and would have been the envy of any concert hall. Although the general public was still on ration cards, and food was not at all plentiful, the restaurant was always well supplied and the cuisine was excellent. The clientele was made up of people who could afford to pay a hundred roubles or more for dinner or supper. Foreigners found it very cheap as the rate of exchange was so favourable then. There was always a hetero-geneous crowd of actors, writers, embezzlers, thieves, con-men, pimps and their prostitutes. Most of these people I came to know and I had many friends among them.

Our band was a great success, and when the month was up the management decided to prolong our stay. But this was impossible as three of our musicians played in the Maryinsky or Kirov Opera House and had to be back for the opening of the season. A fierce row resulted, and when we left the Managing Director swore we would never set foot in his hotel again. Although I had no intention of playing in a Moscow restaurant all my life, I felt this was an unfortunate start. I had come to like the busier atmosphere of Moscow and believed there were greater opportunities here. I decided I must move to the capital in the future, but did not expect this to happen as quickly as now turned out.

On our arrival back in Leningrad, an extremely unpleasant shock awaited us. The musicians of the Utesov Jazz Revue, after quarrelling violently with their leader, had quit. They had taken our places at the Astoria and at the October Cinema. Just as we were about to take the matter up with the Trade Union, the orchestraless Art Director of the Utesov Jazz Revue, Arnold, approached us proposing we should take the places of the 'mutineers' in the Revue.

This seemed to be a piquant way of getting our own back, so we agreed, picked up our still unpacked cases and returned to Moscow. We were to take part in the film *Jolly Fellows* which had already started shooting down in the Caucasus. Utesov was to play the leading role. Arnold had not heard of our row with the Director of the Metropole and signed a contract for us to play in the restaurant and live in the Hotel. We arrived and stood in the foyer waiting to be shown to our rooms. I could not help feeling worried when I saw the Director's broad smile turn into a snarl when he saw who we were. A heated argument ensued. The Director was adamant. We had to go. Arnold looked at him calmly, lifted the phone without a word and asked to be put through to the Director of the National Hotel, only a couple of blocks away at the end of Gorky Street. Referring to an earlier conversation, he told him that he was prepared to sign a contract for our band to play in his restaurant. The Director of the Metropole soon realized that he was making a big mistake. Our orchestra was among the best in the country and had already proved to be an attraction. He had enough sense to lay his hand on the receiver, and truculently agreed to recognize the existing contract. Many years later, Arnold told me he had never spoken to the Director of the National at all, but had rung up a friend, also a theatrical manager, who had caught on to the trick and played up to it.

And so I renewed my acquaintance with the high life of Moscow. I soon learned to recognize the part-time KGB agents in this motley circle, especially the top-class prostitutes, men and women, who centred their attention on the foreign diplomats and businessmen who frequented the hotel. In those days the restaurant presented a fascinating spectacle, and with a little imagination and inside knowledge, it was not difficult to guess what was going on at this or that table.

One man treating half a dozen people to a feast of lavish pre-Revolutionary proportions might have just served a sentence in the notorious Solovki Island Prison, and judging from the scale of the banquet and the size of the waiter's tip had 'struck gold' again. Another man I saw, a young Belgian diplomat who seemed so overwhelmed at his luck in wining and dining such a beautiful companion, by chance introduced to him at a party, couldn't have known that neither the party nor the introduction was likely to have had any element of chance. There was the white-haired writer, who took such pride in parading his lovely young wife (the fifth) in front of the élite Metropole public. He didn't know that she was having an affair with our guitar-player.

I had many strange admirers in the Metropole. None of their professions would have made them eligible for Moscow drawing-rooms. I never played cards but I did at one time acquire a passion for billiards. I used to spend hours with a cue in the basement, where all the professionals and suckers would gather along with the *urki*, the high-class criminals. One of the professionals, a man of about forty called Karapet, seemed to be rather proud of our friendship. He was one of the finest billiard players I have ever seen, and he taught me a lot about the game, especially its seamier side. Karapet was always very elegantly dressed. He won his clothes from foreigners. They had about as much chance of winning a game against him as of getting into the Kremlin. Some years later, while on tour, I was walking along a street in Saratov on the Volga when the clicking of billiard balls drew me like a magnet to the nearby hall. Play was in progress on three or four tables. Some of the local fly-boys were taking the mickey out of an elderly peasant in a *tujhurka*, a coarse padded jacket, felt boots and a well-worn fur hat, from which unkempt hair stuck out like straw in a dustbin. He was making the boys laugh by suggesting it would be better to play with the thick end of the cue and was telling them what a good day he'd had at the market, showing them a big roll of notes. So they began to cajole him into having a go 'just for fun'. I was laughing at him, too, although I was sorry to see that the old chap was in for a good fleecing. In fact, I was about to advise him to go home when I caught him winking at me from under his scraggy brows. It was the elegant Karapet! He signalled to me to keep my mouth shut.

Only a born actor could have played the part of an old, clumsy peasant with such skill. He made the most unbelievable shots, often missing the ball completely, while the fly-boys roared with laughter. I had to leave to get ready for my show, and by this time he had already lost half of his bank-roll. I returned after the show to find him with a few thousand of the fly-boys' roubles stuck in his felt boots. At about three o'clock in the morning he thanked them all for giving him a valuable lesson in billiards and said he had to go 'as the old woman'll be wondering where I've got to'. We met round the corner and went to his hotel room where, with a bottle of cognac and plenty of tasty *zakuski* (a sort of primitive hors d'oeuvre) we sat until dawn broke while Karapet regaled me with exciting tales of his 'tours'. As he only ever performed one-night stands he left Saratov the following morning. 'Anyway, they'd murder me if they found out who I was.'

Another of my admirers called himself a travelling insurance agent. In reality, Shura was a *medvejhatnic*, the name given in the underworld to safebreakers, the élite of the criminal profession. He adored his wife and it was his unfailing custom to order a table for two every Saturday night 'with champagne'. But I was always a welcome guest at his table, and he would beam with pleasure whenever I invited his wife to dance. When Shura went off on a 'sales trip', he often asked me to look after and take her to supper as usual every Saturday night. He even hinted that he didn't mind sharing her charms with such a good friend while he was away. Once he disappeared for a long time, some six months, and I assumed that he had been caught and was in prison. Many years later I was told by another safe-breaker that Shura had secretly crossed the border into China, broken into an allegedly impenetrable bank-safe and escaped with an immense sum. As the police were on his trail, he couldn't cross over the Soviet border, so he travelled round the world, squandered all the money and found his way back to Russia by working on a ship bound for Odessa.

While Utesov was away filming on the Black Sea coast, our manager signed a contract for us to give a show in between performances at a cinema which bore the hilarious name (at least to an English ear) of Horn. The cinema stood on Triumphal Square, named in memory of Napoleon's retreat from Moscow. It has since been renamed Mayakovsky Square, after the poet, a poor exchange, despite Stalin's declaration that Mayakovsky was 'the greatest poet of the century'. Perhaps the square should more accurately have been called Theatrical Square. To the right of the cinema was the Satirical Theatre, where a whole galaxy of splendid actors performed. Across the street was the Moscow Operetta. Little did I know that there was a lovely ballerina there who, three years later, was to become my partner, on the stage and off. The theatre's Art Director, Grigory Yaron, was a fine comic who was consistently under criticism for his productions of Calman, Offenbach and Lehar in which the players were dressed in the traditional tailcoats and top hats. This style aroused the ire of the Party. The top hat was reviled as a symbol of capitalism. Soviet musical comedies and operettas should portray the working class and reflect their industrial achievements! I remember the first 'pure' production of this kind, in which the actors and actresses appeared on the stage in dungarees and wellington boots. Most of the audience stalked out of the theatre after the first act. They could have saved their energy. They were doomed to see many more such spectacles. What came to be known as Soviet musical comedies and operettas were written by cunning authors who catered to the demands of the Party and re-dressed the old themes of classical operettas, calling them proletarian realism. The only real difference was that the players cavorted in boiler-suits and cloth caps.

Beside the Operetta Theatre was the Moscow Music Hall. It had a permanent company, the cream of light entertainment. They too had to put on plays and revues of an anti-capitalist character. Circus and variety numbers were invited to leaven the dull loaf of propaganda, but even these artistes were subject to the demands of the Party. The funnyman on the flying trapeze had to don a capitalist tailcoat, and in the slapstick comedy act the apple pies were flung into the faces of Chamberlain and Poincaré. Whenever the revue was too crudely political and the house half-empty, Utesov's Jazz Revue was called in to fill the seats, and so the Music Hall became a second home to us during that winter.

At the top of the theatre were about a dozen rooms, along a long corridor, where, owing to the housing shortage, some of the permanent company had to live. Many were the noisy and jolly parties I enjoyed there. I remember one incident from which I was lucky to emerge intact.

One of our most ardent admirers was a young performer called Masha. She would always stand in the wings to hear my rendering of a popular favourite, 'Masha and Me at the Samovar'. Perhaps she felt I was singing the song for her and that endeared me to her. Much to my embarrassment she took to me in a big way. She was a circus artiste, what they called a 'heavy juggler'. The word heavy was apt. Masha juggled with a number of steel balls, each weighing about a stone. She rolled the balls across her shoulders and bosom, over head and along her arms, and her finale was most effective. She would throw each ball into the air and, leaning forward, would catch them, one after the other, on the nape of her neck!

How Masha came to the circus and invented such an act I never discovered. But I did find out that she came of peasant stock and had worked in the fields from an early age. She escaped from death by starvation during the terrible famine on the Volga. Some wandering tinker took her in tow and deprived her of her virginity at the age of eleven. She must have been pretty hefty even before she became a circus performer but the effect of juggling those immense steel balls for three to four hours a day had worked a drastic effect on her physique. She was gargantuan: even though only just over medium height, she looked like a champion weightlifter. Her hair was cropped short, and she had a square, peasant face with a wide mouth. Her neck, naturally, was thick, and her shoulders broad, with muscles like an Irish navvy's.

Masha was shy and was quite inarticulate when it came to conversation. Everybody laughed at her behind her back, but never to her face. Once during a rehearsal, a burly stage-hand made some rude remark about her. Masha went over to the man and gave him a slight push that sent him flying across the stage into the orchestra pit.

Popularity had brought me many admirers, especially among the opposite sex. Often I would be surrounded by girls after a show and would be thoroughly enjoying myself when everything would be spoilt by the silent appearance of Masha. Gradually the other girls would melt away before her cold gaze. In her courting, Masha was persistent. No matter what subterfuges I resorted to, she was always there waiting, silently reproachful. In a way I liked her, probably because we always like those who like us. She reminded me of a St Bernard. I was scared stiff of being left alone with her. Once, in a conscience-stricken moment, I invited her to supper at the Metropole after the show. That clinched matters for her. From then on I was her young man. She wanted to stay the night, but I managed to convince her that it was against hotel regulations.

Finally there came a night when I lowered my guard and paid for it. I was invited to a party in a room at the top of the Music Hall. It was a hard-drinking affair and there came a moment when I needed to go to the lavatory at the end of the corridor. It was about three o'clock and I was sure Masha would be fast asleep in her room. Nevertheless, I tiptoed past her door so as not to disturb her. My precautions were in vain. All of a sudden the door opened and I saw Masha gazing at me intently. I mumbled some excuse and was about to beat a hasty retreat when her hand shot out and gripped my shoulder. I was yanked unceremoniously into her room where I found myself locked in a tight embrace.

At last she released me. I started to tell her how pleased I was to see her and hoped she was keeping well in this cold weather. I stopped in mid-sentence and stood as if hypnotized. She had thrown off her dressing-gown, in a second had pulled her night-gown over her head and now appeared completely naked, a female Hercules. There was something magnificent about her well-built body, in spite of its dimensions. Her muscles rippled exquisitely, her movements were as graceful as those of a racehorse. I gazed at her in fearful admiration.

She made a little step towards me, towering over me as I stepped backwards to the door. I wanted to call out for help, but refrained. I realized that I would be the laughing-stock of the entire theatrical world if the story got round. I groped behind me, searching for the door handle, and began to bleat something like, 'Well, my friends will be wondering where I've got to . . .' Masha was a big girl but she was extremely agile. In a second she had her arms around me. I flew across the room and landed on the bed. To my horror I saw her locking the door. As I lay helpless I remembered how the American Central Intelligence Agency always instructed their women agents, if the object of their surveillance became too violent in his sexual desires, to 'relax, open your legs and enjoy yourself'. I had no option but to follow suit.

For such a powerful girl, Masha was gentle. Unfortunately she didn't know her own strength. In the ecstasy of her many climaxes, she flung me about like one of her steel weights and when she wound her arms and legs around me, I could hear my bones cracking under the strain. When the first rays of the dawn broke through the frost-covered window, I rose quietly, gathered my clothes, and tiptoed towards the door. 'Stop!' came the command from Masha, and I obeyed.

This energetic affair lasted for a few weeks and then Masha was unexpectedly recalled to the circus to go on tour. Our parting was not a tearful one. Masha never cried. A smacking kiss and a friendly slap on the back and off she marched. I never saw her again, but I did hear that she got married to a circus wrestler, appropriately billed as 'The Northern Bear'.

In those years Moscow was the Mecca of the theatrical world. The Revolution had stirred up the melting-pot of art. It was a time of new ideas and experiments, many of them idiotic, some of them brilliant. New creative talent seemed over-abundant. There were theatre directors like Meyerhold, Vakhtangov, Sulerjhitsky; writers such as Bulgakov, Paustovsky; the cinema directors Eisenstein, Pudovkin, and composers such as Shostakovich and Prokofiev. They have all gone now. Some went to their deaths in the camps, others were hounded and their creations destroyed by Stalin's henchmen. Many died of broken hearts. The New Enthusiasm has perished and a grey, Party-approved art has taken its place. Stalin has gone too, but his disciples remain, dictating and browbeating, herding men of ideas into the camps or the mental homes. 'The Stalinist crimes shall never happen again', said the 'angry' young poet Yevtushenko, but they are happening. The middle-aged Yevtushenko is still alive, but no longer the 'angry' poet of the old days.

Curiously enough, the Music Hall was probably the most interesting of all the experimental theatres of those days. It attracted many who had new ideas. In one anti-clerical play, trapeze acrobats flew over the stage in white gowns, with wings attached to their backs, and conjurers put a stop to the nefarious activities of the snake in the Garden of Eden by shoving it into a box and producing a wriggling rabbit instead. In another production the chorus girls were dressed to look like the new assembly line in the automobile plant.

This kind of nonsense was soon banished from the repertoire when it came under the creative eye of that brilliant and most versatile choreographer, Kasyan Golizovsky. It was more out of necessity than from choice that Golizovsky accepted the proposal made by the Music Hall Theatre, to take the chorus girls under his wing. He had been hounded for his ideas and experiments in ballet by every State and Party organization concerned with the arts.

His productions of the classical ballets in the Bolshoi Theatre are performed to this day. His concert programmes were a carnival where we saw such great ballerinas and dancers as Ulanova, Semyonova, Plisetskaya, Maximova and Vasiliev, for whom Golizovsky created images and qualities of which they themselves were unaware. Unfortunately, his intractability in refusing to obey the orders of Party officials brought him into confrontation with the Ministry of Culture and the Party, with whom he was always on the worst of terms. Despite the pleas of the Bolshoi Ballet Company he was forced to resign his post. The Music Hall had always been offensive to the authorities, because of the Western flavour of the revues and shows, no matter how proletarian the theme, and it was eventually closed down. The theatre was handed over to the People's Folk and Amateur Arts. The galaxy of brilliant artistes gave way to folk singers and dancers.

Golizovsky still managed to eke out a fairly decent living. He was a gifted artist and sculptor and his exhibitions were invariably packed. His books on the dance—classical, modern and folk—are standard textbooks to all teachers and choreographers to this day. But the ballet theatres were closed to him and it was only after Stalin's death that he was invited to create the production of the magnificent *Leili and Medjnun*. When sickness forced him to retire, this genius of the ballet was granted a State pension amounting to the magnificent sum of seventy roubles a month, which is about the same as a charwoman would receive. Only through the efforts of a group of Bolshoi Ballet dancers headed by Vladimir Vasiliev was this pension reluctantly raised to one hundred and twenty roubles. Kasyan Golizovsky died a poor man but defiant to the end. He is now hailed as the 'Father of the Modern Dance'.

I had the misfortune to know and play alongside one of the least talented of the new breed of the People's Folk and Amateur Arts, Misha Philipov. He was a small man, unintelligent but cunning. He had served a sentence for raping a ten-year-old girl. For good behaviour he was transferred to a prison colony called Bolshevo just outside Moscow. At Bolshevo, criminals went through a period of 're-education', according to communist ideals, and were released when considered fit to mix in society. Misha joined the colony's folk song and dance group not because he had any gifts but because the group was allowed to travel and give concerts outside the prison. The choreographer did his best for Misha and managed to teach him a number in which he played a street sweeper and performed a dance with a broom. When Misha finally received his freedom he was asked what he would like to do. The Soviet authorities are a great deal kinder to criminals than to political prisoners. Misha said that he would like to be an artiste. He had heard that artistes earned a lot of money, and didn't get up until midday. The officer handed him a letter of recommendation typed on the official paper of the NKVD, the People's Commissariat for Internal Affairs. It was addressed to the Director of the Moscow State Variety Artistes Organization with the request to do all in his power to assist M. Philipov to find work. No mention was made of his immediate past. The Director, assuming that Misha was a KGB agent, accepted him immediately.

Misha was registered as a staff artiste at full wages, a position normally won through stiff competition. But no audition was demanded, and no one asked what he could do. The concert manager was given strict orders to include him in all the shows. The whisper went round that Misha was a KGB *stukach*, an informer, so everybody went out of their way to express their devotion to the Party, the Government and the KGB. All went well for Misha for the first few months. He was earning a lot of money performing twice a day. He was on the bill with us several times and he was simply awful. But his luck didn't last for long. Complaints began to pour into Head Office from the managers of the theatres and clubs where we performed. The Director tried to put him on the special 'secret' list of people with inexplicable jobs, but the Head Book-keeper would not hear of it. There were far too many on the list as it was. So Misha was transferred from the permanent staff to the 'piecework' list, where the artistes were paid only by actual performance. Here the competition was fierce and Misha gradually found himself on the rocks. By now, his real story had become known, and as artistes are a soft-hearted lot and they felt the joke had been on them too, Misha managed to survive on the roubles slipped into his pocket. Where he slept nobody knew. He still had ideas about becoming an artiste, turned up every day and hung around in the big courtyard outside the office on the offchance of finding an engagement.

Then came the turning-point in his life. The old Agency doorman died and the artistes advised Misha to take the job. 'You're here all day anyway. At least you'll have some kind of a wage and maybe they'll find you some place to live.' So Misha became a doorman. Meanwhile, a commission had been set up, headed by the film director Grigory Alexandrov, to promote a new idea, the State Amateur Folk Arts Theatre.

Someone advised Misha to enter a contest announced by the commission. He performed his old Charlie Chaplin act and created a sensation. A simple doorman dancing a Charlie Chaplin act! Proletarian art! Talent from the depth of the masses! These and other effusive slogans appeared in the papers, accompanied by photographs of Misha with a tiny moustache, bowler hat and baggy trousers. Alexandrov announced that he would engage the extraordinary doorman in his new film. Misha was transferred from his tiny cubicle below the Agency stairs to a swanky room in the Peking Hotel, just across the road from the new Amateur Theatre. He was in clover again.

After long preparations, with endless rehearsals conducted by the finest directors and choreographers, the night of the première of the new State Amateur Folk Arts Theatre was announced. Vast sums of money were spent by the Government on the décor and costumes, and naturally the critics went into raptures over the show. In fact it was better than might have been expected. Some of the amateurs were very good, some were mediocre and some were just poor. Misha was the worst of all. The compère gave him a big introduction, announcing that he was a simple doorman but so gifted that Alexandrov had already engaged him for his new film and so on. I will not try to describe his act. The best efforts of the choreographer had not been sufficient to improve his dancing or even make him look like an artiste. The audience was polite, but the compère had to rush the next number on to fill the unexpected vacuum when Misha's expected encore did not materialize.

Nevertheless, Alexandrov stuck to his guns and took Misha off to the city of Gorky on the Volga where the greater part of his film *Volga, Volga* was to be shot. I played the part of a singing and dancing cook. Misha was tried in every possible role, medium and minor, but all he did was to make the Assistant Director wring his hands in despair.

One evening after a long day of filming, we were sitting in the crowded hotel restaurant when Misha, blind drunk, came staggering down the steps and approached the table where Alexandrov and his gifted, lovely wife, the actress Lyubov Orlova, were sitting. Misha began to curse Alexandrov for his failure to make a star of him. When the waiters and hefty doormen tried to grab him, Misha seized bottle after bottle from the nearby tables and systematically began to smash the mirrors. The whole place was in pandemonium, with women screaming, half-drunk men roaring with laughter, and shouts of 'Grab him!'

Misha was eventually hustled away, Alexandrov managed to hush up the whole affair and the bill for the damage was footed by the Mosfilm Studios. He also used his influence with the militia, and a very crumpled, downcast Misha was freed from his cell and put on a train for Moscow. After that Misha was fired from the State Amateur Folk Arts Theatre and couldn't even get his old doorman's job back again at the Agency. When last I heard of him he had a job as a porter in a vodka shop.

I have digressed. No account of the Moscow theatrical scene of the thirties would be complete without a mention of the Tchaikovsky Hall on the corner of Triumphal Square and Gorky Street. While I was performing in the Horn cinema, work on the Hall was nearing completion and it promised to be one of the most original theatres in the world. Vsevolod Meyerhold was making history in the production of drama, and this theatre was his brain-child. Like most of his ideas, it was revolutionary at the time. He wanted to destroy the proscenium arch and bring the action right into the middle of the audience. The scenery was to be suspended from movable rails. The idea was dropped for the simple reason that the theatre never became the one it was intended to be. The arrest, and subsequent death in the camps, of Meyerhold, one of the world's most eminent theatrical directors and innovators, was among the many heinous crimes committed by Stalin. The designs for the Meyerhold Theatre were destroyed.

The publication of Meyerhold's valuable notes and theories on drama would have been a fine monument to this great man. Many attempts were made to publish them, but to no avail. In the few tolerant years after Stalin's death, many letters were sent to the press protesting that the manuscripts were being suppressed and Meyerhold's memory condemned to oblivion. Under pressure, the then chief editor of *Izvestia*, Khrushchev's son-in-law, Adjubei, wrote a scurrilous article castigating those who had found the nerve to campaign for the book. He told a deliberate lie, saying that the book was already on the printing press and would soon appear in the shops. No one has ever seen that book to this day.

About a month after we started at the Metropole, the star and leader of the Jazz Revue, Leonid Utesov, arrived back from filming by the Black Sea. Leonid Utesov was a clever and strong-willed man and he was the first to break through the barrier of official disapproval of 'decadent' music with his Jazz Revue. He once told me of a minor clash he had with the Minister of Culture. After a show he was invited to the salon behind the Government Box where the Tsar used to receive artistes and where now the Bolshevik leaders did exactly the same. The Minister asserted that all light entertainment was rubbish, especially music hall and variety. Utesov plucked up his courage, of which he had plenty, and went into battle.

'Excuse me, Comrade People's Commissar, but Lenin held an opposite opinion about music hall artistes!'

The Minister asked him in a condescending manner, 'How do you know what Lenin thought about it?'

'From his wife, Nadejhda Krupskaya. In her memoirs she recalls how she and Lenin used to go to Montmartre to listen to Monegeuse, the great music hall artiste. Lenin liked him and considered him to be extremely talented.'

The Minister smiled sardonically. 'That may be so. But you are not Monegeuse.'

To which Utesov, typically daredevil, replied, 'And you, comrade, are not Lenin.'

Jazz in those days was what is called 'traditional'. The jazz orchestra consisted of between twelve and forty high-class musicians with a proper musical education. As a rule, the musicians sat in three to four rows with the conductor in front. The performance consisted of the playing of popular jazz music and songs, and the only artistes to move about the stage were the singers and dancers. It has to be said that jazz music was condemned as highly decadent by the older generations, just as pop music in Russia is today. Maxim Gorky described jazz as the 'music for the fat men', that is, the capitalists, although jazz was more popular among the revolutionary youth than it was among the aristocrats. The top jazz band leaders in the West were Jack Hylton, Billy Cotton, with whom my sister Millie sang, the American Paul Whiteman (his orchestra's rendering of Gershwin's 'Rhapsody in Blue' is a classic to this day), Duke Ellington and many others.

Utesov, with his theatrical upbringing, jettisoned this traditional musical approach. His revues had a theme motif running through them and his musicians played parts in appropriate costumes. For that reason, Utesov chose young musicians (we were all in our twenties) on the grounds that they were more adaptable. Even the instruments served a dramatic purpose apart. Acrobats leaped over the double-bass, tap-dancers performed on the piano, conjurers pulled squirming rabbits out of saxophones. In one revue I played the part of an old bearded man who got in everybody's way. The basis of it all was still the orchestra playing popular music while moving about the stage. I don't know whether it was his policy or not, but Utesov insisted on including plenty of Soviet songs in the programme. This obviously helped to appease the anti-jazz Party bureaucrats and save the company from extinction.

Utesov was born in Odessa which is famous for the originality of its citizens. Nowhere else do people juggle with the grammar and pronunciation of Russian to such peculiar effect. Their sense of humour is unique. Odessa probably heads the list of all Russian cities in the numbers of gifted writers and poets it has produced, men like Babel, Paustovsky and Bagritsky. Famous violinists like Heifitz, Tsimbalist and Oistrakh got their early musical education in the Children's School run by Stolyarsky. Utesov was among a troupe of brilliant actors and actresses who became the backbone of the country's finest theatres. He was born at the end of the last century, and his childhood and adolescence were darkened by the anti-Jewish pogroms, when the 'Black Hundreds', as they were called, thugs and hoodlums carrying portraits of the Tsar and the image of Christ, rampaged through the streets.

Utesov arrived from the Black Sea coast in the late autumn of

1933 after finishing the first scenes of the new film *Jolly Fellows*. He greeted me cordially when we met, said he was glad to have me in the show and hoped that we would learn something from one another. I am afraid I learned little from him and this made my two-and-a-half years of work in the Revue extremely frustrating. It was a pity that Utesov was so envious of the success of others; with those numbers I did perform, I had to fight tooth and nail to ensure their inclusion in the programme.

When I read his memoirs I realized that having a Western artiste in the Revue was against his policy of singing and playing Soviet songs by Soviet composers. Indeed he was a pioneer of many songs like 'Polushka, Polya' that became popular even in the West. He was a splendid actor and sang well in a throaty way. ('Have no voice and never had one', he would announce to his admirers.) He would put the same sob into his voice my mother so detested. I didn't like it either, the musicians loathed it, but the audiences loved it.

His relations with the musicians were always strained. Utesov had a minimal musical education, gained mostly from violin lessons in his boyhood, and although he had a good feeling for music, he could never express himself technically. This led to misunder-standings and quarrels. One of them in particular could have ended badly. Our pianist, Simon Kagan, who has now managed to emigrate to the West, was a highly educated musician, a child prodigy who never became a concert artiste because of his love for jazz. He, in fact, was the Musical Director of the orchestra, a post which Utesov had grudgingly to hand over to him. Although he was entirely dependent upon Kagan for his arrangements, Utesov was invariably caustic in his criticism of the pianist's playing on the accordion, an instrument which Kagan abhorred.

The Soviet authorities considered the accordion to be one more 'belch of imperialism', and although it was tolerated in Moscow and Leningrad, it was strictly forbidden all over the provinces. There were very few accordions and each one of them was worth its weight in gold. Utesov had managed to procure this one with the help of a friend in the Confiscation Department of the KGB. Its unfortunate owner had probably brought it from abroad.

Noisy quarrels always followed any show where Kagan had to accompany Utesov in songs about the bluff and hearty Soviet sailor. Things came to a head during one of the rehearsals. After a particularly uncalled-for remonstration from Utesov, Kagan sna-tched the accordion and threw it with all his might at Utesov's head.

For a split second our star could not decide which was best, to save the accordion or his head. He ducked. A hapless saxophone player took the full impact of the instrument on his chest. 'My accordion, my accordion! Is it broken?' was the plaintive wail.

The final scenes of the film *Jolly Fellows* were to be shot at the Mosfilm Studios. We travelled there in a lorry that had been transformed into a bus, with planks for seats, driving along the south bank of the Moskva River, to a point where the magnificent Novodevichy Monastery stands on the farther bank. Then we wound our way up among greenery and trees to what used to be called the Vorobieva Hills but which are now named after Lenin. In the middle of this open, uninhabited countryside stood the Mosfilm Studios. No more ridiculous site could possibly have been chosen. Nobody had thought about the problems of transporting scenery, timber, coal for heating and all the other materials needed for a giant studio. Even the river could not be used as it lay at the bottom of the hills. The nearest railway depot was only a couple of kilometres away, but no connecting road had been built. To make matters worse, this great barracks, standing on the edge of a cliff, was open to all the icy winds that blew. No form of heating could warm the place. When it was twenty-five degrees below zero outside, it was fifteen degrees below inside. We suffered terribly from the cold in our thin costumes.

I was impressed by our director, Grigory Alexandrov, and he and I became very good friends. He was not a tall man but his bushy mane of hair gave him added stature. His blue eyes always seemed to be a little sad, even in moments of exultation. He had begun his career as a circus acrobat and later became involved in avant-garde theatre. This led in turn to the infant cinema where he met Sergei Eisenstein. There he became his co-director for many years. Together they made the classic *The Battleship Potemkin*.

When I met them, they had just returned from America where, for four years, they had been making the picture *Que Viva Mexico*. Eisenstein was under a cloud, as Stalin had ordered a vicious campaign against him. Stalin did not like a genius, the only one he recognized was Iosif Vissiaronovich Djugashvilli (Stalin's real name). *Que Viva Mexico* had been financed by the American writer Upton Sinclair, but he had died before it was finished. According to Eisenstein, he had been promised that the film would be developed and sent to Russia. So he went home in 1931. The film never arrived. It was cut and edited in Hollywood and shown all over the world to great acclaim. Eisenstein had made a brilliant job of depicting a popular revolution, but the Hollywood version, which was called *Thunder Over Mexico*, portrayed a neo-Fascist nationalist uprising. Eisenstein found it difficult to prove that he had been deceived, so he was accused of treachery to the Soviet Homeland and to his art. For a few years, before making his great films *Alexander Nevsky* and *Ivan the Terrible*, he did nothing but teach. *Ivan the Terrible* put him in trouble again, as Stalin saw it as a covert allusion to himself.

I knew Eisenstein quite well and spent many a pleasant evening in his flat, a modest establishment belonging to the Studios. The conversations, discussions and arguments taught me more than any university could. Our conversations were confined to the arts—the cinema, music, literature—never involving politics. This subject was always avoided in such a mixed company. Nor did Eisenstein ever discuss or comment on Stalin's witch-hunts—he was a loyal Russian and only wanted to make pictures in and about his Motherland. Strange to say, Eisenstein did not disappear into the camps. He died in his prime, of heart failure.

Alexandrov, whom I also knew well at this time, was a man of natural charm, able to get along with anyone. I remember one morning, during the shooting of the film, he was having difficulty in keeping his eyes open. I asked him if he was feeling well. He said he was all right, just tired—he hadn't had a wink of sleep that night. I suggested the old remedy for insomnia, counting sheep. He laughed, and said that his problem was not insomnia. Then he told me how the night before a phone call had come from the Kremlin. Stalin was bored and wanted Alexandrov to come along and cheer him up, a task he was only too used to performing. During his four years in Mexico, he had learned a lot of Spanish folk songs which he sang beautifully, accompanying himself on the guitar. And so the weary film director, after a hard day's work, had no option but to pick up his guitar and go off to entertain His Majesty, Comrade Stalin.

SIX

Circus Days

The talented film director Konstantine Mints once opened a speech in the Moscow Cinema Workers' House with the following words, 'Tovarischi, when the talk turns to the problems of Soviet comedy, there is nothing to laugh at!' This was said in 1939 when Stalin was at the height of his power. Mints was sacked immediately and had to take his talent to the State Circus. I mention his wise words because I was to discover the truth of them when I began to act in films.

The Party hierarchy like to see comedy films behind closed doors, so they will not be observed by the population laughing their heads off like ordinary human beings. Comedians are loved by the people but shunned by responsible Party officials. To them, comedians are a dubious lot. They can never be sure that the fun isn't being poked at them, or if there isn't some hidden meaning behind the comic antics.

It is a different thing with 'heroes'. In Soviet films 'heroes' always say and do the right thing, are always one hundred per cent for Soviet power and the Party. When the Honours List is published every now and again, the actors who play heroic parts invariably head the list of orders and titles. If a comic slips in, you can bet your last rouble that he has a friend in the Central Committee or the Ministry of Culture.

I played about a dozen film roles during my acting career but all of them were small parts when a comic episode was required. The only lead role I played was in a children's film, where the scripts and verses were written by the now famous Sergei Mikhalkov, a Party stooge and a millionaire.

The minute I stepped into the Mosfilm Studios, I felt at home, despite the dust and rubbish, and the unapproachable Director, sitting in his special chair like Rodin's Thinker. I did not seem to need much coaching to acquire the techniques of acting in front of a camera—slowing down movements and gestures, changing facial expressions, and above all, being friendly with the cameramen.

Life in the Soviet cinema world, with all its intrigues and jealousies, is no better or worse than that in the Western cinema except that in the West stars become millionaires while in Soviet Russia, stars do not. If you see a girl being placed nearer the camera in a group scene, you can bet your boots that she hopped into bed with the cameraman or the Assistant Director the night before.

During the filming of *Jolly Fellows*, Alexandrov fell in love with an actress who had a tiny role, so work was suspended while they went off on their honeymoon. When they returned, the script had been rewritten and his new wife had become the co-star. It has to be said that Lyubov Orlova, in contrast to many directors' wives, was a talented and versatile actress. The film was a great success. When the Honours List appeared, Alexandrov was decorated with the Order of Lenin, the highest award at the time, and Lyubov Orlova was given the cherished title of Honoured Artiste of the Republic. The star, Utesov, was presented with a camera!

One reason why Utesov was not recognized was that, apart from the fact that he was a comic, he was on the black list. The then President of the Soviet Union, Kliment Voroshilov, struck Utesov's name off the Honours List without bothering to check the truth of an absurd rumour that he had been arrested while crawling across the border, carrying a stolen copy of *Jolly Fellows*. It was ridiculous: many years later, the world champion weightlifter, Yury Vlasov, managed to lift the ten cans of film, but could only stagger about a dozen steps.

Concern for the life and health of people in a Soviet film studio is no more or less marked than in any studio in the world. I once played in a film called *Circus*. It was a touching drama about an American circus performer who has to flee from the USA because she has had a baby whose father is black. Performing in Moscow, she keeps the child hidden, fearing public condemnation. The climax comes when her German manager, an obnoxious character, comes dashing on to the arena holding on high the weeping child so that all can see what kind of a fallen woman she is. All this is his futile attempt to estrange her from the handsome Russian artiste with whom she has fallen in love. To his dismay the great-hearted

Soviet audience reacts in an unexpected way and takes the child to its bosom, thus proving the superiority of communism over capitalism.

'So what if he is black?' bawls a stout Ukrainian lady. 'We don't care if he's green with pink spots.'

As the child is passed from one to another, each person sings a lullaby in their own language, since by an amazing coincidence each happens to be a representative of the various nationalities in the USSR—Russian, Ukrainian, Uzbek, Tartar, and even a Jew played by that brilliant actor, Mikhoels. (That was before the war, when anti-Semitism was not so rife.)

During my life I have known many great people and I have come to the conclusion that the greater the man, the simpler he is in his relationships with others. Such a man was Mikhoels, one of the greatest I have ever known, whom I met during the filming of *Circus*. It is said that Gordon Craig, Ellen Terry's son and Isadora Duncan's lover, was persuaded against his will to see *King Lear* at the Jewish Theatre in Moscow. He requested a seat at the end of a row, so that he could slip away quietly unseen if necessary. Mikhoels played Lear. His conviction and artistic mastery in portraying the lonely tragedy of the King was so superb that Craig stayed to the end and dashed backstage to embrace the great Jewish actor. He was crucial to the success of *Circus*.

According to the script, when the child was safe in the embraces of the Soviet audience, his tears were supposed to disappear and he was transformed into a laughing bundle of joy. I never saw a child that slept so much as this one, and if he was wakened he made no secret of his displeasure. As children are not allowed to be filmed for more than four hours, everything depended on whether he would laugh heartily or, if the gods were kind, perhaps emit a gurgle of delight. Then we could all go home. But no. He refused to express the slightest pleasure, even when he was offered ice-cream, or chocolate, or shown a dancing monkey. When the otherwise stolid cameraman tried the old gag about 'the little birdie' the four-year-old boy looked at him with disdain and went back to sleep.

At the slightest flicker of a smile on the child's impassive face, everybody shrieked 'Full lights!' but before the electricians could stretch out a hand, the flicker would vanish. The Production Manager rushed up and down the studio shrieking 'The Plan, the Plan!' and accused everyone else of not trying their best to make the child laugh. The cameraman lost his temper and yelled back at him,

'If you're so bloody clever why don't *you* try to make him laugh. Show him your Plan.'

'I will, I'll show you,' the Manager retorted. He went over to the boy, brief-case in hand, and began to emit the most unintelligible baby sounds. The boy remained unmoved. The Manager screwed up his nose and mouth and his glasses fell off. The episode was turning into a brilliant satire. Bending down in search of them, he continued to make what he thought were funny grimaces through his legs. Everybody in the studio stood motionless, afraid to breathe, when a tiny look of interest appeared in the boy's eyes. Anticipating success, the Manager began to perform something like an African war dance, holding one finger on his head, gyrating and leaping. The boy's eyes began to close again. The Manager redoubled his efforts and in doing so tripped over one of the hundreds of cables that clutter up the floors of film studios. Falling, he struck his head on an iron transformer-box and lost consciousness. The boy began to shriek with laughter. It took everyone a split second to realize what had happened. Then they burst into action. The head cameraman bawled, 'Full lights! Full lights, damn you!' But the boy laughed so long that they were able to shoot about a dozen takes. Nobody noticed the ambulance-men when they placed the Manager on a stretcher and carried him off to hospital, where he lay for about a month with concussion. A delegation from the Party and Trade Union branch visited him in hospital, bringing him a bag of oranges and an official recommendation for bravery in the line of duty.

In this film, I played the part of a retired artiste who does odd jobs around the circus. My big scene comes when the American star doesn't turn up for the show. The Circus Manager calls on the elderly lady cashier and myself to revive our old bicycle act, the Flying Trio, to appease the audience. In a trice we come flying on to the arena all togged up in our flashy costumes, which looked as if they had come in with the Mongolian invasion. In reality, my partners were middle-aged and had no cycling experience. So they were mounted on tricycles while I, being young, was perched on top of an ancient penny-farthing made of cast-iron and weighing about half a ton. To get the pedals moving required Herculean strength. That bike nearly brought my young life to a painful conclusion. The following day was the seventh of the week, the only free day. (I say the seventh day because it was decided after the Revolution to abolish the names of days and give them numbers instead. You can imagine the confusions that could arise.) Remembering that I could sleep in the next morning I went to a birthday party on Saturday evening and came staggering home around four o'clock in the morning. Two hours later, I felt someone trying to wake me up. Through a haze I heard the Production Manager telling me the Plan had not been fulfilled and so they had decided to call off the free day. A cold shower and several cups of black coffee woke me and soon I was off to the Lenin Hills, feeling tired, unsteady and sorry for myself.

One of the tricks I had to perform was to leap up in the air with my penny-farthing, twist round like a ballerina, land back and carry on round the arena. A harness, as used by trapeze artists, was attached, with a long rope going up to a block-and-tackle near the ceiling. I relied on five burly men who held the end of the rope, waiting to haul me up at the appropriate moment.

'Up!' came the order from the Assistant Director.

'What?' shouted the leader of the hauling team, cupping his hand to his ear.

'Up! Up, I said!' the assistant bawled.

'Did you say up?'

'I said "Up" twice, you . . .'

'Right! Up twice!'

They jerked me into the air so suddenly that the bike was torn out of my hands and I was left twisting helplessly in the air. Then down I came, with a rush, and hit the floor. Then I was hauled up again for the second time. Everybody shouted to one another. It was worse than my most awful nightmare.

'But you said lift him up twice!'

'I didn't say lift him twice, I said I had said "Up" twice!'

Nobody took the slightest notice of me dangling in mid-air. What with the hangover and the belt squeezing my stomach, I felt ghastly. Then they decided to tie the heavy bike to the belt around my waist. I had found I couldn't hold it during the leap. To a series of 'Ups' and 'Whats?' I was pulled up and down and twisted in mid-air and began to lose all sense of time and place. The final shot nearly ended my career. I was jerked up so abruptly that the belt slipped up around my chest and the weight of the heavy bike squeezed so tight on my abdomen that I couldn't breathe. To make matters worse, the block-and-tackle jammed. That was when I underwent the experience of being hanged. Perhaps the story has a salutary ending for I decided then and there that, if I lived to tell the tale, I would always vote for the abolition of capital punishment.

Someone finally had the sense to fetch a step-ladder, climb up and untie the bike. But the belt was so tight that it was impossible to unfasten it, so I had to be held up while someone else clambered up to the ceiling to unravel the rope. Eventually I was lowered and as I dashed off to the lavatory, I heard the Director say: 'I think we'll use that last take—it was the best one.' The man who said, 'Art demands sacrifices' knew what he was talking about.

In the course of *Circus* I came to know Mikhoels quite well and I remember one occasion that shows exactly what sort of an artiste he was. We had all gathered in a large recording studio to perform the celebrated lullaby. The microphone was unknown in theatres and concert halls, and certainly in the Opera House. So most of the singers had not the faintest notion of how to sing to a 'mike'. There was a sense of great anticipation.

The first to start was a Russian, a soloist from the Bolshoi Opera House whose reputation there was untainted. Standing about a foot from the microphone, in the traditional pose, with his hand on his chest, he filled his lungs and delivered the first notes of the lullaby. Someone grabbed the microphone as it fell, but the whole place rang and re-echoed to the notes. Dunayevsky, the composer and one of the finest writers of Soviet songs, dashed out of the recording room. He was an extremely irascible man with no respect for reputation or titles.

'What the hell do you think you're singing?' he shrieked. 'A call to the revolutionary uprising?'

I saw the Party Secretary wince, but he remained silent. It was better not to cross Dunayevsky at such moments.

'This is a lullaby, d'ye understand? A lullaby. You're supposed to be quietening a weeping child. You sound like a mother elephant trumpeting to her young in the jungle!'

The offender declared he was a singer and not a baby-sitter, and that he was a pupil of the great Sobinoff. After each take, he was moved another step away from the microphone until eventually he ended up in a far corner of the studio. The result was that he sounded as if he was singing in a barrel.

It was therefore with a butterfly stomach that I approached the mike to sing my English lullaby. I have not got a strong voice, but was fortunate enough to have had some experience of singing to a microphone. When I finished Dunayevsky came barging out of the recording room. My heart sank. I shut my eyes and waited for the worst. Then I heard him saying, in a broken voice, 'That's what I want. Learn from this lad, you . . .' The string of expletives described what he thought of the Bolshoi Opera House and its singers. When they in their turn stamped out in a huff a break was announced for diplomatic talks.

I walked out into the corridor for the break; Mikhoels was waiting for me, wanting to know if I could spare him a few minutes. Could I just sing a few bars of the song to show him how I did it? I could hardly believe my ears, and in my confusion I could only nod my head. To think that such a great actor could ask me to teach him how to sing a lullaby!

I sang for him in a quiet corner and it didn't take him long to catch on to the trick. It was mainly a question of technique. He thanked me profusely and told me I could ask him for any favour within his power. I told him how much I wanted to see his King Lear but couldn't because of the difficulty in getting tickets. He wrote my name down and said I could come any day I liked and there would always be two tickets 'for you and your girlfriend'. I grieved when I heard of his tragic death under the wheels of a lorry in Minsk, and even more so when I heard, after the Stalin disclosures, that this kind, gentle man had been murdered by the KGB. There are few men like him in Russia now.

The eight months during the winter of 1933–4 proved to be my introduction to big-time Soviet show business. Working in the Utesov Jazz Revue, filming at the Mosfilm Studios and living in the Hotel Metropole I learned how important it was to have friends in the Central Committee and the People's Commissariats, as the Ministries were called then. It was only when I went to live in Moscow permanently, in an ordinary house, that I came into contact with the working class and all their troubles and privations.

There had been notable unrest in the factories, and even an unheard-of strike at the famous Putilov Plant. The workers were angry at the prospect of having to continue pulling in their belts during the Second Five Year Plan. Many of the ringleaders disappeared but Stalin took the hint. He resorted to a trusty gimmick. The order was given in 1933 to open what were called 'commercial shops' where food was easier to procure, but at a much higher price. So rationing continued, but in a subtler way, while Stalin was praised by the media for his 'care of the people'.

Streamers appeared on street corners proclaiming 'Thank you, Comrade Stalin, for the Happy Life.'

Apart from food the main problem was housing. Few people could boast of having their own flats in those days. In 1917, the population of Moscow was only about a million. The influx into the capital of people in search of better opportunities had increased the population to five million by the time I first came there in 1933. To relieve the acute housing shortage, families were squeezed into one room. The spare space was given to the homeless. And so rich and poor, actors and plumbers, professors and street-cleaners lived under the same roof sharing all the tribulations of a hectic commune.

The good-hearted Russians would always share what food they had, but living in a large communal flat was a sterner test of patience and good neighbourliness. I never ceased to be amazed at people's ingenuity in trying to secure some kind of privacy at home. The way a room with three or four adults living in it could be divided into separate cubicles, with the aid of cupboards and wardrobes, curtains and screens, was a masterpiece of planning.

On every door of the ordinary six- or seven-roomed flat hung separate electric meters, to avoid any arguments about paying the bill. Naturally there could not be six or seven gas meters in a communal flat, so a big chart hung on the wall in every kitchen. Each tenant had to mark down the length of time a gas appliance was used. To take a bath, where a majestic Ascot provided the hot water, cost a standard ten kopeks.

One of our neighbours was a man of tremendous size and he produced this amazing proposal. 'Owing to the undisputed fact,' he declared, 'that I am twice the size of anyone else in this flat' (he looked at me pointedly), 'I need half the amount of water necessary to take a bath. I have therefore decided to pay for half the gas, that is five kopeks.' In all seriousness we demanded tests. He sat in the bath dressed only in a pair of swimming trunks and it was proved that he really did need only half the amount of hot water for a bath.

One never could estimate the living conditions of people by the way they dressed. I became friendly with a man called Volodya who often spent an evening in the Metropole Restaurant. He and his wife were exceptionally well dressed, though in a somewhat *nouveau riche* style. The cloak-room attendant would bow down deferentially when Volodya handed in his wife's mink or her astrakhan coat. Her advent into the restaurant, decked out in fabulously valuable diamond rings, necklaces and bracelets, was a sight to be seen. The source of all these riches was a tiny shop in an archway on Stoleshnikov Pereulok, Moscow's Bond Street, where the only goods on sale were men's collars. Private enterprise, on a small scale, was still allowed in big cities.

One night, after a jovial supper, Volodya invited me to go to their place on Stoleshnikov Pereulok for a drink. Judging from the diamonds and mink coat, I expected something pretty swanky. We went down some steps into the basement area of a magnificent house. Volodya opened the front door of a flat and we walked along a long corridor, lit only by a small, dim lamp. It was cramped and very stuffy: the walls were festooned with bicycles and big zinc washing tubs. As we felt our way, I accidentally clattered into one of the tubs. A door opened and an angry voice shouted something about capitalist bastards who would never learn to come home at night quietly. At last, Volodya opened a door and we entered a room, the only room they had. It was a large one, divided into two. The only window was high up and looked out on to a dismal, claustrophobic courtyard. However, the place was crammed with rare antique furniture, Louis Quinze bureaux and Chippendale chairs. In one half there was a magnificent mahogany bedroom suite and I have no doubt that many a member of the former royal family had slept on it. Looking into an exquisite glass cabinet, I saw a collection of bibelots including a coffee set with the letter N on every cup, a relic of Napoleon's retreat from Moscow, and two vodka *shtoffs* decanters with the letter E in different scripts. 'This one,' said Volodya, 'came from Ekaterina the Great's table, and the other came from Tsaritsa Elizaveta's.' Everything in the cabinet had some Russian history to tell. All that my collar merchant could say about the unique collection was that it had cost a mint of money. I believed him. An hour or two later I emerged on to the Petrovka feeling as if I had been visiting some underground treasure-house. In my hotel room I drank some water from a plebeian glass and brought myself back to reality.

The main form of public transport in those days was the tramcar. The network of tramlines began outside the Metropole on Theatrical Square. For those whose rooms in the Metropole faced out on the square, the perpetual clanging of the tram bells and the screeching of their wheels as they went round in a giant circle was unbearable. From here, the trams trundled their way to the outskirts, no great distance in those days. A three-mile walk took you to the edge of the city.

I could not be lonely in Moscow: there were always diversions. About a fortnight after I arrived I went for a stroll. Emerging on to the Square, I heard the sound of shouting and screaming coming from a crowd milling around a tram-car. I went over to see what had happened and was told that some drunk had fallen under the tram and they couldn't get him out. Everybody around the tram was supervising the operation. (Russians love to supervise.) Somebody shouted, 'There's a leg over there but I can't see the rest of him.' This started an argument, 'It isn't a leg, it's an arm.' Two camps immediately took up the debate, which was at its height when the fire-engines arrived. After much advice from the crowd, the firemen's captain decided that the tram would have to be lifted by a large jack. But they didn't have one with them. A fire-engine was dispatched post-haste to the tram depot where there was one. Half an hour later, the jack was placed under the tram and the slow job of lifting began, to the accompaniment of the words from the 'Song of the Volga Boatmen', 'Ei, ukhniem, Ei, ukhniem'.

At last the captain cried, 'Stop, I can see him . . . get him out.' Strong men paled and women screamed, though they all pushed forward to see the fearful sight of arms and legs lying in different places. I opened my eyes when I heard roars of laughter. I looked under the tram and there was an emaciated drunk, lying between the rails, fast asleep and absolutely intact. When the firemen and militia dragged him out, he squared up to them, with clenched fists, cursing them roundly for interrupting his dreams.

It was in the winter of 1934 that I witnessed the advent of two new means of transport into Moscow that were to oust the tram from the city centre—the trolley-bus and the Metro. The first line of the Metro from Sokolniky Park to the Gorky Park of Culture was completed that year to blaring headlines. By chance, our band became very friendly with the workers who built the Metro. We used to finish at three o'clock in the morning and usually went for a walk, to get some fresh air before going to bed. It was at this hour that the Metro workers came out of the bowels of the earth through a shaft beside the ancient Chinese Wall. When they learned we were the actors from the film *Jolly Fellows*, they dragged us along to their canteen where we had to tell them all about the film and the trick photography in it. On my initiative we gave them many an impromptu concert. They told us about the lives that had been lost and the accidents that had occurred either from the inexperience of the builders or from sheer negligence. When a huge crevice split Okhotny Ryad down the middle, from Theatrical Square to the end of Gorky Street, it was because the designers had not taken into consideration two tremendous buildings, the Hotel Moskva and the Council of People's Commissars, that stood over the line at its most shallow point. There is no doubt that now the Moscow Metro is the cleanest and best-serviced in the world with its airy halls and hanging chandeliers. But no monument will ever be erected to the fine young men who gave their lives in building it.

At first the Metro was not popular. 'I'll be buried under the ground for a long time after I'm dead, so I don't want to go there before my time,' was the general view. The mere sight of the moving stairs was enough to make the peasants and the older folks go back to the ticket-office to demand a refund. To this day there is still an operator at the bottom of the escalators with a hand on the emergency lever for those peasants who still cannot learn. This was a must in the early days. More than once I have seen peasants thrown off at the bottom of the stairs covered in milk and with smashed potatoes rolling all over the platform. I remember peasants with sacks on their backs wandering about stations trying to get out. On a tram they could see where to get off, but on the Metro, with the stations' names giving no indication of location, they were lost. For instance, the three main railway terminals stand on what used to be called, appropriately enough, Vokzalny Square or Railway Station Square. It has been renamed Komsomolsky or Young Communist Square which doesn't mean a thing—especially to the young communist from the provinces himself, searching for the appropriate Metro station with half an hour left before his train leaves for Kazan or Tashkent.

The winter passed and spring came with welcome rays of sunshine which melted the big heaps of snow and ice. We rejoiced at its appearance as we waded through the slush. I had now been in Russia for two years and was beginning to feel well established. *Jolly Fellows* was nearing completion, and we were getting ready to leave on a summer tour of the Ukraine. I had resigned myself to never seeing my family again so it was quite a shock to receive an unexpected letter from my mother announcing her arrival in Leningrad in a few days' time. I was ordered to meet her at the boat. As I stood on the dock watching the ship tie up, I gazed at the passengers standing on the deck. To my mixed pleasure and dismay, I saw that Mother was accompanied by my three sisters who had grown so quickly since I saw them last.

'I have come to stay,' my mother announced. 'I have turned my back on capitalism and am going to help the good cause of building communism!'

Suddenly I realized what I had done. In my letters home, I had been too exuberant about my success in show business and Mother, judging by Western standards, assumed that I had become rich, and would be able to keep the whole family. She had stayed in Moscow before, during the year when my stepfather was Deputy Chairman of the Communist International and, of course, she had lived in VIP conditions. She hadn't the faintest idea what life was like outside the Hotel Luxe on Gorky Street, where leading foreign communists lived. (My only encounter with Marshal Tito occurred in 1939 when I bumped into him in a corridor of the Hotel Luxe and just escaped being scalded by the boiling water he was carrying in a kettle from the communal kitchen.)

What on earth was I going to do with my mother and sisters? I had no place of my own, so where were they going to live? I suggested that she should approach the Comintern with a request for a room. Mother replied that she wanted no privileges and would live like the rest of the people. My God, I thought, what is she going to say when she discovers the truth about the way the Soviet people live? I managed to wangle a double room for them in the Metropole.

The sumptuousness of the splendid restaurant and its symphony orchestra, conducted by the celebrated violinist, Ferdinand Krish, impressed my mother. I squirmed in my seat when mother told me to ask Krish to play Strauss's 'Blue Danube'. It was hard to tell her that Strauss was forbidden and that Krish was a famous musician and not a restaurant *labukh*. I mentioned the problem to a friend in the orchestra. Krish played the 'Blue Danube' on condition that my mother wrote the request in English and signed it, so that he could prove it was a foreigner who had asked for it. I introduced the family to Utesov, and to the band. When my three sisters, Jean (aged eight), Millie (ten) and Alma (seventeen), sang a trio, my colleagues were delighted and impressed. Millie, incidentally became a popular singer in England, as 'Kilts Campbell' with Jack Hylton, Roy Fox and other top band-leaders of the thirties and forties.

As the day approached for the band to go on tour, I could not think what to do. My mother was no fool, and although she didn't admit it, was aware of the grim truth about life in the Soviet Union.

She solved the problem for me by announcing, peremptorily as ever, that she was going home. 'But,' she declared, 'I am doing so only to hasten the downfall of capitalism!' I expressed the hope that she would be in time. 'But,' she went on, 'so that you won't be lonely, I am going to leave Alma with you.' This loneliness was a figment of my mother's imagination and I certainly didn't welcome the prospect of having to look after a seventeen-year-old sister. But I did look after her for a year, until it became impossible, when I packed her off back home. Later, she married an American who became a leading scientist and gave her a comfortable life. She could thank her lucky stars that I didn't let her stay in Moscow.

Our first engagement in the Ukraine was in Kharkov, where we played a month in the Summer Theatre in the lovely Park of Culture named after Postyshev, the first Secretary of the Ukrainian Communist Party. (Postyshev's immense popularity displeased Stalin, so he had him exterminated.)

I was glad to see Eddie and Kyril Sinelnikov again. Kyril was now an Academician, while Eddie had just finished a long course of treatment and had achieved her cherished dream, to have a baby. Despite her love for her husband and his homeland, she decided to have her baby in her native Liverpool. They were both glad to have the few kilos of coffee, sugar and rice I brought with me. The brutal collectivization campaign was dying out, but life was by no means easy. On our way from Moscow, we no longer saw the outstretched hands and pleas for a piece of bread. The platforms of the country stations were empty, guarded by poker-faced militiamen. Here and there lonely figures could be seen working on the land. The Sinelnikovs' house-worker (the word servant was strictly forbidden) Oksana avoided any discussion about what had happened, but once I was in the kitchen with her father who had come up from the country. A couple of glasses of *gorilka*, Ukrainian vodka, loosened his tongue, and he told me of the terrible plight of the defiant peasants.

'The worst thing of all,' he said, 'was the way the land cried. You are a city chap so you wouldn't understand what that means. To us the land is both the mother that feeds us and the child we nurse and fuss over. We don't know what communism means and we have nothing against the Bolsheviks. Lenin gave us the land free of charge and for always. Now these bandits' (Oksana banged some plates on to the table) 'take it away from us. Stalin doesn't know anything about what's going on, I'm sure. Our village elder wrote to him and the next thing was they came and arrested him. So we didn't work. Our land cried pitifully . . . but what mother can stand by and do nothing when she hears her baby crying? So we went back.' The old peasant looked at me, with tears in his eyes, while his big, strong hands clenched and unclenched. I felt he was trying to tell me that they had not lost the battle, that they were not cowards who had given in easily. No, it was because the land cried.

From Kharkov we travelled to the capital, Kiev, and then to Odessa, that glamorous cosmopolitan port on the Black Sea, city of the *khokhma*, the inimitable joke, where a fiddle is placed in the hands of every new-born baby. In every other city in the world you may find signs in the buses or trams saying: 'Do not engage the driver in conversation while in motion.' In Odessa, the equivalent sign should, according to the citizens, read 'Have you got no one else to talk to?' During the summer, when all buses and trams have their windows open, a sign appears saying, 'It is dangerous to lean out of the windows.' The Odessites translate this into the following: 'Shove your head out of the window and you are going to look a terrible mess.'

After Odessa, we had a month's holiday, so our enterprising Manager arranged for us to go to a seaside resort, Anapa, where we gave ten performances. We received no money but were given two return railway tickets, free meals and accommodation. In the absence of our leader, Utesov, I took over his place and was the star of the show. I enjoyed this as Utesov had not been very liberal when handing out parts in the main show. I revived all my song and dance acts that had made me popular before joining the Revue. The applause and the writing of autographs for adoring young girls gave a great boost to my confidence. Anapa is a children's resort because of the shallow bay and the medicinal waters. Young mothers used to bring their children here for the whole summer, so the few men at Anapa were very much in demand. It was just my luck to have a seventeen-year-old sister with me!

In fact, it was Alma who gave me the fright of my life. Although we lived in a private house, we had our meals in a convalescent home not far away. Sitting at the table with us was a pleasant man called Igor. When he heard I had a rehearsal after the midday meal, he invited Alma to go with him for a half-hour flight in a plane, to which she readily agreed. On my way home from the rehearsals, I was met by Nina, our young landlady, who was in such a state of fright that she could hardly speak. 'Alma! Alma!' was all I could get out of her. Eventually the story burst out like a flood.

'I was sitting in the front room when I heard a knock at the door. I opened it and nearly fainted. A full-blown colonel of the KGB, in uniform, asked if Alma lived here. I wanted to say no, but I heard Alma shouting excitedly, "Coming, coming". They left together. I followed them a long way until we came to a military place with a sentry on duty. He saluted and let them pass. Alma has been arrested. I'm sure of it. Come on and I'll show you the place.'

I too began to feel terrified, and as we dashed along the dusty road, I racked my brains to think what Alma might have said or done. Then we turned a corner and there she was walking arm-in-arm with our table companion, Igor, complete in the full uniform of the Border Guards, a section of the KGB. Alma's words tumbled over one another as she described the flight over the town and the nearby mountain valleys. It was the first time she had ever been up in a plane. Igor stood by, looking very strange in his uniform. Up to now, I had only seen him in white trousers and open-necked shirts.

The summer season was over, and at eight o'clock on a sunny morning in September 1934 our train, carrying us back from the Black Sea, puffed into the Moskovsky Station at the far end of the Nevsky Prospekt in Leningrad. This was the autumn of the fatal year in which a chain of events showed Stalin in his true colours. Twenty years were to pass before we learned that the Great Teacher and Father, the Friend of All Children, was one of the tyrants of history. At the time, Stalin was the least of my worries. I was concerned about where Alma and I were going to live. Travelling with us on the train was our guitarist and tap dancer who bore the inappropriate name of Kolya Shicker. In Yiddish, *shicker* means 'drunkard'. Kolya drank no more than the others in the orchestra, nor was he Jewish but 100 per cent Ukrainian. He was only thirty-five but was referred to as 'starik', 'the old man', because all the other musicians were still in their twenties. When he married a seventeen-year-old girl, some practical jokers gave them as a wedding present a reproduction of a well-known painting called 'The Unequal Marriage' by the Russian artist Makovsky. This depicts a decrepit old man being wedded to a girl of about fourteen. Behind them can be seen the faces of a couple of young dandies preparing to help the ancient bridegroom with his marital duties. The result of this joke was a perpetual suspicion in Kolya's mind that his lovely young wife was cavorting with someone younger than he. Actually, Tonya was a virtuous and faithful wife and never gave her husband any grounds for his accusations.

Alma and I went to Kolya's place for a couple of days until we could find a room. He had two rooms in a communal flat overlooking the Fontanka Canal. We survived it for a day and a night but then gave up. Sober or tipsy, Kolya's language was lurid, though not devoid of humour. But luck was with us, for as soon as Mrs Lawson, an old English friend of Mother's, learned that we were back in Leningrad, she told us that if we didn't come to her at once we need never step across her threshold again. I was glad. Alma was picking up Kolya's foul language quicker than proper Russian.

The Jazz Revue was engaged for the whole of the winter season, 1934–5, in the Leningrad Music Hall Theatre on the Nevsky Prospekt. A new statute had been passed forbidding artistes and actors to work freelance, so that everyone now became an employee of a State theatre or agency. We were registered as employees of the Music Hall Theatre, and all performances, concerts, radio or gramophone recordings were negotiated by the management who received the whole fee. We were given a fixed salary; mine was 800 roubles a month. I had been earning as much as 5,000 roubles a month and this was a big blow to my pocket. After paying for rent, food, taxes and Trade Union dues, I was left with 100 roubles spending money, which certainly didn't allow for suppers in restaurants after the show. Instead we used to frequent a bar, in a basement just round the corner from the theatre, called the Bochka or 'Barrels' Bar, where the walls were decorated with barrel ends. After the show we would have a couple of beers each and engage in the Russian custom of chewing pieces of *vobla*, smoked roach from the Caspian Sea. The fish was hard and stiff and the ritual was to bang it on the table to soften it up. Sitting in a fog of tobacco smoke and listening to the music of an ancient fiddler and pianist seemed to me the height of bliss. I was an actor among actors and I experienced a wonderful sensation of belonging there. We delighted in back-stage gossip, and would listen for hours to extravagant tales of how many curtain-calls the company got in Vologda or Astrakhan. I loved it, and to this day I believe there is no better company than actors talking over a few bottles of beer after a show.

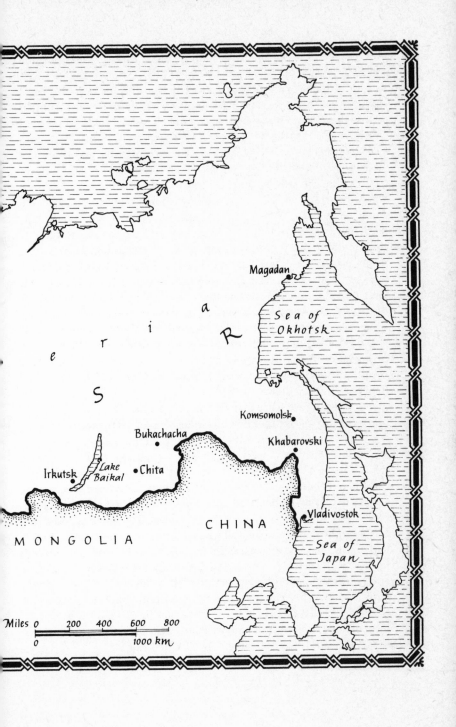

Magadan

*Sea of
Okhotsk*

S i b e r i a

R

S

Bukachacha

Komsomolsk

Khabarovski

Irkutsk   *Lake
Baikal*   Chita

Vladivostok

CHINA

MONGOLIA

*Sea of
Japan*

Miles 0   200   400   600   800

0   1000 km

The State Circus was only a few minutes' walk from the bar, and most of the performers came along to 'bang a *vobla*'. In Russia the circus is undoubtedly the most popular of all entertainments and it is certainly not primarily for children, as in the West. Every town and city has a permanent brick-built circus with a well-equipped arena. I renewed my acquaintance with an artiste I had met the previous year in Moscow. Everybody called him Sasha Lyotchik, which means 'aviator'. He had been a trapeze acrobat all his life and his group was called 'The Avios'. When I met him he had given up high flying. He was getting on in years and was beginning to lose his touch. His decision to come down to earth occurred after he missed a few catches and sent his partners diving down into the net, something no trapeze artiste can enjoy. The circus management helped him to buy a group of trained animals, including a camel, and Sasha became Sa Sha Khan, the Wonder Trainer from the Orient.

It was a good act. Sasha entered the arena perched on top of the camel, accompanied by the wailing of Eastern music and the beating of drums. He was dressed like an Indian maharaja, complete with long cape and white turban. He jumped down off the camel's back and proceeded to put his animals through their tricks. There were no tigers or lions, just a few monkeys, small Himalayan bears, a couple of llamas and the camel. His daughter performed a solo dance with a big snake.

One evening we were gathered in the Bochka Bar after the show and were surprised to see that no circus people had turned up. It was not until after midnight that a group of them finally came down the steps, looking very upset. We sensed something awful had happened. It was only after they had drunk their first jar of beer that we questioned them. All that Koko, the clown, could say was 'Sasha Lyotchik'. Then he burst into tears. The others just sat and gulped their beer. We had to wait for the full story. Sasha had entered the arena on the camel as usual, to the sound of the music and drums, had halted, waved his hand in his Eastern greeting and leaped lightly off the camel. As he did so, his foot got stuck in the long cape and before he could save himself, he fell on his head. He was dead, with a broken neck, when they touched him. Such is the circus. Sasha had fallen dozens of times from the Big Top, *na kopchik* (on his rear end) as circus folk say, with only a broken arm or leg to show for it. But a fall from a camel's back killed him.

'At least he died in the arena,' said Koko, which summed up perfectly the spirit of the circus troupe.

On another occasion, we were all escorted from the Bochka Bar to the local militia station. In fact it was through no fault of ours. It was the day before pay-day, and we had only enough roubles for one bottle of beer each. After we had drunk that, there was a vacuum. Conversation didn't seem to click without that second bottle. Suddenly, the street door banged open and down the steps, shaking the snow from his sheepskin coat, came Boris Kornilov, the famous poet. Tossing his coat aside, he slumped into a chair at our table and bawled at the top of his voice, 'Hail to ye, the Muses, the sons of Zeus and Mnemosyne!'

Boris Kornilov was a peasant like his great compatriot and fellow-poet, Sergei Esenin. Both were examples of the kind of genius that occasionally emerges from the peasant masses of Russia. Boris was a fine poet, with immense talent, but little or no education. He enjoyed addressing people with flamboyant declarations, probably picked up in a newspaper article or magazine.

'I have just earned 200 roubles for reading my verses at the Children's Pioneer Palace,' he shouted. 'The money burns my pocket like Vesuvius in eruption. Chelovek! Beer for all my friends. Musicians! Play up! I am paying for everything tonight.' Boris had evidently seen Chekhov's *The Cherry Orchard* and was repeating the outbursts of the *parvenu* merchant, Lopahin.

We didn't mind. Boris had come like the answer to a prayer. It was after the fourth or fifth round that someone asked a question which was our undoing.

'What did you read to the kids?' was the fatal question.

Kornilov screwed up his face as if the beer had turned to vinegar.

'Oh, a load of *govno*,' he said. The word *govno* means shit. The Russians apply it to anything under the sun from rotten food to government bureaucrats. 'You know what they want,' the poet continued. 'The task of the literary worker—can you imagine Pushkin being called a literary worker?—is to educate youth to become responsible citizens! So we give them the *govno*.'

The poet's voice could hardly be heard above the din and noise in the bar which, I thought, was lucky for him. *Stukachi*, informers, in bars are like cockroaches in a communal kitchen.

'You didn't read *My Africa* did you?' was the next unfortunate question.

Kornilov banged his mug of beer down on the table, and leaning towards the speaker aggressively, cried, 'What are you saying? That

My Africa is a piece of *govno*? Is that what you are trying to infer, you miserable swine?'

I edged away from the table. In case of an emergency, and it looked as if there was going to be trouble, I wanted to skip out as quickly as possible. Boris was roaring by now. 'I am going to read *My Africa* right now and anyone who says it is *govno* will have their heads bashed in!'

And he began to read the poem. It was a masterpiece, a great poem which, if it had not been for the banality of the theme (that only Soviet communism could solve the problems of black Africa or understand her people's sufferings and aspirations) might have become a classic. As Boris read it the bar became quiet and the musicians stopped playing. Any noise, no matter how slight, was met with a muffled 'sh-sh-sh'. Boris would never have won a prize for elocution, but his powerful conviction moved the crowd. When Boris ended the reading silence reigned, until a bleary-eyed customer sighed deeply and said, '*Zdorovo!* Fine!'

'Is that *govno*? Is that shit?' Boris demanded, looking round the bar. Evidently Boris did not take the silence as a sign of agreement, for before anyone could stop him, he seized a bottle from among the few dozen on the table and hurled it through the window. The rest of the bottles followed in quick succession. It was like a scene from a Western. Everyone, including myself, dived under the tables. Within a few minutes, a posse of militiamen came thumping down the stairs of the bar and we were all marched off to the station. Despite our protests of innocence, we were fined five roubles each for breach of the peace—all except Boris Kornilov! His fame as a poet had penetrated even the whitewashed precincts of the militia station. We demanded that he pay all of our fines which, to give him his due, he did after a certain amount of persuasion.

As we passed the grand old building on the Nevsky which to this day houses the Kniga bookshop, Kornilov demanded that we should all kiss the handle of the door which had been opened many a time by the greatest of all Russian poets, Alexander Pushkin. We did as he asked, with reverence, and then staggered home to our beds with the first streaks of dawn lighting our way.

SEVEN

Married to the KGB

Our new production of the Utesov Jazz Revue in the late autumn of 1934 was a great success. *Jolly Fellows* had been released and was being shown to packed cinemas. Utesov himself had reached the zenith of his fame, and only the notoriety he once gained during his early career for his rendering of *blatnie* songs, ballads of the *urki*, the criminal elements, prevented him from being honoured by the Government. After a performance in the Kremlin, where Stalin was present, we were invited to a banquet there, a sumptuous affair where caviare was eaten with spoons and champagne flowed in the proverbial rivers. Stalin was in a benevolent mood and, addressing Utesov said, 'How about letting us hear the forbidden Odessa songs?' Utesov sang the 'Odessa Kichman', a touching ballad of a young man writing to his mother on the eve of his execution for killing his unfaithful wife. 'You can tell them all, Mama, that your son died like a man,' were the last words. When Utesov finished, there was a profound silence which was broken by Stalin who said, 'They were correct to forbid such songs.'

The last curtain went down on the show one night in December 1934. Everybody was still on stage when the Theatre Manager walked on and told everyone to stay behind as he had a special announcement to make. Standing on a chair, he said in a broken voice, 'Comrades, Sergei Mironovich Kirov has been foully murdered!' Sergei Kirov was the popular Leningrad Party leader: it was widely known that in the Politburo (the Communist Party's leading body of which Kirov was a member) Stalin was master-minding a fierce power struggle. For a few seconds all the actors and musicians in their gaudy costumes and wigs stood as if stunned. Then everyone without exception wept like a little child. Tears of disbelief ran down their cheeks. The Manager continued, raising his voice above the weeping, 'A cowardly assassin from some counter-Revolutionary group of former aristocrats and rich merchants' (Stalin had cunningly prepared the ground by accusing these innocent people) 'waylaid our Mironich in the corridor of the Smolny Institute and shot him dead. We shall have revenge upon these dastardly criminals for the loss of our Mironich!' The Manager could say no more as he was overcome with grief.

There was hardly a single citizen of Leningrad, regardless of their attitude to the regime, who did not support Kirov. He was a stocky, broad-shouldered man with a charming smile. He did much to alleviate the hardships of the First Five Year Plan, especially for children. I met him once when he visited the Lenfilm Studios. He was a modest man who forbade any pomp or ceremony in everything he did. For example, whenever he visited a factory, the only one who knew his destination was his driver, who was informed as Kirov climbed into the car. He did not want anyone to telephone ahead and give the management and Party officials the time to stage-manage anything.

Once I was playing a small part in a film where a Soviet soldier speaks English. I was quite surprised when a quiet man, standing among the group of rubber-neckers, asked me where I had learned to speak English so fluently. When he heard I was an *anglichanin* he began to ply me with questions about life in Britain and about the people. When I was called away to the camera he said we must meet again. He didn't say who he was, but I was curious and someone told me: 'That was our Mironich—you know, Kirov.' We did not meet again and the next time I saw Kirov he was in his coffin, lying in state, in the Tavrichesky Palace. Our company joined the queue after the show at about midnight in a heavy snow storm in December 1934. We passed his coffin at eight o'clock the next morning. I have never seen anything to compare with the emotional scenes displayed by the people. They came from the city, from the countryside and from far-off towns. Mironich was truly loved and that, of course, was why he lost his life. Stalin—and not only Stalin but any man who becomes Party ruler—would not tolerate any threat to his power. The feeling among the delegates to the Seventeenth Party Congress was that they should elect Kirov to the post of General Secretary in Stalin's place. Not only did Stalin exterminate Kirov; the majority of those delegates were to meet the same fate. No one can know what Kirov would have been like if he had become the Party leader—Soviet history has shown that absolute power creates tyrants—but as the Party boss in Leningrad, he proved himself to be kind and considerate, with the people's interests genuinely at heart. He was a great man and a great loss to Russia: it seems odd that in the West he is known only because his name was given to the famous ballet company.

It was just after this that I first became aware of the massive purges that had begun with the 1917 Revolution and periodically, like a smouldering fire, would still burst into flame with greater ferocity. When I heard that the *byvshies*, the former aristocrats and rich, had been given twenty-four hours to gather together what they could carry of their possessions and report to a deserted railway depot beyond the city borders, I was completely bewildered. I could believe that some kind of small counter-Revolutionary group did exist. It was out of the question that all these people could have been involved. These innocent men and women were bundled into cattle trucks and, after untold suffering, were brought to what were called *peresylnie punkty*, exile distribution centres, in the Urals, Siberia and the Kazakhstan desert. In the summer of 1935 the band made a big tour of all these places and met many friends and colleagues eking out a miserable existence.   If you look at the map of the Soviet Union you can see a small town called Polunochnoye above Sverdlovsk. It is the last station on the branch line from the Trans-Siberian line. After Polunochnoye there is nothing but thousands of square miles of uninhabited tundra. When we visited the town it was called Kabanovsky, named after the First Secretary of the Sverdlovsk Regional Party Committee. A further example of the megalomania of this tin-pot Party boss (First Secretaries are to be counted in their hundreds) was a giant banner that stretched across the stage over the heads of the actors. On the banner were the words: 'Glory to the communist cause of comrades Marx, Lenin, Stalin and Kabanov.'

Comrade Kabanov's presumptuousness cost him his life. Two years later during the 1937 Stalin purges, he was executed. Kabanovsky reverted to its old name, the much more poetical Polunochnoye, which means Northern Midnight.

Polunochnoye was typical of thousands of small provincial towns dotted all over Russia. Only its administrative buildings were made of brick, some of which might reach the dizzy height of three storeys. All the other houses were log structures lining muddy, unpaved streets that wound their way to the edge of the tundra.

There were no pavements except on the one main street which (as in all such towns) bore the name of Lenin. The drab shops added little colour to the scene with their monosyllabic, dilapidated signs announcing the wares which they were supposed to sell, 'Meat', 'Fish', 'Butter'. The locals called these wares *Uletuchy*, things that vanished the moment they appeared on the shelves.

When we visited it, there was nothing poetical about the place. Polunochnoye had now become the Exile Distribution Centre for *byvshies*. I was staggered when a man stopped me in the street and said, 'Have you been dragged into this nightmare, too, Villi?'

I hastened to assure this man whom I barely recognized that I was not an exile but a member of the Utesov Jazz Revue.

'Don't you remember me? I am Victor Arnfeld. I was an actor in the Moscow Operetta Theatre.'

Victor was an extremely interesting man. He came from an aristocratic family and bore the title of Baron before the Revolution. He was a naval cadet when the 1917 Revolution erupted. When the famous ballerina, Kschessinskaya, escaped in the night with her child and all the valuables she could stuff into a doctor's handbag, it was Victor who carried the bag. A complete Russian patriot, the young Baron Arnfeld remained in his homeland. He had a good voice and became an operetta star. Now he was an exile. Eventually he landed up in the Gulag camps. Released during the war, he became a member of an artistes' group, and performed for the troops. For his service to his Motherland he was arrested again in 1945, returned to the camps and was released only after the death of Stalin. The suffering and horror he experienced broke his health and he was bedridden for many years. Finally, he came to live next door to us in Moscow and I was a constant visitor until he died.

There was a similar chance meeting a year later, when I had quit the Jazz Revue and teamed up with my future wife Elena. We were on a tour of the Urals and Siberia and had to get to Tobolsk which, like Polunochnoye, is on the edge of the tundra. We arrived without our pianist who, whether by accident or on purpose had missed the train. I remember setting out in a bone-shaking lorry. Elena, the only woman in our ten-man group, was given the questionable pleasure of sitting in the driver's cabin. At least she was spared the merciless rays of the broiling sun and the attacks of giant mosquitoes. On the way, we stopped in a tiny village to look over the log house where Rasputin had been born. Tobolsk was a desolate, sullen place. The sight of the fortlike guard-house where we had to show our travel documents to be stamped with an exit pass so that we could leave freely had a depressing effect on us.

The only guest-house was a doss-house for peasants bringing their products to market. The men were given a large barn of a room, while Elena was invited to another large dormitory for peasant women. She returned immediately, declaring that she preferred to stay with us men. The stench, apparently, was unbearable. Russian peasant women have no idea about letting fresh air into their houses. Windows are for watching the neighbours through and are not to be opened. So a large wardrobe was moved into a corner and Elena's bed was placed behind it to give her some privacy.

Our major problem, however, was to find a pianist. There was no theatrical agency, of course, and the only person responsible for show business in Tobolsk was the manager-cum-caretaker of the summer theatre. He scratched his head until he remembered a lady pianist who taught at a children's music circle in the security guards' club. Off we went to find her. Trudging around Tobolsk was no joke. It had been raining heavily and the absence of drainage had turned the unpaved streets into a quagmire. As the Russians say, we had to 'tie our galoshes to our ears'. In the end we found the lady, but when we asked her to play in the show that evening, she shied away. However, she told us about one of the local exiles, a good pianist from the mainland (they called everything beyond Tobolsk 'the mainland'), who was forbidden even to practise. We found this man and his wife living in a tiny room built on to a log house. Our compère gasped when he saw him. He was Boris T., a well-known concert pianist. When his wife, an aristocrat's daughter, was banished, he declared he would go with her. In retaliation the KGB put a black mark against his name, and this meant that he was no longer allowed to practise his profession. In desperation, Boris T. was forced to take a job in a carpenter's shop. He showed us his calloused hands.

The Commandant gave grudging consent for Boris to accompany our show that evening. A Moscow show was a rarity and he was interested in getting a free performance for his garrison. Boris practised our music all day and it was heart-rending to see the look of anguish on his face as his fingers refused to obey. By the evening, however, he had warmed up sufficiently to accompany us exceptionally well.

At the opening of the show, our compère announced that we had the pleasure of being accompanied by the laureate of an international contest for pianists in Paris, Boris T. Many years later, I met Boris again and he told me that our arrival had been a godsend. The little musical group for children was changed into a school, for which a large house was allotted. He was appointed headmaster and given a room and a kitchen at the back. So life became easier for the international laureate in exile.

One of the biggest Exile Distribution Centres was Orenburg, a town on the edge of the Kazakhstan desert, where the exiles were forced to live in the *auls*, the nomad villages. Orenburg was typical of any small town on the Volga River, except that it had some of the style of the Orient as well. There were camels instead of horses and it was a common sight to see these docile, long-suffering animals, with their absurd faces, plodding along a street and carrying the merchandise that had been brought by a modern goods train into the desert. Orenburg later became famous for its Military Aviation School where Yuri Gagarin, the first man ever to fly in outer space, graduated. In the thirties it was notorious for its terrible Gulag labour camps which were being erected when I was there. Life in the town seemed to comprise a succession of human tragedies. One, especially, I shall never forget.

When we arrived at the hotel in Orenburg, a rambling building with Spartan facilities, we were told not to walk in the streets at night, and even in the daytime to go around in groups. The reason for this was the invasion of the *urki*, robbers, who had come from all over the country to strip the *byvshies* of their valuables. Many an ex-courtier with a gold watch died in the dark streets of Orenburg at the hands of the *urki*. The KGB did nothing to stop these robbers— what difference did it make whether the *byvshies* died in the dark streets or out in the desert?

The theatre where we performed was a large wooden building in the town gardens, extravagantly called the Park of Culture. In the evening the youth of the town strolled to and fro in front of the theatre and engaged in the thoroughly cultural activity of bottom-pinching. As usual, all the local KGB men came to our shows, and their Chief threw a grand party for our star, Utesov. The other ranks swarmed around the rest of the band. One of my fans was a Captain who introduced himself as Vasya. He was a tall, fair-haired man with gentle blue eyes and an honest, open face. The pouches under his eyes told of excessive drinking. I happened to be sitting on a bench, watching the bum-pinching parade before the show, when Vasya sat down beside me. I remarked on the hilarious spectacle before us.

'Bah!' said the Captain. 'A lot of cows and yokels. Now if you and a few of your lads would like to come to my place after the show, I can promise you a good time. I'll have some of the *byvshy* women along and they'll show you a thing or two.'

His face became more and more flushed as he described the 'thing or two'. I wanted to refuse, but when I considered the alternative, a drab restaurant with the badly cooked food that had to be washed down with vodka to drown the taste, I agreed and said I would tell my friends. However, I suggested that he shouldn't bother to invite the *byvshy* women. I was afraid that I might know some of them.

'Are you fellows eunuchs or something?' he said, with the hint of a sneer in his voice.

'What if the girls don't want to come?'

'Don't want to come! That's a good one! They'll come running. They know what'll happen to them if they don't.'

Vasya met us after the show with a couple of *drojhkies*, and ordered the drivers to go along the high street so that the town could see he was doing the 'Jolly Fellows' proud. At last we arrived at his house, a two-storeyed log building that had once belonged to a rich merchant. We were led into a large drawing-room decorated in the oriental style with low divans and thick carpets. When our host threw off his tunic and slumped down on one of the divans, I thought that he had only to don a fez and a flowing gown to complete the picture of the sultan with his harem. There were several women in the room, some sitting, some half-lying on the divans. Two of them introduced themselves as Maria and Tatiana. They were both in their early thirties, simply and elegantly dressed, and their manners spoke of good breeding. They were obviously *byvshies*. Maria told me afterwards that she had run away from a noble home to become a ballerina but was expelled from the Marinsky School after the Revolution. Tatiana was dark and laughed when I suggested she might be a gypsy. 'I wouldn't be surprised if I really were a gypsy. It used to be quite the fashion in the aristocracy to have a gypsy woman for a mistress.'

The two other women were nearer forty, and with their loud dresses and coarse manners were obviously not of good breeding. One answered coyly to the name Tossia, and the other, a hefty peroxide blonde, demanded to be known by what her friends called her, Malyutka. Her friends must have had a quaint sense of humour: Malyutka means 'little one'. The last of the women was a nice-looking young girl with hazel eyes and chestnut hair who had done her best to give her well-worn clothes some semblance of taste. There was nothing of the peasant in her, to judge from the perfection of her arms and legs, while her slender fingers, although coarsened by heavy work, showed that none of her forebears had ever handled a plough. She sat upright on the edge of one of the divans, looking completely out of place. The set smile on her face reflected how hard she was trying to be polite.

'Come on! Take your pick.' The Captain-Sultan waved his hand expansively to indicate that he didn't mind sharing his harem with friends.

I sat down beside the shy girl, who moved away so quickly that she nearly fell off the divan. I mustered my most charming smile, and what I thought was a reassuring expression. Evidently the girl interpreted my look as a lecherous leer. She appeared to be more terrified than ever. I racked my brains for something to say—an unusual state for me. After what seemed ages I managed to come up with, 'It's been a nice day today, hasn't it?' and, 'This is a charming town, isn't it?' The girl could hardly have agreed with these banal remarks since for her neither was remotely true. I was just beginning to wish that I had never come to this party when Vasya's orderly announced supper. With undisguised relief the girl and I joined in the stampede for the dining-room. The abundance and variety of the food was truly mouth-watering. As the Russians say, there was everything on the table except birds' milk: smoked salmon, caviare, pickled cucumbers, boiled ham 'with a tear in its eye', raw herring soaked in red wine, *pirojhki* of all sorts, minced meat, chopped eggs and decanters filled with vodka.

'What will you have to start with?' The shy girl had at last found her voice, a soft, husky voice with a cultivated accent. I thanked her and said I would choose what she chose—I trusted her taste. She looked at me in alarm and stammered as she spoke again, 'You are not Russian, you are a foreigner!'

I hastened to reassure her it was safe to talk to me.

'Oh, I'm not worried about that . . . I couldn't be worse off than I am now.'

She told me her name was Sonia and, while I was introducing myself, Vasya called on everyone to fill their glasses for the first toast. In a voice full of emotion our host cried out, 'I raise this glass to the Great Father, our Teacher and Benefactor, Comrade Stalin!' Throwing back his head, he emptied the vodka down his throat and then grabbed a pickled cucumber, sniffed it and pushed it into his mouth. Everyone followed suit, being careful to turn their glasses upside-down, *do dna*, to demonstrate their complete agreement with the toastmaster. Then came toasts to Soviet power and the Soviet people, the noise in the room grew, and the smoke thickened. The time had come for jokes, each becoming more lurid than the last. Malyutka made the locals laugh with a story about a local Party leader whom they knew. 'He was so fat,' she said, 'he couldn't do anything with me. When he wanted to take back the food and brandy he'd brought, I chucked him down the stairs.'

The story seemed to excite everyone, and one by one they disappeared into the bedrooms. Soon only Sonia and I were left, sitting at the table. The muffled sounds of laughter and squeals seemed to make Sonia retreat more and more into herself. After a while Vasya reappeared with a pink-faced Maria trailing behind him. 'What are you two doing here?' he shouted. 'Are all the rooms engaged? Come on, in you go. Enjoy yourselves. If you don't take her in there, I will!'

Neither of us moved. I was just thinking up an excuse when Sonia suddenly seized my hand and said in a surprisingly merry voice, 'Why not? Come on! Let's go and enjoy ourselves.'

I was taken aback and rather angry. I pushed Vasya roughly aside, and putting my arm round Sonia's waist, almost dragged her into one of the bedrooms. The minute we were alone she whispered urgently, 'Please, please, don't touch me . . . please!'

This made me even angrier. She was making a fool of me. 'What's the matter with you? You're the one that wanted to come in here. You said you wanted to enjoy yourself.'

'I had to, I had to! Don't you understand? We are in the hands of the Captain. If he had taken me into this room, heaven knows what he would have done to me. He's a beast! And then I have to tell you . . . I am a virgin.'

I really was out of my depth by now. My anger had evaporated. Then I saw the look of terror in Sonia's eyes, and tried to calm her. 'All right, Sonia, don't worry. I won't touch you. But I think we should spend the night together, so it looks like the real thing. Come on, lie down beside me on the divan and huddle up. Don't be afraid. I won't touch you. It's all right.'

And so we spent the night innocently together. It was a severe test of my fortitude. After this, we began to meet every evening. What Sonia did during the day or where she worked I never discovered, but her red and roughened hands suggested hard manual labour. She rented a small lean-to attached to the main building but with a separate entrance. The rent swallowed up half her wages but she valued her independence above everything. We would sit together on a bench, under the bright moonlight, and talk and talk.

The troupe's engagement at the theatre was extended for a further week and the nearer the final Sunday approached, the more pensive Sonia became. When I mentioned that our next stand was in Kuibishev, she suddenly jumped up and went and stood at the tiny window, her back turned to me. She kept repeating '*Bojhe moi, Bojhe moi . . .*' ('Oh God, Oh God . . .') Then abruptly she threw herself on her knees and grasped my hands.

'You cannot go away! You must not go away and leave me. What am I to do? What's going to happen to me?'

The more I tried to console her, the more she shivered, as if in a fever. I put my arms around her and she quietened down. We sat silent for what must have been ages. I don't know why but suddenly I asked her, 'How old are you, Sonia?'

'I am only nineteen, but I feel as if I've been living for ever.'

I was puzzled. 'Only nineteen? But you can't possibly be a Byvshi! You can only have been a year old when the Revolution began. Why have you been exiled?'

And then she began to tell me her story. 'I was born of an aristocratic family. My ancestors made Russian history. My name is Muravieva.'*

Although my knowledge of Russian history was scanty, I knew that this name had been a powerful one before the Revolution. Many of the Muravievs had been staunch pillars of the Tsarist regime while, paradoxically, others had been its most bitter opponents. I asked Sonia whether one of her ancestors had been banished to the Siberian copper mines, at the beginning of the nineteenth century, along with a group of rebels called the Decembrists. She sighed and answered with a wry smile, 'Yes, isn't it droll? I told the KGB about it, but they said they had never heard of the Decembrists, that I was lying to save my skin.' She paused for a moment and then went on: 'My parents were young and rich and,

* This was not her real name. For various reasons I prefer not to reveal her true identity.

like most of their kind, I suppose, pretty frivolous. I was their first-born, and was sent to our country mansion at Gatchina, with my nanny, while they went off to the Ukraine to inspect an estate. When the 1917 Revolution came they were probably afraid to return to Petrograd. I never heard anything from them again. My nanny took me to her home village to live with her family, but she died when I was five. I was sent to an orphanage where I was brought up as a proper communist. So much so that when I went to my Teachers' Training College I actually applied for membership of the Young Communist League. That was the beginning of my misfortunes. I appeared before a mixed Party and Komsomol Commission and I had to tell them the story of my life. You should have seen the horror on their faces when they learned I was an offspring of the Muravievs. Both Party and Komsomol secretaries were sacked and I was expelled from the college. I was working in a factory when I was ordered to quit Leningrad. And so now I am here.'

I thought for a moment she was going to cry again. I was stunned by the cruelty she had suffered. With an effort she straightened her back and continued her tale. 'So now you know my story. I am called a *byvshy* and yet I never knew what it was like to be an aristocrat. I am just as communist-educated as any other girl. Why do I have to suffer when I have done nothing wrong? That's why I feel old, so old.'

All the next day I racked my brains to find a way to help Sonia but to no avail. At supper that night she was silent. She seemed to have something on her mind which she could not express. Later, in her room, I asked her what I could do to help her, pointing out that she knew more about these things than I did. 'There is a way,' she said at last. 'It's a slender chance, so slender I don't know whether it is worth trying.'

'I'll be the judge of that.'

She closed her eyes, and almost in a whisper she said, 'I might be saved . . . if . . . if . . . you were to marry me. Please, don't think badly of me . . . I won't be a burden to you. I'll cook for you—I am a good cook—I'll wash for you, scrub the floors. If you get tired of me, I'll go away. We can easily get a divorce. Please help me. I'll die in the desert . . . it is terrible there. It's not my fault my parents were aristocrats. Please help me . . .'

She raised my hands and kissed them, and the tears poured down her cheeks. I took her by the shoulders and told her to stop crying, saying that I was a stupid idiot for not having thought of it myself.

'Of course, we shall get married,' I cried. 'I'll go to the Registry Office tomorrow and find out what I have to do.'

The next day brought a disappointment. I was told at the Registry Office that I had to have special permission from Moscow to´marry a Soviet citizen. The lady in the red headscarf was coldly polite and advised me to take my fiancée to Moscow where I would find it much easier. By the smirk on her face I knew she had guessed this was a marriage of convenience. It is a ruse which remains popular even today. We had a matinée that day, and after the show I approached our band inspector, Alfred, a wise man whom we called our Rabbi. He considered the problem in silence for a few minutes and then spoke quietly.

'This is going to be hard for you to understand. That you want to help Sonia is commendable; my heart, too, goes out to these unfortunate people. But the KGB will never let her go, even if she is here by mistake. They won't let you marry her either. You'll only get into trouble yourself and they will send Sonia into the desert immediately to get rid of her. As for smuggling her out with us on the train—forget it. There will be a thousand eyes watching. The KGB know all the tricks. The only advice I can give you is to wait until we get back to Moscow. Maybe your British Party representative can do something.'

We parted at that. I remained on the bench in the gardens where, so as not to be overheard, Alfred had taken me. With a sigh I rose and walked towards the gate, and there, as if to confirm my dismal thoughts, stood Captain Vasya. He greeted me effusively, 'Well, well, look who's here. I haven't seen you for ages.'

After some small talk, he suddenly asked me, 'How is your affair with that girl getting on? What's her name? Oh yes, Sonia. What's she like in bed? You are a lad, aren't you . . . I'll bet you've taught her a thing or two. You artistes know all the tricks!'

I tried to get him off the subject by telling him that I had not been sleeping with Sonia, that I was not interested in her. He simply guffawed. 'Not interested, eh? Then what have you been doing in her room until three or four o'clock in the morning? Playing tiddlywinks? And why do you want to marry her? Huh!'

Vasya slapped me on the back with more vigour than simple friendliness required. There was something of a warning in it. 'Now don't try to be smart,' he said genially. 'We know all about you. We know you wanted to register your marriage, and that was foolish. I like you, you're a good artiste and I'd hate to see you get into trouble because of a bitch of a girl. Forget Sonia. And don't even dream of smuggling her on to the train. I'd pull you both in.'

He seemed to be saying all this in a good-humoured, easy way, without the slightest hint of severity or harshness. He continued, 'I got into trouble once for taking pity on someone and got demoted for my trouble. I know that it's no fault of Sonia's that she's here. It's just one of those mistakes; I didn't make it but I have to answer for her. She's here now, and this is where she stays. All I can do—don't get excited, it isn't much—is keep her in town as long as I can. And don't worry, I won't touch her!' I had no option but to thank him grudgingly. As we left the gardens he put his arm round my shoulders like an old pal.

When Sonia and I went to her room after supper that night, she guessed from my doleful expression that nothing had come of the marriage idea. She did not sigh or weep, in fact she tried to brighten me up with a funny story. Seeing that I was still upset, she began to talk in a more serious vein. 'Listen to me, my dear. Don't be so down-hearted. I was almost sure nothing would come of it, it was just a faint hope, that's all. I know you'll do all you can to help me when you get to Moscow. Please God, you'll find a way. I just want to tell you that I really like you, very much.'

She laughed when I told her that Vasya thought we had been sleeping together. 'Maybe we should have. I might have become pregnant. It would have been your baby and maybe saved me from the camps in the desert. That would have been grand.'

When I left her, she said she could not come to see me off at the station. 'I'd probably have hysterics. I don't want anyone to see that, especially the KGB men.' And taking my face in her hands, she kissed me tenderly on the lips, gazing into my eyes for a long time. Then, with a sudden movement, she released me and said hurriedly, 'You had better go now or my landlord will have something real to report. Goodbye, my dear, and please, don't ever forget Sonia, your *byvshy* girl-friend.'

And that was that. I never did forget her. I went to Moscow in late autumn and did everything to get permission to marry her, but nothing came of it. Already in 1935 the rumblings of the approaching 1937 purges could be felt and the midnight arrests were beginning. Who cared for a lonely girl on the edge of the desert? I wrote to Sonia but got no reply. I never saw or heard of her again.

From Orenburg, we travelled to Kuibishev and on up to the Urals. Once again I was to discover the price being paid by the Russian people in the relentless drive towards industrialization.

Our first venue was Magnitogorsk where one of the many giant projects of the First Five Year Plan was under way. A sleepy agricultural village was being transformed by a gigantic iron and steel plant. Throughout Russia appeals had gone out to join in 'laying the foundations of communism' by working in the new scheme. It was obvious from the town's growth that the propaganda machine had achieved the desired results but social planning had lagged far behind the pace set by the industrialists in the Kremlin and there was a severe housing shortage. It was late autumn when we arrived; the hot, dry winds from the surrounding steppe had changed into cold blasts, and relentless rain had turned the scorched earth into a sea of mud. A township of canvas tents and dug-outs had sprung up where the workers and their families lived, ate and slept. The only new brick buildings were the administration centre and the so-called 'Palace of Culture' which might have been more aptly described 'Palace of Propaganda' with its printing press, radio studio and theatre. This did not deter our audiences. They filled the theatre to capacity each night. They would arrive wrapped in their rough working clothes, and use the cloakrooms to change into suits and brightly coloured dresses, determined to celebrate fully such a rare diversion.

I had now been with the Utesov Jazz Revue for nearly three years and I felt it was time to quit. I was ambitious and felt pretty confident I had the makings of a star. At least that was what my friends and admirers told me. And with all the self-assurance of a young artiste who has never had his fingers burned, I considered that stardom was just around the corner.

On the way back from this tour in the autumn of 1935, I read in the papers that the Fifth Comintern Congress was about to open in Moscow, and among the list of delegations coming from all over the world was a British one including my stepfather, J. R. Campbell, and the General Secretary, Harry Pollitt. Here's luck, I thought, maybe Father or Harry can put in a good word for me so that I can be allocated a room in Moscow and fulfil my dream of living permanently in the capital. Immediately on my arrival in Moscow I started a hopeless search to find out where they were staying. 'No information is given to strangers,' was the answer I got.

'But,' I cried, 'I am not a stranger, I am Comrade Campbell's stepson.'

'Have you anything to prove it?'

'Here is my passport. You can see our names are the same.'

'Having the same name is not proof.' And bang went the window.

My luck improved when I met an English girl, Kate, who lived with her mother in a communal flat and invited me to sleep on her floor. Kate was the daughter of a Latvian called Peters, who had been in Lenin's bodyguard before the Revolution. When Lenin was in exile in London, Peters met and married Kate's mother, an Englishwoman. After the Revolution, he became one of the heads of the KGB but, finding them an inconvenience, he left his English wife and daughter to eke out a meagre living for themselves. After Lenin's death, Peters fell into disfavour and was demoted to the post of Commandant of the Kremlin, where he cultivated his allegiance to the Great Teacher, managed to escape the purges and died in his bed. After the Second World War Kate and her mother were arrested and went into the camps where the older woman died. Kate was released after Stalin's death and received permission to return to London. I do not know if she is still alive.

The Congress of the Communist International was due to open on the evening of the third day after my arrival back in Moscow, and I had still not found my stepfather. I was standing disconsolately among the crowd near the Hall of Columns where the Congress was to be held. Suddenly I saw Harry Pollitt strolling towards the hall. Harry and my stepfather were the closest friends. He was more of an uncle to our family than were our true uncles. Forgetting that I was surrounded by militia and plain-clothed KGB men, I shouted, 'Uncle Harry! Uncle Harry!' and pushed my way to the front of the crowd. I was immediately grabbed, but, struggling, continued to shout. I was overjoyed when I saw Harry cross the street. When he showed his delegates' mandate to the militia, they released me.

'Where the hell have you been?' Harry bawled at me. 'Your old man has been looking for you and he's going to give you a kick up the arse for not finding him!'

'I've been looking for him everywhere, but the stupid bastards in the Central Committee won't tell me which hotel he's in.'

'He's in the Hotel Europe. Room 234.' I burst out laughing. This hotel was just round the corner from Kate's place.

My stepfather greeted me warmly. I did not refer to his prediction that I wouldn't be able to stick life in Russia. He had been right about its hardness and right to warn me, and I suspect he was proud that I had managed to stick it.

Next morning, on the front page of the paper, was a large photograph of Stalin with J. R. Campbell on his right and on his left, Georgy Dimitrov, the Bulgarian communist. Dimitrov had been elected President of the Comintern and Campbell, his First Deputy. I did not talk to Father about helping me get a room in Moscow as I thought this photograph would be enough to impress any bureaucrat. I was mistaken. If Campbell had been a petty official in a District Party Committee his name would have carried more weight than as the leader of the biggest communist organization in the non-Soviet world. But by then the Congress had closed and Father had gone, so I could get no help from him.

In spite of everything I decided to stay in Moscow but needed a lot of dogged persistence to do so. I found that band leaders were not falling over each other to engage me, so I had to swallow my pride and chase after them. During 1936 I must have performed with five or six different bands, mostly in the foyers of cinemas. The most promising of them was a Swedish band led by Mackie Berg. I performed with them only once, in the Revolution Theatre, and we brought the house down. My programme was made up of popular traditional jazz music from compositions by Gershwin, Duke Ellington and others. But the greatest applause came when I sang in Russian an old gypsy song called 'Caravan'. Russians love it when foreign artistes sing their favourite songs in Russian and I often exploited this patriotic eccentricity, as did many other visitors. Still the expected contracts did not materialize.

My biggest problem, as always, was to find a place to live. One evening I went home to Kate's feeling very despondent after another disappointing audition, to find a young fellow sitting with my friends at what looked like a festive table. He was introduced as Volodya, an old schoolfriend of Kate's, who had returned to Moscow after a long absence, and had come along to celebrate the renewal of an old friendship.

How much it must have cost Kate to tell me this remarkable lie. A few years later I happened to be walking near the notorious Lubyanka, the headquarters of the KGB, when I saw Volodya, in the full uniform of a KGB major! But by that time I had lost touch with him and he had no interest in me.

In the meantime we became very friendly. He was learning English, and was grateful for any help I could give him. He introduced me to a young couple, Tonia and Yasha, who kept open house every Saturday evening. The guests brought their own vodka while the hosts provided pieces of sausages boiled in a tomato sauce. There were always a couple of dozen people and that alone ought to have made me suspicious. Regular gatherings in private flats were taboo. If Tonia and Yasha could entertain openly, then obviously they had permission from the authorities. Tonia took to me as if she had known me all her life, would sit with me in a cosy corner and coax me to tell her all my troubles, what I was doing and where I went and to whom I talked. And in my naivety and loneliness I confided in her. In retrospect I imagine that Volodya was delighted with her comprehensive reports.

On another evening at Kate's I met a blonde and extremely attractive nineteen-year-old girl called Maya. Her job was in the Personnel Department of the Grand Hotel. At the time I did not realize that an official in any personnel department (Maya was the secretary in charge of staff files) is appointed by the KGB. If I had, I could have saved myself a few years of frustration and trouble. Kate went so far as to warn me openly not to have anything to do with Maya, but I put it down to jealousy. Volodya said nothing, but ignored her completely. Years later I was told by a close friend in the KGB that the biggest 'sin' for a KGB officer was to reveal the identity of an informer or agent. 'Two different departments were interested in you,' my friend explained. 'Kate and Volodya were assigned to you by one department, Maya by the other. Obviously Kate, Volodya and Tonia took a liking to you and tried to warn you as best as they could, without risking the dire penalties for revealing Maya's real intentions.' I was dumbstruck, as you will appreciate when you hear the rest of this story.

The day came when Kate told me I couldn't stay in her room any more. A neighbour in the flat had written an anonymous letter of complaint to the militia about me (writing anonymous letters is a popular hobby in Russia). My residence permit was expiring and I had only a week to find myself a room or return to Leningrad, maybe even leave the country. Maya suggested that if the worst came to the worst, we could get married and she could register me officially in her room as her husband. I leaped at the idea, and we dashed along to the Registry Office. It was as sudden and as casual as that. The room where Maya lived had been given to her mother by the Tuberculosis Hospital on Bojhedomka Street, near the Square of the Commune, where she worked as a medical sister. The room in the dilapidated house was worse even than the Glasgow slums of my boyhood. I vowed I would get out as soon as possible. As it turned out I lived there for three years. In 1939 the whole house was demolished to clear a site for the Soviet Army Theatre.

There were five of us in the room—myself, Maya, her mother, her twin sister and brother. There was no bathroom, one lavatory for about fifty people, and one communal kitchen. Maya's brother, a lad of seventeen, came home drunk twice a week and became so abusive that he had to be tied up. The noise of quarrelling in the kitchen, and other rooms, where the hospital nurses lived with their families, became so unbearable that I used to wander the streets to escape from it all. I would gaze into some basement and see a family sitting cosily round a samovar and envy them. Gradually I became more and more depressed: one morning, I thought I'd go mad. I grabbed my coat and jumped on to a tram-car which took me outside the city to a place called Pokrovsky Vstrechny. The morning was bleak and grey, and as I sat on the banks of the lake, I began to ponder whether it wouldn't be better to tie a stone round my neck and finish everything off. Life had become a series of disasters. I couldn't find regular work in show business, my part in *Circus* had been small and brought me little money and satisfaction. I had performed with half a dozen jazz bands, but although I was popular with audiences, band leaders would announce, without being able to look me in the eyes, that I wasn't needed. Why? Maya had given up her job at the Grand Hotel and followed me wherever I went. I realized the mistake I had made in marrying her, but there was nothing I could do about it because of my need for an official residence registration. Why not finish it all? There was no one near the lake to see me, and it would be weeks before anyone found my body. I woke up as if from a nightmare. What was I thinking of? I jumped to my feet and ran and ran, stopping only when I reached a busy road and mingled with the crowd on the pavement. Only then, among people, did I feel calm and safe.

It was a good thing I did not choose a watery grave, because on returning home I found a letter from the manager of the Udarnik Cinema, one of the largest, inviting me to come and have a business talk. The next morning, I put on my best Sunday suit and was in his office on the dot of twelve. He had seen a preview of *Circus* which he was to première and he wanted to have a grand circus programme in the foyer for as long as the picture ran. I was to do my clown act from the film. This was the act where I did comic work on bicycles.

And that was my début as a clown on the stage and in the arena.

The film ran for three months and I earned quite a decent sum of money, most of which went in paying debts. The experience of working as a clown was of great value to me, and widened my abilities as a performer. A clown, and I mean a good clown, is probably the most difficult role in the art of theatre. An actor who can play a clown can play anything. A clown has to be intelligent, versatile and agile. No one can write a script for him—he has to do it all himself.

During my engagement at the Udarnik Cinema something significant happened which seemed to warn of bad things to come. Maxim Gorky died at the age of sixty-eight. He had been a close friend and comrade-in-arms of Lenin, but in the first years after the Revolution had fallen into disfavour among the Bolsheviks, including Lenin, who condemned him strongly for his defence of the intellectuals. Although many historians extol Lenin as a mastermind and genius, he was often no less ruthless than Stalin. Gorky was so disgusted by this ruthlessness that he resigned from the Communist Party and left the Soviet Union to live on the island of Capri. This was never forgiven or forgotten, even when he returned to the Soviet Union in 1928. Ominously, when Gorky died no order was given to close down places of entertainment for a period of mourning. The funeral was not a public event. We knew nothing about it until we saw the militia clearing the streets of traffic and pedestrians from Nikitsky Vorota where Gorky lived, down through Arbat Square to the Bolshoi Kamenny Bridge, past the Udarnik Cinema, and on to the crematorium in the Donskoe Monastery. We artistes climbed on to the roof of the cinema in our clowns' costumes and watched the solemn procession from above. The coffin, draped in a red banner, lay on an open car. In the procession were Molotov, Voroshilov and other leaders, but Stalin was not there. His obsession about popular heroes was so strong that even in a world-renowned writer like Maxim Gorky he saw an enemy. This is not hearsay. It was revealed in the Stalin Disclosures of 1956.

My engagement in the Udarnik Cinema ended and I was out of work again. Two fellow clowns, whom I had taken into the show with me, on the understanding that we would continue working together, let me down. The State Agency, they said, had refused to include me in the act as a trio was too expensive. I did get an engagement with a twelve-man jazz orchestra in the Coliseum

Cinema and, as well as singing and dancing, I had to compère a half-hour show in the foyer. I looked out a bunch of jokes and my act seemed to go over well with the public. I was stunned when, three days later, I was taken off the programme and ordered to appear at the Censor's Office. Next morning, I had to listen to a poker-faced official as he described the 'crime' I had committed—performing unscripted material. I was told what would happen to me if I ever opened my mouth again on the Soviet stage without a properly visa'ed typewritten script in quadruplicate. This stipulation is still in force wherever the spoken word is performed anywhere, and it means that disc jockeys do not and could not exist. Radio announcers are only allowed to say the name of the music or song and the composer. One of the best television programmes was 'Cinema Panorama' conducted by Alexei Kapler, a talented script-writer with many excellent films to his credit. (He also gained fame for falling in love with Stalin's daughter, Svetlana Alliluyeva.) Kapler originated this television programme during the liberal period after the death of Stalin, and the reason for its great popularity, apart from Kapler's professional knowledge of the cinema, was the informal way in which he conducted it. Needless to say, he had no prepared script. All went well until the beginning of the seventies when the Kremlin decided to clamp down on the freedom of speech guaranteed by the Soviet Constitution. Kapler was ordered to submit typewritten script for every word he pronounced. He refused and explained rightly that the programme would lose the charm of its informality. He was told, 'Script or get out.' He went, and with him the best programme on Soviet television.

On my way home from the Censor's Office I dropped in at the café in the Hotel National where theatrical agents, managers, actors and performers gathered to talk business. As I walked in I saw Arnold, the Art Director of the Utesov Jazz Revue, waving to me to sit down at his table. For a second, I thought of leaving without my coffee, fearing he might want me to return to the Revue.

'Where the devil have you been hiding? I've been searching for you high and low,' he cried. 'What are you doing now?'

I went to great lengths to tell him how the Mosfilm Studios, the big showbiz agents, and the jazz band leaders were all fighting among themselves to engage me. I might have saved my breath as Arnold was an intelligent man and an old trouper himself. He interrupted my exaggerations. 'Well, I'm glad you have become so famous,' he said slyly. 'No point in wasting your time with the magnificent proposal I had to make.'

I realized I had overstepped the mark and remarked nonchalantly that no artiste ever refuses to listen to one more offer. It appeared that Lev Rogatsky, the Head of the Foreign Department of the State Circus, had a grand idea for a big 'attraction' in which his wife, Elena, a splendid ballerina, and Tamara, a music-hall dancer who had married Kalmanovich, the Minister for State Farms, were to play the leading roles. Arnold had been engaged to direct and choreograph the act. I was the only artiste he knew of who could play the singing, dancing clown needed to complete the act which, he declared effusively, would be a sensation. After getting my 'grudging' consent, Arnold rang Rogatsky and arranged for us to meet the next evening at seven o'clock in the Minister's flat on Gertzen Street.

Dressed in my best three-piece suit, and with my shoes shining like stars, I rang the bell at exactly seven o'clock. I waited for the door to open, thrilled but apprehensive, little realizing as I stepped over the threshold that that meeting was to change my destiny.

I was ushered into the Minister's study and invited to take a seat. Sitting opposite me was a beautiful young woman who studied me with dark, thoughtful eyes. I was struck by the elegance with which she wore an exquisitely tailored checked costume, a white frilly blouse, a tiny white hat and black shoes. But most of all I liked her eyes. I was aware that she was curious to see this song-and-dance clown that her husband, Rogatsky, was foisting on her, a classical ballerina. Nevertheless, I could see a kindness intended to soften my awkward and nervous state. This was Elena.

With her was Tamara, the Minister's wife, attractive in a typically Russian way, and the handsome, dark-haired Rogatsky. Rogatsky was voluble and persuasive. The new act was a grand idea; the General Director of the entire State Circus, Alexander Dankman, had promised to allot a large sum; the girls would enter on white horses, Elena poised on points; we would all play musical instruments; we would travel the world. I liked the sound of world travel, but I had my doubts about working with girls, especially a Minister's wife. We agreed to meet again in a few days, when Rogatsky had prepared the contracts.

I returned home to find a young fellow waiting for me in the communal kitchen. He introduced himself as Sasha, a musician from the English Jazz Orchestra whose leader was a man called

Barton who had been arrested by the KGB and accused of spying. Barton was expelled from the country and the rest of the English musicians left as fast as they could. But Barton had already recruited some Russians and now they wanted me to take the orchestra over and create a jazz revue. I thought this was a miracle which would save me from working with girls. I left for Leningrad a few days later, with the last of my money. When I arrived I rang Sasha immediately, but got no answer. From then I lived with that phone. Only once did I get an answer, from a woman who said tearfully that Sasha had gone away. Where? She didn't know and hung up abruptly. I was in a mess, the last of my money almost gone. I went for a walk along the Nevsky Prospekt and was so engrossed in my anxious thoughts that I hardly looked at a young fellow who asked me for a match. Automatically I searched for the box in my pocket and handed it to him. As he lit his cigarette he addressed me in a whisper. 'Don't take any notice of me. Go round the corner into the Sadovaya and wait for me beyond the cinema!'

In wonder, and some apprehension, I did as he asked. Standing in the shadow beyond the cinema I waited for him.

'Sorry for the cloak-and-dagger stuff, but I'm afraid I am being watched,' he said, continually glancing over his shoulder. 'I am Sasha's brother. He and the other musicians were taken the night after they arrived back home. Sasha told me to find you and warn you. You'd better get back to Moscow and forget all about it.'

'Yes, but what if they're released? After all, they couldn't possibly have had anything to do with the spying business.' I was clutching at a final straw and must have sounded naive.

'They won't be released! Once the KGB takes anyone they never let him go. They'll cook up something. You'd better go before they find out about you.'

And without another word he disappeared into the darkness. I was in a quandary. Was he really Sasha's brother or an *agent provocateur* from the KGB? One way or the other, I realized that the only thing to do was to get back to Moscow.

On my return I rang Elena immediately. I didn't tell her of my attempt to escape. She was glad to hear from me and told me to come along to dinner. And that suited perfectly. I had not eaten for two days.

We started rehearsals. To earn money, I did an act in a Charlie

Chaplin costume which was popular at children's concerts. Elena had a partner from the Bolshoi Ballet, Sergei, and danced *pas de deux* at clubs and halls. Tamara had no act, since she didn't need to work, and was a nuisance, often coming late or not at all. Elena, on the other hand, as a fully trained classical ballerina, was entirely professional. We became great friends.

EIGHT

The Stalin Purges

We entered 1937, that fateful, dreadful year, and already the whispers of arrests were to be heard. The first blow came in February. For the first time Elena was late for rehearsal. She arrived looking pale, with dark rings under her eyes. She excused herself and without a word joined in the rehearsal. When we had finished she asked me to wait behind after everyone had gone. Her voice sounded tired and broken. 'They took Rogatsky in the night. It was horrible. We were asleep when they hammered on the door. They ransacked the place.'

I was amazed at her self-control; only a slight quiver betrayed the tremendous strain she must have been suffering. She laughed bitterly. 'They found the box with all my theatrical jewellery and almost danced with glee—they had unearthed a hidden criminal hoard! When I tried to explain to them that it was all imitation, they roared at me, "We've heard that one before." They didn't arrest me. Our marriage is not registered and I'm not officially Rogatsky's wife.'

Hardly had we recovered from this shock when Alexander Dankman, the General Director of the State Circus, who had promised to finance us, was arrested. The General Director of the Mosfilm Studios and the Chief of the State Repertoire Committee were arrested at the same time and it was put about that they had been discovered crawling towards the Kremlin walls, with a box of dynamite. This was absurd—all three were so stout!

And so we were left with neither a manager nor any finance. Eventually we were given a loan to cover our expenses, breathed a sigh of relief and went on rehearsing. Then, about the middle of April, Tamara's husband, the Minister, was relieved of his post.

This was an ominous sign. A few weeks later, a discreet phone call informed Elena that her partner Sergei had been arrested in the night. Many years later, we found out that he had died in the camps. He was a splendid dancer, dedicated entirely to the ballet, and had no interest in politics. But he had been on a five-year tour abroad—and that was his crime.

We finally managed to complete our act and the audition was so successful that we were booked into most of the top variety theatres. First, we went to Tbilisi in Georgia and topped the bill for a month in the Summer Gardens. We were fêted everywhere by Stalin's exuberant compatriots. After the tension of the last few months, we all felt relaxed until a telegram came with the news that our partner, Tamara's husband, 'had gone away on a long trip', which meant that he too had been arrested. As we had only a few days of our contract left, Tamara worked to the end, although it must have been hell for her. The former Minister was executed as an 'enemy of the people'.

We performed for a month in the Moscow Hermitage Gardens, the Mecca for all artists in Russia, and as soon as we had finished there was another important engagement to begin. I rang Elena to make arrangements and was flabbergasted to hear her say, 'Tamara has gone off on holiday.'

'What do you mean, holiday? Where has she gone?'

Elena's calm voice answered, 'Come over and I'll tell you all about it.'

When I arrived, Elena told me that Tamara had been taken the night before. Her five-year-old son was in the care of her parents. We never heard of Tamara again, and only assume that she too must have died in the camps.

All that day Elena and I rehearsed in her room, humming our music, and transforming our act from a trio into a duet. Standing in the wings that evening, I kissed her good luck as she waited for our music to begin. She now had to open the act alone. Tears of admiration were in my eyes as I watched her dance. All that is beautiful and courageous in the Russian people I saw in Elena that night, and I fell in love with her.

The new act was well received and seemed to work better as a duet. Describing a comic routine is no fun, you have to see it. But to give you an idea of what Elena and I did to become Soviet showbiz stars, here is an approximate description.

The scene is set in a picture gallery. I am a slightly inebriate clown-attendant imitating the faces and poses in the portraits. I draw aside the curtain that hangs in front of me to reveal Elena in a rosy crinoline and white wig. When I lie down to sleep at side-stage Elena comes to life and dances a minuet. Then she returns to the picture-frame and I wake up. I draw the curtain and, thinking it was a dream, I open the curtain again. This time Elena is in a blue costume with a mini-skirt. She does a dance-moderne and, dodging under her high kicks and sliding away from her whirlwind twists, I dance with her. Into the frame she jumps again. Then I sing a comic song about the dangers of drinking at work and follow this with a dance based on the unsteady movements of drunks. I open the curtain to see Elena standing elegantly dressed in evening tails and wearing a top hat. As a show-stopping finale we dance a tap dance *à la* Fred Astaire and Ginger Rogers. All this would have been splendid but for the subtle terror of the Stalin purges.

The man whom Stalin had appointed as Head of the KGB was called Yezhov. This was a grimly appropriate name: there is an old Russian expression *yezhovykh rukavitsakh*, meaning 'one who rules with a rod of iron'. Yezhov did that with a vengeance. Yezhov and his subordinates added to Stalin's orders their own particular brand of horror. They never arrested anyone in the daytime. People who lived in blocks of flats where the lifts were closed at midnight would listen fearfully to the stamping of jack-boots on the stairs and heave a sigh of relief when they did not stop on their landing. But nobody ever asked who had been taken in the night, on the principle that 'Curiosity killed the cat.'

Stalin was concerned to exterminate all those who had deviated from the Party line and those who, like Sergei Kirov, presented a threat to his ascendancy. But as the purges went down the ranks, political 'crimes' became as lowly and paltry as the vigilant informers who disclosed them. A charwoman in the local KGB offices lived in the communal flat next to ours. Her humble connection with the KGB was enough for her to terrorize all the tenants in the flat. Whenever she appeared in the kitchen the other tenants would disappear into their rooms until the coast was clear. An old lady who lived in the tiny room next to the kitchen had a trivial quarrel with her one day about matches or primus fuel. High words ensued and the upshot was that the old lady was arrested, accused of 'desecrating the image of Comrade Stalin'. She had washed the floor of her room and covered it with old newspapers. Virtually every Soviet newspaper carried a large photograph of

Stalin on the front page, and the old lady could hardly help, as the charwoman put it, 'digging her dirty heels into the beloved features of our Great Teacher'. She was kept in prison for six months without trial until someone realized the absurdity of the whole thing and set her free. The 'crime' was too ridiculous even for KGB judges.

Then came the Kamenev–Zinoviev trials, the high point of the purges, and the signal for massive reprisals. Kamenev and Zinoviev had criticized and even opposed Lenin at one time. Although they had since behaved themselves, they were now to pay for their old sins. More accurately, Stalin had found a pretext to get them out of the way. The arrests and executions reached such gigantic proportions that it became a little difficult to explain how half the membership of the Communist Party, including most of the leaders (except for a few stooges like Molotov, Kaganovich and Voroshilov), all the People's Commissars, and hundreds of thousands of Party and Government executives were international spies and agents of Imperialism! Stalin solved the problem by putting Yezhov up against his own wall and executing him. Yezhov was not accused of spying, he was accused of being an alcoholic, a homosexual and a schizophrenic. Everybody sighed with relief, and said, *skatertyu yemo doroga*, good riddance to bad rubbish. Stalin appointed a fellow Georgian, Lavrenty Beria, as Head of the KGB. The atmosphere of suspicion and terror in the capital was now all pervading.

Soon, rumours about Beria's penchant for raping small girls began to circulate. I was friendly with the four Btorov sisters, the Soviet swimming champions. The youngest, Tonia, was training in the Black Sea for a marathon when a motor-boat crossed her path. She recognized the occupant as Beria and was flattered when he stopped to ask questions about her swimming achievements and records. She had not heard the rumours and unsuspectingly agreed to rest for a while on his boat. The moment she was on board he tore off her costume and although she was a strong girl she was unable to stop him. Her cries for help were useless. The only other boat nearby contained Beria's bodyguards and they just turned their backs. When the horror was over, Beria ordered Tonia back into the water and threatened life imprisonment if she ever told what had happened. How she managed to swim to the shore is a mystery. Her injuries were so severe, and the psychological trauma so great, that she gave up swimming for ever. Beria lasted for sixteen years, until

Stalin's death in 1953. Molotov, Khrushchev and the new leaders had him executed as an international spy and agent of Imperialism. This was very much in their own interests as he might otherwise have revealed how many death sentences they themselves had signed.

Elena and I performed in Moscow all through the winter of 1937 and into the beginning of 1938. Our act was such a success that we were instructed to prepare for a concert in the St George Hall of the Kremlin, in the presence of Stalin. I had performed for Stalin once before with the Utesov Jazz Revue and although it was a unique experience, it was not one that I enjoyed, even though we did not see the Great Teacher, who always sat at the back of his box, in the dark. For Elena, after the nightmare of her husband's arrest, the thought of performing for Stalin was appalling. But, of course, we had no choice.

Command concerts always included famous acts and top artistes, but even these normally ebullient personalities sat in silence in the dressing-rooms to which we were conducted in convoy, through a myriad of check-points. Poker-faced officers examined our passes with microscopic thoroughness. We were ordered not to wander about backstage but to stay in our dressing-rooms and wait for our call. We were told not to expect any encores and to return to our dressing-rooms immediately after the performance to wait for the convoy to escort us back to the outer world. Although we could not see Stalin we felt his awesome presence, which added to the feeling of claustrophobia created by the security men.

I could never understand the need for such performances. The applause sounded mechanical, as if by command. No one seemed to be enjoying themselves, neither the audience nor the artistes. On and off the stage, we felt the suspicious eyes of the security guards. Conjurers had to prepare their tricks and apparatus under the supervision of stony-faced guards who never betrayed any natural curiosity. During our act Elena had to change costumes twice, and it was my job to hang them on chairs behind the back curtain. The first time we performed in the Kremlin, I prepared everything as usual and returned to the dressing-room. When we went behind scenes to warm up, I found to my horror that the costumes had disappeared. When I asked one of the guards where they were, he took me to a side-room where the costumes were being thoroughly scrutinized. The guards took no notice of me when I asked to have the costumes returned, even though we were due next on stage. I was reprimanded for not calling a guard to watch me set up the costumes, but 'as it was the first time', we were allowed to perform. We were glad to get home that night.

In the spring of 1938 Elena and I left on our first tour together as a duet. By this time we had become the closest of friends, with a brotherly-sisterly affection for each other. It was the first time in my life that I had someone in whom I could confide all my worries and troubles—my mother considered anything of that kind to be a sign of weakness. Although I appreciated Elena's loveliness and perfect figure I never allowed myself to think of her as a desirable young woman. We dressed and made up in the same dressing-room, often we shared the same room in a hotel, we got to know one another as well if not better than husbands and wives, but Elena was my *partner* and a better one I could not have found. Husbands can leave their wives, or vice versa, if anything goes wrong, but partners in show business have to stick by each other. They have to work together, live together on tour, create new acts and rehearse together, argue and agree, quarrel and make it up.

As we toured the Urals and Siberia I could still detect a flicker of fear in Elena's eyes now and again. She had not recovered from the trauma of Rogatsky's arrest. What was worse, she did not know where he was, as the KGB refused to accept any parcels from her, or even a note since she was not his registered wife. It was no wonder that Elena took a long time to recover from that horrible night. All her life she had suffered from the attentions of the secret police. She came from a well-to-do family and her father had been a prominent civil engineer. They had lived in a large six-roomed flat on Spiridonov Street, in the fashionable quarter near the Nikitsky Gates. Many of the street battles of the 1917 uprising took place around these Gates where the Cadets, who were loyal to the Provisional Government, had their headquarters. It was during one such affray that Red Guard worker-soldiers smashed down the front door of Elena's flat, suspecting the family of harbouring Cadets. They marched through the rooms, smashing anything that got in their way, shouting at Elena's father and threatening to 'slap him against the wall', a favourite expression among Bolsheviks. When they levelled their Mausers at the family and ordered them to get out and go to hell or wherever they liked, until the fighting was over, tiny Elena looked up at the Commander with her serious eyes and asked him, 'Please, sir, may I take my dolly with me?' Perhaps this reminded the man that he was a father himself, and a human being, because he barked grumpily, 'All right. You can all stay, but don't dare go near the windows or . . .'

One by one their rooms were requisitioned, leaving the family of four with two rooms. A couple of years later, one of the new tenants wrote an anonymous letter to the KGB and the pack of lies was enough to have Elena's sister, Vera, arrested and held in prison without charge. She was a dancer and many of the great ballet stars, among them Mordkin, were her partners. In prison she had a nervous breakdown and became paralyzed in both legs. She never danced again. Only after requests were made by famous actors who knew Vera did the KGB really investigate the accusations and find them to be entirely false. Vera was released, though no apologies were made. Nothing happened to the woman who wrote the letter, and she continued to live in the flat.

Soviet show business had this in common with the West: there was the same competition to get good engagements, and the way to the top for a young actress was often the same as in Hollywood. The Director of our State Agency had a large divan in his office 'for testing female singers' voices', as the artistes put it. He met his Waterloo with a hefty folk-singer who responded to his advances with a half-nelson and then gave him a good thrashing. He might have been saved by the unexpected entrance of a man from the Ministry who could have hushed up the whole affair. But a large group of artistes were looking over his shoulder. The Director was sacked and went back to his true vocation— van-driving.

Naturally, a lovely dancer like Elena came in for her share of unwelcome attention. Whenever we arrived in a new place or travelled with a new group, her appearance always created a stir among the men. Elena enjoyed the admiration but she always managed to keep the wolves at bay with the greatest of tact. 'Better to lose a potential lover and keep a good friend', was her motto. I became adept at helping her out in tricky situations. We had a secret sign which Elena used whenever she wanted me to come to the rescue. Many a would-be suitor must have hated it when, like the proverbial little brother, I would appear, apparently out of the blue, to sit it out into the small hours. They could not possibly take offence either. Elena and I were so polite and considerate, asking after the health of their wives and children—'Perhaps you have a photograph of them?' was one of our favourites.

Once, in Erevan, in Armenia, the People's Commissar of Forestry introduced himself to Elena after the show and invited her to supper in the restaurant. As usual, she told him she couldn't go without her partner, which did the trick. Neither of us liked Ministers or Generals, partly because they were almost always bores, with no interests apart from their own particular spheres, and partly out of respect for the wise old Russian saying: 'From Tsars you must keep far away, to keep your head for another day.' However, this particular Minister was persistent and politely asked me to join them. A wink from Elena persuaded me to agree. He turned out to be reasonably good company. He was intelligent and well-read and as the next day was Sunday, he invited us to go for a ride in his car up to Lake Sevan in the mountains. It was a perfect day, warm and cloudless, as we climbed the twisting roads, often little better than tracks, and when we finally stopped at the summit we gasped in wonder. There are many beautiful lakes in the Caucasus but this one surpassed them all. Its breathtaking span was held in the cradle of the surrounding mountains. When we gazed into the diamond-clear water we had the feeling that we could see down and beyond, right to the other side of the planet. A lonely medieval monastery was perched on a tiny island in the middle of the lake and in the distance we could see Mount Ararat, its peak eternally hidden in cloud.

The waters of the lake were glacially cold, so we contented ourselves with sunbathing. The People's Commissar expressed doubt about this. Although he was a Russian he had lived long enough among the Armenians to respect their antipathy to anyone's undressing in public, especially women. We made fun of him and decided to confound Armenian conventions. We paid for it dearly. We forgot that the clear mountain air did not filter the sun's ultra-violet rays and on our way back we began to burn like stoves. The worst of it was that we had to perform our act that night and Elena had three lightning costume changes. I was on stage but I could hear her stifled groans as she dragged one costume off her scorched skin and pulled on a new one.

The People's Commissar became infatuated with Elena and later travelled to Moscow to propose to her. I had been making so much caustic fun of him before he arrived that she couldn't look at him without a smile. I was jubilant when she refused him, and he returned to his Armenian forests.

The following year, 1939, was one of the most eventful in my life, a mixture of unprecedented joy, sadness, and even tragedy. I started it off by committing one of the most mindless blunders I have ever made. I applied for Soviet citizenship.

The Russians have a saying: 'The greatest misfortune that can befall a man is when nature deprives him of wisdom.' I was sure that I was doing the right thing and I wouldn't listen to any advice. There was nothing political about my decision, I was far too engrossed in my profession to think about ideology. Our act had become popular and I felt that my career in the Soviet Union was on the upswing. An equally deciding factor at the time was the procedure which I found increasingly irksome of having to renew the residence permit every three months. When the Managing Director of our Agency signed the necessary request for a continuation of my stay, he looked as if he was signing his own death warrant; the same was true of the Manager of the house where I lived. The new restrictions of movement for foreigners were an added frustration. I had to have a travel permit, which meant registering my entry and exit in every town where we played. Often the local militia would have nothing to do with me and refused to sign my permit. Finally, the Party Secretary of our Agency persistently lectured me on my short-sightedness in holding on to my British passport when my whole life and destiny lay with the Soviet Union and her people.

Elena tried to dissuade me, saying that I would never be able to go home again. I rejected this argument. After all, I was British-born, and the authorities could not prevent me from going home for a holiday now and again, which was all I needed. How wrong I proved to be. Nineteen years passed before I went back to London in 1958, and only after Stalin had been dead for five years.

Elena did not give up and we had many more arguments. Although we were close friends, her fear of the KGB was still powerful and she couldn't tell me openly that I would immediately become a second-rate citizen, and that I would lose even the few privileges I had as a foreigner. A month after I tendered my application, my stepfather arrived in Moscow to take up his duties as Deputy Chairman of the Communist International for the year.

Even he was not at all pleased when I told him I had applied for
Soviet citizenship. He came to see our act at the Summer Theatre in
Gorky Park and after careful consideration (he always weighed his
words before giving an opinion) he declared that Elena was 'a very
beautiful young woman and a splendid dancer'.

'Your act,' he said, 'would be just as great a success in the West.'

This was an eye-opener to me as I had never thought of
performing anywhere else but Russia. But it was too late to withdraw
my application. The only one who favoured my becoming a Soviet
citizen was my wife, Maya. By now our relationship had lost all
interest for her. I had not brought her expensive clothes from the
West as she had expected. I could neither afford nor did I have the
inclination to go restaurant-crawling all night. I was working so
hard that I often had less than four hours' sleep a night. So I was
hardly surprised, still less upset, when I came home one night to find
my wife in the passionate arms of a new lover. He was a well-known
and affluent playwright and she no doubt considered him a better
bet than me. I sincerely hoped she would be right. My sole concern
was to keep my house registration intact.

Then the blow fell. The house where we lived was to be
demolished to make way for the new Red Army Theatre. The law
laid down that in such cases the tenants had to be found other
accommodation, a minimum of eight square metres per person. This
would have meant building a skyscraper. A bureaucratic squabble
ensued in which the Army insisted that the Moscow Soviet should
provide new housing, while the Moscow Soviet declared in turn
that it was the Red Army's problem. In the end, Stalin signed a most
inhuman order rescinding the previous law. Instead of living-space,
evicted tenants were to be given 2,500 roubles (about £200) each to
build their own homes. The money was just about enough to build a
privy.

The authorities allotted the evicted tenants plots of lands, and
shanty towns, made of plywood boxes, mushroomed in the fields. It
took me over an hour to find one family who were living in a field
some forty kilometres down the Belorussky Railway Line. I was
shocked to see that they were living in a tent, in the dead of winter,
with temperatures fluctuating between fifteen and twenty-five
degrees below zero. Their only water supply was a frozen rivulet.
They had to hack out pieces of ice and melt them in a pail. Before
anyone in a democratic state condemns the Russians for what seems
to be cowardice and servility, they must remember that the purge

was still operating efficiently. To complain or protest was sufficient reason to be accused of anti-Sovietism—a straight road into the camps.

It was a bitter winter. Enthusiasm for the building of the new society appeared to be on the wane. Absenteeism and lateness for work were rife; drunkenness was reaching epidemic proportions. Workers were throwing up their jobs and searching for better ones, a new expression called them 'transmigrators'. Stalin signed a new law. Anyone committing the 'crimes' of absenteeism or lateness was sent to prison. The courts were packed. Sentences of three months in jail were passed for being half an hour late for work. I had a friend whose telephone number was almost the same as that of the speaking clock. He became so infuriated at being woken up in the early hours to hear someone at the other end waiting to be told the time that he evolved a cruel way of teaching them to dial the number properly. As an actor he easily learned to imitate the toneless voice of the clock, and if the time was in fact 6.30 a.m., would announce it as 8.30 a.m. He got great satisfaction when he heard an anguished wail, 'Oh, my God!' He imagined his victim in the pale rays of dawn dashing down into the street, pulling on his trousers over his long johns, while his wife ran beside him, holding his coat and hat.

Maya and I received a notice ordering us to collect our 2,500 roubles and quit the premises no later than 1 October 1939. This was particularly heartless since that is when the first snows begin to fall in Moscow. I refused to accept the money and began to bombard every possible organization from the Central Committee of the Party to the Red Cross, demanding to be given a room. Eventually I received a letter informing us we had been included on a waiting list, and I discovered by chance and good luck that the Secretary of the Moscow Housing Department was married to a man with whom I had been friendly, the *maître d'hôtel* of the Metropole. She promised to do her best to push my name up the list. Even so it took a year and a half before this desperate hope came true.

In the meantime, Elena and I went on tour, first to Odessa and then to Leningrad. This was the first time we had performed together in either city and naturally we were anxious to know how these two very different audiences would receive us.

The Odessites call themselves *khokhmachi*, meaning 'jokers', from the Yiddish word *khokhma*. They consider their theatrical traditions to be unrivalled in the Soviet Union, and to a certain extent, it is true. When they say, 'That's no act for Odessa,' you can be sure you have failed.

We played in the 10,000-seat Green Theatre in the picturesque Central Park. The compère, a local artiste, had never seen us, so he put us somewhere in the middle of the programme. After the show was over, he stormed into our dressing-room and demanded to know whether we were *mishugini*—'crazy', in Yiddish. The ensuing dialogue proceeded in the approved Odessa style, in which questions are always answered with questions.

'What makes you think we are *mishugini*?' we asked.

'What do you mean by bringing a *shlager*, a big hit, to Odessa and saying nothing so I look like a *pots* [indecent Yiddish for 'a fool'] in front of the whole town?'

'How did we know our act would be a *shlager* for Odessa?'

'Am I asking you or are you asking me? What makes you think I won't put you down to the last on the programme as nobody wants to go on after you?'

'And what makes you think we will refuse to be the last act on the programme as nobody wants to go on after us?'

Another illustration of our success with the Odessites was that whenever I strolled along the main Derebasovsky Street without Elena, the shoe-shine boys and the *khokhmachi* sipping their coffee in the pavement cafés would call out, 'Hey, Villi, where's Elena?' To which I would answer, 'She's gone for a swim across the Black Sea to Turkey. She'll be back in time for breakfast!'

Odessa accepted us, and had taken us to their hearts.

Leningraders are the absolute opposite of Odessites: they are calm and dignified. They like to behave in what is popularly believed to be the English manner. Proud of their former aristocratic traditions, they have never forgiven the Soviet rulers for transferring the capital to Moscow. Even the old name St Petersburg is still revered. The citizens still refer to their city fondly as 'Peter'. Leningrad is virtually the only city in the Soviet Union where passengers stand in orderly queues for buses and trams. If someone tries to jump the queue, you will hear someone remark disdainfully, 'He's probably a Muscovite.'

Neither Elena nor I were newcomers to Leningrad. She had been extremely popular there with other partners, in classical ballet duets, while my popularity was still remembered on the Nevsky Prospekt. Our new combination was welcomed by our admirers, but they were a minority. How would the very demanding

Leningrad audiences react? You could almost hear them saying, 'We are quite prepared to agree to your act being good for other cities, but for Peter . . .!'

The programme was an excellent one, the orchestra was conducted by Isaac Dunayevsky, at that time among the best song-writers in the Soviet Union. Despite his explosive temper, this slight, wiry man was inspirational. He was a friend of Elena's of many years' standing, while he remembered my own performances in the Jazz Revue and the film *Circus*. If he hadn't been Jewish his 'Song of the Motherland' would almost certainly have become the Soviet National Anthem. Today, it is the signature tune of Radio Moscow and far more popular than the official choice! The compère was a young straight actor called Arkady Raikin, who had sprung from obscurity in the Theatre of the Young Audience to a modest success on the variety stage. This was his professional début.

Our first meeting was rather a stormy one, as often happens in show business. The act before ours had just finished and Arkady Raikin was filling in the pause before announcing us. As I stood in the wings I could hardly believe my eyes when I saw him performing a little act which was almost identical to ours. In the theatre this is considered to display ethics of the worst variety. After the show, I am afraid I went up to him in a very belligerent mood, and if it had not been for Raikin's own extraordinary personality, the affair might have assumed the dimensions of a Sicilian feud. But Arkady was so obviously upset and so profuse in his apologies that I had to change my tune. An amicable outcome was reached in the restaurant of the Actors' Club where, after a good supper and a great deal of wine, we drank the toast *bruderschaft*, and with tears in our eyes, linking arms and swallowing a little glass of vodka, we vowed to be eternal friends. And so we have remained ever since. Today Arkady Raikin has become a legend, the most popular artiste in the Soviet Union, and the only satirist who dares to pillory the vices of bureaucrats, bribe-takers and toadies. The hierarchy hate his guts, while the people adore him. The Government has been forced to award him, very grudgingly, the highest possible honour for an actor, People's Artiste of the Soviet Union.

Raikin makes people laugh, but when they leave the theatre, they stop to think about what made them laugh. I have read his fan mail and I doubt whether many artistes receive letters like this one, from a mill girl in Ivanova.

Dear Arkady,
    Please show up our managing director on stage or TV. He
drinks, and mucks about with tarts, and doesn't do his work
properly so we don't fulfill the Plan and don't get our annual
bonus, all because of this rascal . . .

Raikin is, among other things, the Art Director of the Leningrad
Miniature Theatre, which he founded. When we arrived back in
Moscow in November 1939, we were told by our Directors that if
we could show our new act within a week, we would be included in
the winter programme at the Moscow Variety Theatre. We had
been rehearsing our new act all the time but despite this, it took a
week of sleepless nights before we would declare it ready and perfect. The idea for the act was Elena's and it was based on music from
The Nutcracker Suite. A toy shop comes to life at night and the
clown dances and sings with all sorts of lovely toys and dolls (Elena
did three of her lightning changes in the wings). The audition went
down well and we were in red letters on the bill. At the same time,
the first-ever All Union Contest of Variety Artistes was announced,
so we entered our names.

    The only actors who were decorated by the Government before
the war were film stars. The straight theatre, such as the Maly and
Moscow Art Theatre, got scant attention. Variety was absolutely
ignored, and this gave rise to considerable dissatisfaction among a
number of gifted performers. One morning in December 1939, a
friend woke me up at an appallingly early hour. When I told him
that I did not appreciate practical jokes like this he told me to shut
up and read the morning's news in *Pravda*. Intrigued, I did
as he said. There was a two-page list of circus performers who
had been decorated by the Government, and there in the group
awarded the Medal 'For Distinguished Labour' was my name.
I could hardly believe my eyes. To think that I, a young foreigner,
had been given such an honour, and for my performances as
a clown!

    To this day I feel ashamed of the unforgivable blunder I then
proceeded to commit. Without checking the list, I rang up Elena to
congratulate her. Elena answered by congratulating me, quietly
adding that her name was not on the list! I didn't know what to say. I
mumbled something idiotic about how it was an award not for me
alone but for us both. It was then that the beauty of her nature was
fully revealed to me, as she reassured me that she was truly happy

about the award. 'Only,' she declared, 'we are not going to wear the medal in turns.'

Later, I learned that Elena's name *had* been included on the list but the responsible Party official in the Central Committee had struck it off because her husband was languishing in the camps as an 'enemy of the people'.

My own joy was shortlived; I was naïve enough to imagine that everybody would share my excitement. When I went to the theatre that evening nobody spoke to me. Half a dozen stars who had been so friendly the day before now walked past me without even a nod. It was not difficult to understand their attitude. They had been big names for many years. I had only just reached the top of the ladder, and was a foreigner into the bargain.

Then came the All Union Contest for Variety Artistes and I had no time to brood. We passed through the preliminary rounds easily and entered the finals. And that is when the row started. The speech in our favour was given by Mikhail Zoschenko, the eminent writer-humorist. Opposed to us was one of the stars of show business, Smirnov-Sokolsky, an extremely gifted artiste who wrote his own material but was also notorious as an arrogant bully. He had been one of the most insulting to me about my award. A stormy quarrel ensued between him and Zoschenko, the result of which was that Zoschenko stalked out of the room declaring that he had come to judge a contest, not to take part in a bullfight. His missing vote cost us a prize. As it was, we were awarded the Honourable Diploma, though to be among the twelve best Soviet performers was in itself an honour. Winning contests and being awarded medals means very little to most performers. The audience is the true judge and the magical shout 'Encore' is worth more than any medal or title.

Such disputes and wranglings among show business people were, however, the pettiest of storms in tea-cups compared with what was happening in the world. On 23 August 1939 the notorious Nazi–Soviet Pact was signed. To say that this astounded people is to put it mildly. In all the seven years I had been living in the Soviet Union, I had heard nothing but anti-Nazi propaganda: 'Prepare to Defend the Motherland against the Fascist Invasion.' It had been made perfectly clear that Hitler and his brown-shirt troops were the most vicious enemies of the First Workers' State. Yet now, apparently, we were pals and cronies! After the Pact had been signed, sickening photographs appeared in the papers showing Molotov and Ribbentrop embracing one another. The mealy mouthed explanation from the Kremlin assured us that the Pact was necessary to gain time, that it was a counter-move against the British–French plan to incite Germany to attack the Soviet Union. None of these arguments convinced the Soviet people, especially when eleven days after the signing of the Pact, Britain and France declared war on Germany!

Worse, the Red Army crossed the Polish borders from the east, while the Nazis came in from the west, and together they destroyed the greater part of the small Polish Army. The official explanation was that it was vital to push Soviet borders further west against the enemy. But now that the Nazis were our friends, where was the enemy? One of the most brilliant Soviet generals, Tukhachevsky, was executed for reporting that, as a result of his observations on a visit to Germany, he was convinced of Hitler's intention to take the war eastwards. What were we to believe?

And then the Red Army attacked Finland. Very few accounts have been written of the courage of the Finns, who met the might of the Red Army with hatchets, pitchforks and knives. The Finnish men, women and children fought like tigers for three months and, despite a barrage of anti-Finnish propaganda, the Soviet people had more than a sneaking admiration for their staunch resistance. I met very few officers or men who were proud of what they were doing in that particular war.

A friend of mine from my Leningrad days, a well-known champion skier, returned wounded from the Finnish front. I was present at a small party given to welcome him home from hospital. He told the story of a sniper, a lovely Finnish girl with platinum hair, who held up his company's advance for a day and a half. She was eventually surrounded, taken down from her tree-top sniper nest, her clothes soaked in blood from a wound. The SMERSH (Army KGB) officer ordered her to be hanged. He stood by as the soldiers prepared to put a rope round her neck. But before anyone could stop her, she pulled out a knife hidden in her clothing and stabbed the SMERSH officer in the heart. Taking advantage of the confusion, she grabbed a pair of skis and was away. 'And,' said my friend the champion skier, 'although we gave chase, somehow we couldn't catch up with her. Strange, isn't it?'

What did the ordinary Soviet people think about these events? The answer is that they didn't think. They stood stolidly in queues waiting to buy food which had suddenly become even scarcer. As for my colleagues in show business, their behaviour was no less self-interested. Groups of artistes had gone into occupied Poland behind the 'victorious' Red Army and were now returning home, their suitcases packed with new clothes. Patriotic artistes were scrambling to perform for the troops so that they could replenish their wardrobes. The propaganda machine boomed about 'stretching out a hand of brotherly friendship to the people freed from the capitalist yoke'. One of my actor friends, an excessively stout man, when asked why he did not apply to be sent to Poland, replied: 'I would be overjoyed to stretch out a hand of brotherly friendship to the people recently freed from the capitalist yoke—but I'm not sure they've got my size in suits and shirts!'

Elena and I did not apply for permission to perform in the 'liberated territories' and the management did not show any great inclination to send us. Although I had become a Soviet citizen in 1939 and had been decorated by the Government, I remained a foreigner, someone not to be trusted. There were things I had better not see.

By the spring of 1940, disgruntled artistes were returning empty-handed from the 'liberated' countries with tales of the hunger and shortages now afflicting the 'freed' peoples. The shops were empty. As one of the artistes, a conjurer, put it, 'Even I couldn't have invented a quicker disappearing trick.'

All through 1940, Elena and I toured the country, from Smolensk to Erevan, Tbilisi, Sukhumi and along the Black Sea coast. We arrived back in Moscow in October. The first thing I did on the morning after our arrival was to visit the Housing Department to see about the room that Maya and I had been promised. I was told that we had been allotted a room in a new house on the other side of the Moskva River, opposite the Kremlin. In normal circumstances I would have been delighted. It was a big room in a modern flat, with only two neighbours, and conveniently placed, only ten minutes from the centre of the city. But the thought of having to share it with Maya filled me with despair. My life seemed to have become a mess. I had no family in Russia but I was in a permanent state of worry about my folks in London. The Soviet media reported almost nothing about the war in Europe. All that the press mentioned, with what seemed to me some callousness, was that London was under continual bombing. Even my work had ceased to be a pleasure. The Directors of our Agency had all been removed, and new ones, Party hacks with no experience of or love for the theatre, had replaced them. The new men wanted to send us off to the Far East, which meant being away from Moscow for six months or more. The dark clouds of war were hanging overhead and everybody realized we would not be able to escape invasion, despite the assurances of Soviet propaganda that the Great Father, in his wisdom, had foreseen the threat from the West and was prepared. Most people wanted to be as near to their homes as possible, and Elena and I were no exceptions. When the new Director ordered us to go to the Far East, to Vladivostok, we quarrelled violently. I told him what I thought of him. It was then that I realized finally I was no longer a foreigner with some freedom, but a Soviet citizen who could be handed over to the courts under new laws against 'disobedience'. While this row was going on I tripped during a performance and fell heavily into the orchestra pit and hurt my back. It wasn't serious, but I realized the possibilities. As they say in Russia, 'A piece of bad luck is often a stroke of good fortune.' In exchange for a packet of Gillette razor blades, my doctor gave me a two-week disability certificate. By the time it expired it was too late to send me East.

I could sense that Elena, too, was depressed. She was pensive and withdrawn, which was not like her. When I asked her what the trouble was, the whole story came out. Some 'well-wishers' had been gossiping to her. According to them I had asked the Director to give me a new partner. In fact, the opposite had happened. He had called me in and suggested that Elena did not suit me, as she was a classical dancer, and even hinted she was 'politically unreliable'. Once again, I gave him a piece of my mind, and he got his own back by spreading the story that it was I who had asked him to replace her. Elena didn't really believe this poppycock, but nevertheless the episode left a sour taste. With the misunderstanding cleared up, Elena and I decided we must leave this State Agency—but how? They might try to split our duet and never allow us to leave the Agency.

When the bells struck at midnight, ringing in 1941, Elena and I were on stage. Returning to our dressing-room, we opened a bottle of champagne, kissed, and wished each other better luck in the New Year. I accompanied her to the Actors' Club where she had been invited to a party by some friends from the Operetta Theatre. I didn't want to go in with her. She coaxed me, but I refused. So off I went, lugging my case of costumes. Back home I was glad to be alone. Maya had gone to a New Year celebration. I made some supper, poured myself a stiff glass of vodka and drank to my own health and happiness. 'And so to bed.'

New Year's morning in 1941 was just the kind I liked most in Moscow in winter. A bright sun shone down from a pale blue sky and the nip in the air sharpened the mind and seemed to make life worthwhile. I was delighted to be alone, and after breakfast, went in search of a phone booth, to ring Elena. A neighbour answered.

'Sorry,' she said, 'Elena can't come to the phone.'

'Why, what's the matter? Hangover . . .?'

'No, no. She can't get up. She thinks she has broken her leg.'

I ran all the way to Elena's place and a quarter of an hour later I was standing in her room looking down at her woebegone face. She immediately calmed my fear.

'Of course I haven't broken my leg. The woman's a fool for scaring you so. I've just sprained my ankle. See? It's beginning to swell. How did it happen? Well, we left the Club about four o'clock. It was really cold and the pavements were icy. I didn't notice a manhole, stepped on to it, slipped and fell. The two idiots who were holding my arms fell with me and thought it was a great joke until they found I couldn't walk. So they had to carry me home. And here I am! *Chort s nimi!* To hell with it! Let's you and I have a New Year party all by ourselves!'

She didn't have to tell me where to find the food and drink, her room was more like home to me than my own. Soon we were laughing and joking merrily as if nothing had happened. Friends who had heard about the accident kept dropping in, bringing bottles of vodka and wine, and a jolly, impromptu party developed. That is what I love in the Russians, they never ask if they can come. They just come and they never ask if you need anything; they just bring it on the principle of the old saying: 'A good hostess never asks guests should she cook a chicken for them or not.' When everyone had gone home I stayed behind to wash up. We began to talk about our future and how to get out of the Agency, where the new Directors' animosity was becoming unbearable, and even threatening. The new law forbade anyone to leave his place of work without special permission, or a watertight excuse. It was then that I had an idiotic idea.

'Suppose you and I were to separate? Tell them we can't work together any more, that you want to return to the ballet?'

We decided that there was no harm in trying. We would hand in our resignations and if the Director, the Party Secretary and the Trade Union Secretary agreed, we could separate for a few months and then join up again. I kissed Elena goodnight and off I went, feeling rather pleased with myself.

The night was frosty, and I drank in the crisp air as I walked down through the empty Arbat Square, into Frunze Street and then across the Bolshoi Kamenny Bridge. But as I walked, a horrible thought began to grow in my mind. Elena had said she would find a partner from the Bolshoi Ballet to dance with during our separation. Suppose that she found her return to the classical ballet more to her liking and didn't want to come back to work with me? I was so upset at this thought that I turned down on to the Embankment, opposite the Kremlin. The more I gazed at the frozen Moskva River, the more panic-stricken I became. I began to speak my thoughts out loud. There was no one around. All Moscow was fast asleep after the New Year festivities. I was alone, with the clouds racing above me, opening and closing the moonlight like the rays from a lighthouse.

'What shall I do if Elena does not come back to work with me? After all, she is a ballerina. Dancing a *pas de deux* with a proper partner is more her style than dancing with an eccentric clown. And if she does go, I won't be seeing much of her any more. I don't want to lose Elena. She's not only a splendid partner but my best friend. I've got no one else in the world but Elena, and if she goes away from me, I don't know what I'll do. I just can't imagine life without her. I mustn't let her go, even for a few months. No, no, no!'

I marched up and down the lonely Embankment waving my hands and shouting to myself. Suddenly I stopped. 'What am I talking about? Can't imagine life without Elena? Nonsense! Of course I can get on without her if she doesn't want to come back to me.'

I had convinced myself by now that Elena was leaving me, and I was angry with her for thinking of doing so—which she hadn't! I was feeling tortured. 'I won't let her leave me! First thing in the morning I'll go and tell her so. She can't get rid of me as easily as that. I'll tell her I can't live without her. I'll tell her she's my only friend, that I love her . . . as a friend, of course.'

At that moment the clouds opened and the moonlight shone again. I stood as if turned to stone. Then I cried out, 'But it's all wrong! It's all wrong! I *do* love her!' I began to beat my head with my clenched fists. 'You bloody fool, you blind idiot. You've been in love with Elena all the time and didn't realize it.' Then I said, 'My God, what am I going to do? This must not be. I must not fall in love with Elena. She's my best and only friend and what's more, my partner. I must not tell her. I would spoil everything. But I have to tell someone and she's the only one I can tell. What am I to do? I know the kind of men she likes and I do not fit in. Maybe she has someone else? No. She told me herself that she was fed up with men hanging around her, "Why do they all want to marry me?" she asked the other day. "I don't want to get married to anyone." I was overjoyed when she said it. Why? Now I know why. And I know why I always feel that twinge of jealousy if I see her with someone else. It's because I'm in love with her. But suppose she doesn't love me? Then what?'

I must have looked like a madman, pacing up and down beside the frozen Moskva River, arguing with myself. I opened my arms to the ancient Kremlin on the other bank, as if beseeching it with its ancient wisdom to help me out of my dilemma. Here I was, a young man who had just discovered he was in love with his own partner, with whom he had been working and travelling and sometimes even sharing the same hotel room, for nearly five years! Comrade Kremlin gazed back at me in majestic silence. Not so the militiaman who had strolled out of the shadows and was observing my antics with deep suspicion. He demanded to know what I was up to. For a second I was tempted to tell him of the glorious discovery I had just made, but one look at his stolid face was enough to deter me. So I merely mumbled, '*Ladno*, it's all right. I'm off home to bed.'

The next morning I put on my best three-piece suit and a bow tie, polished my shoes until I could see my face in them, and brushed my hair carefully. My mother used to say, 'You're well-dressed when your head and feet look good.' The lukewarm rays of the wintry sun shone down on me as I walked blithely across the Bolshoi Kamenny Bridge over the Moskva River, passing the spot where, last night, I had realized I was in love. I raised my fur hat to the Kremlin Gates and walked up the hill to the Arbat Square. 'Now,' I thought, 'it would be grand if I could bring Elena a bunch of flowers.' I was in luck. As I passed the peasants' market on the Arbat an old woman offered me her last bunch of snowdrops. I almost danced the rest of the way up Vorovsky Ulitsa to the apartment house where Elena lived with her sister Vera. My heart was thumping like a steam-hammer as I waited for Elena to open her door.

'My goodness!' she cried admiringly. 'You do look smart. Are you off on a rendezvous with some fair maiden? You've even found some snowdrops for her . . . She is a lucky girl!'

I stood there like a tongue-tied yokel and could only stammer that the flowers were for her.

'For me? Oh, how lovely of you. Just what I wanted . . . I've been lying here with the blues longing for something nice to happen. Spasibo, moi dorogoi!'

When Elena said, 'Thank you, my dear,' I felt I wanted to dash out and bring her baskets and baskets of flowers.

'Elena, that idea about you and I separating,' I blurted out. 'It's mad. I don't want to leave you, even for a few months . . .' I was on the verge of telling her I couldn't live without her, but ended lamely. 'I don't want to work with anyone else but you.'

'Nor do I,' she answered decisively. 'No sooner had you gone last night than I wanted to call you back and tell you it was a crazy idea and wouldn't work anyway. I don't want any other partner but you. So you can go and put the kettle on and we'll have breakfast. I'm starving.'

I jumped up as if the Bolshoi Ivan cannon that stands in the Kremlin courtyard had been fired off in my ear. Elena gazed at me quizzically as I stuttered some apology for not thinking of it myself.

We, or rather she, talked all day while I sat and gazed at her. She was the same Elena, yet she had changed. I could see lots of little things I had never noticed before. She was beautiful, but I had always known that. The first time I ever saw her, I had admired her dark eyes and long, elegant legs. . . . Yes, everything was the same but all so different. This was really not like me. . . . I was in love with her and was afraid to tell her. What would she say? Suddenly she said, 'Why are you looking at me all the time? . . . You're about as conversational as a fish in a bowl. You'd think you had never seen me before. What's the matter with you?'

I tried to evade the question and it must have been the bumbling way I did it that made her put the pointed question: 'You're not in love by any chance, are you?'

I looked at her, terrified. She was so wise, she must have guessed. . . . But no, she was completely calm. How could she have guessed?

'May I be allowed to know who the unfortunate girl is?'

Never had I been in such a situation in all my life. Should I tell her or not? I looked at her imploringly. After a slight pause I saw a light of understanding appear in her eyes. For a few moments she said nothing as if she was not quite sure.

'It's not me, is it?'

All I could do was to nod my head guiltily. She uttered just one word, which sounded like a mixture of wonder and reproach.

'Villichka!'

There was hope for me in that. Adding 'chka' to a name is the Russian way of expressing affection. Elena looked at me thoughtfully while I waited for the axe to fall. I knew that my whole future depended on what she would say that moment.

'I cannot tell you how touched I am. . . . You, of all people, to fall in love with me! You know, I have never said the words "I love you" to anyone, probably because I have never loved anyone, neither husbands nor lovers. Well, you know all about them. It was strange I always wanted to get away from them, to be alone. I could never bear anyone's company for long. You are the only person I've ever felt totally free-and-easy with. I don't have to say anything to you, or try to make conversation. You and I are real friends and no one is nearer and dearer to me than you are, so I don't want to risk losing that friendship. It's too valuable. You know what I've always said, "Better to lose a lover than a good friend."'

'But I don't want to be your lover!' I managed to cry. 'I want you to be my wife, to marry me.'

'I know that. And I don't want to be your mistress. That would be ridiculous. But suppose it doesn't work out? You know me, I am capricious and demanding with men. [I knew that better than anyone. How many ardent suitors had wept on my shoulders after getting a polite but firm refusal of their hands and their hearts from Elena.] If something went wrong we'd lose our act and all the hard work we have put into it.'

I felt as if I was fighting for my life. She held my hand as she listened to my passionate pleas, to my account of the miracle that had happened to me on the Embankment last night.

'I believe you. But we must be careful. It is so risky, and I don't want to lose you. You say that ours could not fail to be a happy marriage. Suppose we go to bed and find we don't suit each other? Don't argue, this has happened to many people. Being friends is not the only thing, sex is just as important. And don't think I'll go to bed with you to find out, oh no. Not until I am absolutely sure of myself.'

This did not seem to me to be very logical but I didn't even press the point. Such was my state that I hadn't even thought of sex.

'Elena, I love you. I have loved you ever since we performed together for the first time without Tamara. I stood in the wings waiting for my cue and watching you as you danced alone . . . you were so beautiful and brave! I loved you from that moment, only I mistook it for brotherly love. It was only last night that I understood that I cannot live without you. And I will not! I don't care if you don't want to marry me, I'm your partner and I'll always be by your side, and God help the man who tries to take my place. So you see, you're on the spot, and you might just as well marry me and have done with it.'

Elena began to laugh so heartily that I had to clamber off my high horse and laugh with her, as of old. She pressed my hand, then released it. 'All right, my little blackmailer! It's time for you to go home. We'll leave things as they are for now. Don't hurry me, give me time to get used to the new you and your love. Who knows, maybe *I* shall fall in love for the first time in my life!'

Five weeks later, on 8 February 1941, we became man and wife, before God, if not at the Registry Office. The Registry Office had to wait for another five years. The world had turned upside-down before we gave our names to a Registry Office girl (suffering from a large gum boil) to certify that the godless Soviet State officially recognized our marriage. The process cost three roubles. Three weeks after our informal marriage we boarded a train for Kharkov.

The Russians have a saying: 'Marriages are born in heaven.' Ours was born on the stage, and our honeymoon was spent on the stage of the Kharkov Variety Theatre where, in 1941, we performed for three months, from March to May, 'Twice daily and a matinée on Sunday' as the bills announced. I recall how people used to say, 'Your act succeeds not only because of its professionalism and fun, but because you see two young people, who like each other, enjoying themselves as if nobody was watching.'

Elena and I were now very much in love and our act seemed to reflect it. We were living in a dream world, as if some deadening weight had been lifted from us. We set up a barrier which it was difficult for reality to penetrate. But these were turbulent times and we soon had to come down to earth.

Performing with us was a mind-reader and hypnotist, Wolf Messing, who had escaped from the Nazis in Poland. His parents had been members of a Jewish sect whose aim, among others, was to revive the acute sense of awareness still powerful in animals but now lost to human beings. Messing was extremely solitary and did not mix with the other artistes. They, in their turn, were afraid of his amazing ability to read other people's minds, especially as the KGB occasionally exploited his gifts for their own purposes. We, particularly Elena, were the only ones he seemed to like. Elena could not be more kind or observant, though she does not parade it. She noticed how tired and thin Messing was becoming, and discovered that he was so absent-minded that he often forgot to eat for days on end. From then on she insisted that he take his meals with us.

I cannot say it was particularly enjoyable sitting at the table with Messing, and trying to keep my mind an absolute blank, but proof of his uncanny gifts came one day when we were sitting in our room after supper and some other artistes dropped in. Messing was in a congenial mood and agreed to Elena's request that he read her mind. He told her to stand in the middle of the room and close her eyes. He just looked at her for a minute or so and before I could leap to save her, she fell straight on her back. At the last moment Messing caught her by the neck just a few inches off the floor. As a professional, I believed he must have had some kind of superhuman faculty. No dancer or acrobat would have fallen without bending one knee to 'soften' the fall. When he woke her, Messing told her something of her past life, all of which was true. One actress, an objectionable woman, laughed scornfully and called it so much nonsense. I thought Messing would burst with anger, but when he calmed down he challenged her to allow him to hypnotize her. She agreed with a sneer. When he began to tell her of all the evils she had committed, of how she had driven her own mother to suicide to get some valuables, she could only scream, 'Stop! Stop!' and rushed from the room.

Eventually, as we came to know him better, he confided his story to us and told us of the horrors he had suffered when he was captured by the Nazis. As he said with bitter humour, 'I don't look like a Jew, all the Jews look like me!' He told us of the terrible sufferings the Jews had endured in Poland under the Germans, and of how he had been beaten up not only by the Fascists but by collaborating Poles as well.

'The worst came when the Nazis found out that I had the gift of mind-reading. They thought I was a charlatan. Often I was called in the middle of the night to entertain some guzzling Germans at a party. Many a time my life hung by a thread when some high-ranking officer would order me to read his mind or hypnotize him. If I had told what I saw there it would have been the end of me. I cursed the day I was born and had had this gift developed in me. I am anathema to everyone—to the Nazis and now to the Soviets.'

I felt he was about to let us into secrets which I preferred not to hear. He had not been long enough in the Soviet Union to learn the sagacious warning which is essential to survival.

> If wisdom's ways you wisely seek,
> Five things observe with care,
> To whom you speak, of whom you speak,
> And how, and when, and where.

Elena immediately complained of a headache and said we could hear the rest of the story when we went for a stroll in the park in the morning. This was March 1941, and although Germany had attacked Poland and was already at war with Britain and France, any mention of a possible attack upon the Soviet Union was forbidden. So the next day we found a bench in a lonely spot and Messing continued his tale.

'Sometimes I had to entertain generals. On one occasion there was a whole group of them. They had just returned from a meeting of the Military Council, with Field Marshal Paulus, and were celebrating something. It was a decision to attack Russia without warning. I read it in the mind of one of them, though I couldn't see a date. I almost gave myself away, and had to invent some incredible rubbish to cover up what I had discovered. Soon I got the opportunity to escape to the Soviet Zone. It took me three days and nights, hiding and crawling, before I crossed the border. The border guards laughed when I asked to see a responsible officer. A week went past before I was interviewed by a Soviet general. When I told him what I had learned, he declared I was an impostor, and handed me over to the KGB, after threatening me with execution if I dared to repeat the "phenomenal lie" as he called it. The KGB eventually freed me, on condition that I would help them in interrogating political prisoners. How could I, when I didn't know Russian? But I told them lies, too. I wanted to write to Stalin, to warn him, but I was afraid, I don't know why. I have told no one, only you, because you are young and happy. But you must be ready. A terrible war is coming, an unthinkable war. Many will die. I will be among them.'

In fact he lived into his seventies, but whenever we met now and again in concerts after the war I never mentioned what he had told us.

At the time we didn't know whether to believe Messing or not. That Hitler was capable of betraying his Pact with Russia, no one doubted for a moment. But there didn't seem to be any sense in his attacking the Soviet Union now. Stalin had put up no resistance to the Nazi conquest of Europe; on the contrary, he had even helped them to capture Poland.

A few days later, we had a further confirmation of Messing's prediction, when a friend of ours, Alexei, arrived in Kharkov on a short visit. When only twenty years old he had been Commander of the division which recaptured the city of Kharkov during the Civil War. He was immediately hailed as a hero and saviour and shortly after was promoted to general. Now his old comrades avoided him, and his brother, the Mayor of Kharkov, did his best to hush up his visit. Alexei had been arrested in 1936 when he was Chief Commander of the Air Defence Forces, because of his support for Marshal Tukhachevsky, that brilliant Commander of the Red Army, who insisted on the leading role aircraft and tanks would play in any future war. He proved to be correct. Stalin counted on his old cronies, Budyenny and Voroshilov, both of whom were cavalry men, and ignored Tukhachevsky, whose opposition to Stalin cost him his life.

Alexei had only just been freed from prison; expelled from the Army, and stripped of all his military orders and medals, he had managed to find a job as Assistant Manager in a taxi depot. (When the war broke out, he volunteered for active service as a private. Such was his talent and ability that he rose to the rank of general once more and won many a new decoration for bravery.)

One night, after supper, he proposed a breath of fresh air. As we strolled along the dark, empty streets, he told us in confidence of Hitler's plan to attack the Soviet Union. He had seen some of his old colleagues on the General Staff, who also knew of the plan but were afraid to discuss it with anyone, let alone Stalin. Alexei warned us to prepare for the worst. He told me that I should be careful as an ex-foreigner not to do anything that might arouse the suspicion of the KGB.

We arrived back in Moscow from Kharkov at the end of May 1941. I wanted to register my divorce from Maya, but the procedure had become more stringent, and it was no longer enough to pay three roubles to have the marriage annulled. The day after my return home, my ex-wife left on a month's holiday to the Crimea, with her playwright, and announced that she would give me the divorce when she came back. In the midst of these problems, Elena and I were pleased to hear that we had been included in the second summer show at the Top Variety Theatre in the Hermitage Gardens in Moscow, to begin on Saturday 21 June 1941. All the tickets had been sold out long before the opening night, and the Gardens were packed with Muscovites in a merry mood. The military band played old waltzes, the restaurants and cafés did a roaring trade, and even the compère, an old enemy of ours, was unusually friendly. He announced us so well that the audience greeted our appearance with applause, which turned into an ovation at the end of the act. We quickly escaped from the celebration party that always follows a first night. We wanted to be alone together, to share our happiness.

I was woken next morning, 22 June, by my neighbours in the communal flat shouting, 'Listen to the radio.' I switched it on to hear the familiar voice of Yuri Levitan, announcing that Russia and Germany were at war. Frivolous though it may sound, the first thing that entered my head was: 'Just our luck when we had got such a good engagement at the Hermitage!'

Later in the day, Levitan came on the air again. 'Govorit Moskva! Listen to Comrade Stalin!'

We listened.

His strong Georgian accent was even more pronounced than usual, his standard gimmick of speaking in slow, measured tones, like the Great Oracle, sounded particularly unconvincing. Fifteen years later, after his death, we learned the reason for his nervousness that day. In the few hours since dawn, thousands of Russians had lost their lives as a direct result of his obstinacy and shortsightedness. Khrushchev, in the famous Stalin Disclosures, declared that the Great Leader hid under the bed when he heard of the invasion. This version has to be taken with a pinch of salt. Stalin had just appointed himself Marshal of the Soviet Union, and had a new and resplendent military uniform made to measure. As there is always dust under any bed, it is not likely that the Leader of the World Proletariat would have risked spoiling his crimson-striped trousers. Khrushchev was never one to spoil a good story.

NINE

With Elena at the Front

The Variety Theatre in the Hermitage was immediately closed down as a war measure and Elena and I were ordered to report to our Agency for further instructions. All artistes who were not called up became members of what came to be called the Artistes' Front Brigade, in the style of the British ENSA. We were declared to be semi-military, taking orders from the Political Administration of the Red Army. Everyone in the Artistes' Front Brigade was given exemption from active service, a White Ticket. I was exempt because of my former British citizenship, so I didn't need one anyway. This situation always made me think of the contradictions of Soviet bureaucracy. As an ex-foreigner I couldn't be a soldier near the Front, yet it was quite feasible for me to be a Front Brigade Artiste travelling to *all* fronts. And this I did, meeting high-ranking generals and officers, many of whom became friends for life. If I had been a British agent I couldn't have had a better opportunity to collect information. Nobody ever questioned my presence. I suppose it never entered anyone's head that a clown could be a spy!

For the first month after the outbreak of war, we dashed from one enlisting point to another. Soviet historians like to paint a picture of unparalleled enthusiasm among the people. That's just make-believe. The only people who get enthusiastic about going to war are generals. The people we saw were shocked and almost incapable of realizing what had hit them. We saw heart-rending scenes: husbands and fathers parting from their loved ones, some standing dry-eyed, staring, others moaning and weeping and clinging to each other. Another popular myth touted around is that the Soviet soldier went into battle shouting, 'Forward for Stalin!' yet Elena and I visited every fighting front, from the Turkish borders to beyond the Arctic Circle, and we never heard of anyone doing such a thing. The propaganda machine did try, at the beginning, to promote the idea with pictures of Stalin, but they soon had to change it for a picture of a simple Russian woman with outstretched hands saying 'Rodina Mat Zobet Tebya!' ('The Motherland calls upon you!'). This did the trick: the Russians are fanatical patriots and will defend their Motherland for ever.

One touching if comic incident illustrates how even the elderly were keen to do their bit for the war effort. Elena and I had arrived from the Volkhov Front, and I went to the Agency to get further orders. In the corridor I saw the familiar face of Kyril Dimitrich, or KD, as we all called him, who had been one of Russia's most popular singers. He was now over eighty and had been retired for years. He was singing to a small group of artistes to prove his voice was still good, which it was. When I expressed my surprise at seeing him there, he replied that he could not bear to potter about in his garden when the country needed every hand: 'And voice!'

The next evening we were to give a concert for the troops near Moscow. When we climbed into the rickety bus, I saw that KD was all wrapped up from head to foot in a vast overcoat. The temperature was twenty-five degrees below zero, and a snowstorm was blowing up. The little bus battled bravely through, and although we arrived late we wasted no time in starting the show. When KD was announced he was met with an ovation. The pianist played the introduction and waited, KD stood gazing at the audience, then turned and nodded to the pianist, who played the introduction again. No response. KD walked over to the pianist and demanded to know why he hadn't started. The pianist shouted back that he had. A look of anguish passed across KD's face and with a terrible cry, 'I've gone deaf!' he dashed off the stage.

It was a subdued troupe that wended its way back to Moscow. KD sat huddled under his greatcoat in the front of the bus and our hearts went out to him in his grief. All of a sudden he began frantically to unwind his big scarf and pluck at his ears. When he began shouting we thought he had gone mad: 'It's my old woman's fault! I'll give it to her when I get back home.' We tried to calm him, but he would have none of it. 'It's cottonwool! Don't you understand?' We certainly didn't. 'It's my old woman. She always stuffs cottonwool in my ears when it's cold. I'm not deaf at all. We were in such a hurry I forgot to take it out when I went on stage!'

What amazed me in the first months of the war was the complete bewilderment, disorganization and chaos. For years, the Soviet people had been forced to go to shooting-ranges to compete for the 'Voroshilov Sharpshooter's Badge'. But when the *Opolchenie* or People's Volunteer Guards was formed a few days after the invasion, most of the men didn't know how to use the rifles. This didn't matter much: there was only one rifle to every ten men. No uniforms had been made for them and they went into battle in their civilian suits, splashing through the mud in ordinary street shoes. A friend of Elena's, a prima ballerina of the Minsk Opera House in Belorussia, escaped from her house in her night-gown with only a coat slung over her shoulders, just before a bomb destroyed her home during the first air attack. It took her a week to get to Moscow walking and riding in goods trains, three of which were bombed. She saw no retaliation in the air, and little on the ground. Shell-shocked and wounded soldiers straggled along the roads to Moscow which throughout the war was rarely bombed; so confident were the Germans of capturing the capital that they deliberately left it intact.

The enemy was advancing so rapidly, or, as the radio put it, 'Our troops are courageously retreating in planned order,' that there was no time for concert brigades, so we were dispatched to the Black Sea resort of Sochi to entertain the wounded. We were given railway tickets, with coach and berth numbers stamped on them, but when we arrived at the Kursky Terminal we found that the original train had been replaced by a 'hard' one, with no compartments. Half the passengers had no tickets at all. Many of them had reserved their places hours before departure time. Even the luggage racks were engaged. It was late in the evening; I persuaded a bleary-eyed tramp to give up his top shelf for a glass of vodka. The smell was so foul that you could have cut it with a knife, but there was nothing else we could do. Elena, at least, had somewhere to sleep. It took us five days to get to Sochi.

The beautiful Black Sea resort was empty. It was yet another example of Soviet mismanagement. We had travelled thousands of miles to perform for the wounded—and found none! Sochi's sanatoria and hotels had been transformed into hospitals, even the excursion buses had been hurriedly painted with red crosses, but all was silent and motionless. The usual crowds of holiday-makers had vanished, but nobody had taken their places. The food that had been laid in for the season was lying on shop shelves in an abundance I had never seen before in Russia. Waiters from restaurants and cafés would waylay passers-by, and beg them to sample their cuisine. Three weeks later, the first hospital trains arrived with the wounded, and the population of Sochi turned the event into a celebration, with brass bands and banners. At last they had some work to do. And so had we.

There were a few serious cases among the thousands of wounded that arrived, but most were suffering from shell-shock and light wounds. They were mainly peasants from the far north or east. They bathed in the sea water in their undershirts and long johns, considering it indecent to show their naked bodies. Vodka flowed and drunken brawls became a common sight. One could hardly blame the men. They had escaped from a bloody nightmare and were celebrating. Later, when things settled down, military police arrived and the streets became safer and quiet.

During the intervals in our concerts at the hospitals, I talked to the men, and from their fragmented accounts I began to get a picture of what had happened.

Forty Nazi divisions had been massed on the borders of Russia. The Border Guards commanders requested that the 'free day', Sunday 22 June, should be cancelled and that the troops should remain on duty. Stalin accused them of panicking and threatened them with reprisals. When the Germans did attack, without warning, most of the Russian troops were asleep. When the alarm was given, they fought in their underwear. How many men lost their lives without firing a shot will never be known. One of the bravest epics was the month-long siege of the Brest Fortress where the garrison—men and women alike—carried on a superhuman battle even when the Germans had passed them by and were on their way to Moscow. Those of the garrison who were taken alive went into concentration camps. When they returned home after the war some were banished to the Gulag camps for 'cowardice in the face of the enemy'!

About the middle of September, some of our troupe's relatives arrived from Moscow and among them was Elena's older sister, Vera. She had been injured during an air-raid, and the evacuation authorities ordered her to leave. She told us that the bombing had not been extensive but that the capital was being slowly evacuated and flats were standing empty. Looting and pillaging had become widespread. Many of our colleagues demanded to be allowed to return home. This was in October. We did not know that the 16th was to be the worst day in history for Muscovites. The Germans had reached Khimki, fifteen miles from Red Square which, their radio boasted, they could see through binoculars. Stalin ordered massive evacuations. Anyone trying to stay behind would be considered to be 'waiting for the enemy', and dealt with accordingly. The Government had transferred to Kuibishev, on the Volga. Stalin allegedly remained in his capital, though whether he did in fact do so remains a mystery. (This 'Man of the People' had a great aversion to mixing with his subjects. Although it was kept a dark secret, we theatrical people knew that a certain Georgian actor, who played the part of Stalin in many films, was often called upon to play the role in real life. I got the shock of my life when I bumped into him once in the corridor of the Mosfilm Studios, resplendent in the Marshal's uniform complete with the Gold Stars of Hero of the Soviet Union.)

We were refused permission to return home to Moscow and instead were ordered to proceed to Tbilisi, the capital of Georgia, and report for duty at the Political Administration of the Caucasian Front. When we arrived—forty artistes and their relations—the Political Commissar would have nothing to do with us. The bureaucratic muddlers had not informed him of our transfer, and he had no accommodation for us, let alone the requisite official orders to feed us. There is a popular saying, born of the Soviet regime: 'A little sparrow can often see further than a big eagle,' so we went in search of a 'sparrow', who turned out to be the Head of the Red Army House, Major Vergassov, a native of the North Caucasian republic of Ossetia. He was a red-haired man of medium height and, like most Caucasians, liked nothing better than to sit down in company with a few bottles of wine and loaves of Georgian bread, *lavash*. He loved showbiz folks, especially the ladies, and did everything he could to make us comfortable. He was in trouble. None of the Georgian artistes wanted to perform at the front because they didn't consider that this was their war. In the early days, Stalin's fellow Georgians did everything to avoid enlistment. It was a source of merriment as well as indignation among the Soviet soldiers that the two soldiers hand-picked to climb to the top of the Reichstag building in Berlin in order to hoist the red flag which was a signal for victory and the destruction of the German Army, were a Russian and a Georgian! I was amazed to hear even Georgian intellectuals reiterate the incredible myth that Hitler's wife was a Georgian, and that for this reason he would never invade Georgia.

Major Vergassov greeted us with open arms. We could fill his quota for the Artistes' Front Brigade. He divided the forty Moscow artistes into four groups of ten and gave each group a number. And so we officially became a Frontal Group of Artistes and were given the honour of being Number One. He cleared a hall in the Red Army House on Rustavelli Prospekt, supplied us with electric cookers, and issued us with civilian ration cards. As the Georgians had declared Tbilisi to be a closed city and no evacuees were allowed to settle there, the shops were still fairly well stocked. The only Muscovites were a leading group of actors from the Moscow Art Theatre, and Tbilisi was treated to the sight of famous actors strolling up and down the Rustavelli Prospekt.

I was witness to a comic scene in the open peasant market. The great director, Nemirovich-Danchenko, had just exchanged a loaf of black bread for some fruit and had given the vendor a ten-rouble note for some eggs. The Georgians consider it beneath their dignity to give small change, so when the great man asked for his change, the heavily-moustachioed peasant threw the small change at him, shouting, 'You bloody Muscovites have been thieving and robbing us all your life but don't like it when someone else earns an honest kopek!'

Another incident happened which I recall with horror to this day. We had just returned from the Front and had managed to get a room in the Intourist Hotel. Next door was a Leningrad couple, Yasha and Vera. Next to them was our pianist Boris's room. He had been given a double bedroom to himself because the windows were broken and as December in Tbilisi is shivery, the room was not in demand. One day, the Hotel Manager asked Boris if he could allow a gifted young pianist, a recent graduate from the Moscow Conservatoire, to share his room for a couple of weeks while he gave solo concerts. We were introduced to Slava, as he was called. A tall, lanky chap, very poorly dressed with trousers too short for his long legs, and a faded policeman's raincoat. His concerts were a great success and one day he told Boris he wouldn't be home that night as he had been invited out by some new admirers. Boris was glad of the opportunity to invite a girl friend to see his family album. About midnight we had just finished supper after the show when we heard someone knocking on Boris's door down the corridor. Whoever it was was trying to get in. But, not surprisingly, Boris had locked himself and his girl in for privacy. Suddenly our own door opened, and in came Slava in his raincoat, carrying a cheap schoolboy's brief-case. We sat paralyzed while he strode through our room. 'Allow me to use your window,' he said, without waiting for permission. He opened the window, climbed out on to the ledge, which was about a foot wide and made of slippery sheet-iron, and continued on his way, walking absolutely without the slightest falter. Elena and I watched him as he went, and I had to catch her hand to prevent her from calling out in horror. We were on the sixth floor and the air was thick with mountain mist and rain. Boris told us the rest of the story. The suitcase with which he had blocked the broken window had fallen to the floor with a bang and a long leg reached into the room. Excusing himself politely to Boris and his girlfriend hiding under the blanket, Slava undressed and in a second was fast asleep. When I told this to my circus pals, tightrope walkers, they declared that it was almost impossible to do such a walk without slipping. I shudder to think that, unwittingly, I might have been responsible for the world losing one of the greatest pianists of the century; Slava was Sviatoslav Richter.

In December 1941, the Red Army, or Soviet Army as it was renamed, in order not to embarrass the Allies, entered Iran to join up with British forces coming from the south. We were sent off to perform for the troops. Our first stop was Tabriz. We were horrified by the poverty of the people. The sight of little boys chained to tables mending shoes in cobblers' shops was heart-rending. By contrast, vast sums were won or lost in the gambling den attached to the restaurant where we had our meals, and the shops and bazaars were packed with British and German goods which even the all-devouring Soviet Army could not exhaust. Gold seemed to be in great demand, and as the daily wage we received was so small, our artistes, especially the ladies, began to sell all sorts of gold trinkets to enable them to buy clothes. I was amused to hear one of our Ukrainian dancers speaking as if he had a potato in his mouth. He confessed to me that he had sold all his gold teeth.

Somewhat to my embarrassment, the Russian Commander took a liking to me and also Yakov Fleer, the well-known concert pianist, and invited our group to a banquet in honour of some captured Iranian generals. The Commander was a typical *moujhik*, a peasant who had risen from the ranks. He elected himself toastmaster and ended every round of toasts by drinking the health, as he put it, 'of the two grains of gold that had floated to the surface, two brilliant talents displaying the mighty potential of the great Russian people' (myself and Yakov). He never knew that one 'grain of gold' was a

Scotsman and the other a Jew, and naturally we made no attempt to disabuse him, especially as he declared that he was going to invest us both with the Order of the Red Star. He was well into his cups by then, and the next day, clear-headed once more, he had forgotten all about us and the award.

It was at this banquet that the British Consul in Tabriz began talking to me. He was delighted when he found out that I was British, and invited Elena and me to have a drink with him later that evening. I had to come up with the usual excuse about giving an early morning concert, but he could have had no inkling of our fear. Instead he proposed dinner the next day which prompted another apology. Throughout our remaining few days there, I had to avoid that poor man who must have been amazed at my insularity, unaware that I was being closely watched by a fellow artiste recruited by the KGB.

Just as we were preparing to leave Tabriz for Teheran, the order came for us to return to the Soviet Union. We were glad to hear this. The prospect of travelling the 600 miles over mountainous roads in a rickety bus, a constant prey to the ambushes of bandits or vengeful Iranian soldiers, was pleasant to no one. We gathered up our luggage and set off for Erevan, in Armenia.

A week's stay in Erevan convinced me that the Armenians had little enthusiasm for the Great Patriotic War, as it was now called. This was probably the only occasion when the Armenians were in agreement with their historic enemies, the Georgians. Usually so smart, the Armenian soldiers looked like punctured balloons in uniforms which always seemed either too small or too big for them. We were once stopped by a sentry somewhere near the front line.

'Halt! Who goes there?'

'Moscow artistes on our way to give a concert for our men.'

'Do you know the password—Mushka?'

'Yes, we know the password. "Mushka".'

'Then pass, Moscow artistes.'

Our next stop, after Erevan, was Leninakan, on the Turkish border, where we celebrated the New Year of 1942. Here we had an experience that could have ended badly. About midnight we were sitting in our hotel room when our accordion player, Yasha, rushed in with the news that a couple of Americans were staying in the hotel, and they had invited us for a drink. The Americans were affable chaps and made us laugh with tales of their long and arduous journey from the Far East. We, too, had travelled along the Trans-

Siberian Line and could sympathize with them. We knew those conductors who could always produce a bottle of vodka at black market price but never a pot of tea. We knew what it was like to go two weeks without a bath, and to share a compartment with a Siberian peasant who declares that the only cure for a cold is 96° proof spirit and garlic. We left them about two o'clock and were just about to go to bed when there was a knock at the door. Two men in plain clothes stood on the threshold, with Yasha standing behind them, looking scared. They showed us their KGB passes and told us to put on our coats and follow them. It was a grim procession that walked through the streets to KGB headquarters, a few blocks away. When I tried to tell Elena, in English, to stick to the truth, I was told to shut up. It was only when we were taken individually to separate rooms that I began to feel scared. I had decided that it was no time for false modesty and I immediately informed my two interrogators that my father was Campbell, the leading inter-national communist. They stopped me and said that they were aware of that. Elena had evidently told them the same thing. In fact, it seemed to do the trick. The upshot was that we were roundly scolded for mixing with unknown foreigners and made to promise that we would give a concert for the KGB garrison. Nothing more was ever said, but I was dumbfounded that we couldn't talk to men who were, after all, our allies at the time.

After a few days back in Tbilisi, our group of ten artistes was dispatched yet again, this time to the Crimea, through Krasnodar. Here we were faced with a further example of bureaucratic bungling. It was January 1942. The Germans had already captured half the Ukraine and were on their way through the narrow strip leading into the Crimean Peninsula. It was only a matter of weeks before it would be in their hands. We crossed the Kerch Straits into the Crimea but on arrival heard the news that the Germans had indeed broken through the Kahovka Strip and were heading towards the naval base at Sevastopol. We gave concerts for a few days but soon the order came for us to return to the Caucasus. Everything was in chaos and confusion. The Black Sea fleet had been sunk and Sevastopol was surrounded but holding out. When we arrived at the port at Kerch, we realized that it was useless to try to find anyone to arrange our crossing. German planes were continually bombing the harbour and people were reduced to using the inner tubes of tyres as life-belts, in daredevil but doomed attempts to swim the few miles across to Taman on the other side.

Most of them were machine-gunned by enemy planes and the icy water took its toll of the rest.

Just when we had given up all hope, frustrated and resigned to falling into the hands of the Germans, Garry, our Political Officer, whom we hadn't seen all day, turned up, wanting to know where we had got to. Garry was a Moscow-born Armenian and he was no exception to the rule that 'an Armenian is worth a hundred cunning Greeks.' 'Grab your cases and follow me,' he commanded. Along with the other eight artistes we trudged about a couple of miles up the shore until we came to a hidden naval base. We were bundled into a small boat, and at dead of night we crossed the Straits to comparative safety. Eventually we managed to hitch-hike to Staff HQ in Krasnodar, where everything appeared to be quiet and calm.

We always recall Garry, our Political Officer, with feelings of gratitude. Without doubt he saved our lives more than once during the year he accompanied our group. In the first year of the war there were few officers who wanted to travel with artistes' groups, as they were called by the derogatory name of *nyanya* or wet nurse. To a certain extent, many artistes were to blame for this. They were a pampered crowd before the war and couldn't get used to the rigours of living and performing at the front. It was only a chance incident in the summer of 1942 that improved the artistes' prestige among the fighting forces.

The eminent pianist, Emil Gilels, was performing in a field to the south of Moscow somewhere near the front lines. Hundreds of troops were standing round the open lorry (our usual stage) listening to Gilels's virtuoso rendering of Chopin when out of the clear blue sky came an enemy plane. Whether it was the spell of Gilels's playing or the fact he did not falter for a split second, no one panicked. A cameraman filmed the whole incident from beginning to end and it was shown on cinema screens all over the country, described as a 'perfect example of cool-headedness and fortitude in the face of danger'.

We returned to Tbilisi in February, to find the city in a carnival mood. The Georgians were secretly rejoicing at the German advance, while the hundreds of officers who had escaped from the Crimea were revelling in the well-stocked wine shops. We had hardly had time to clean our costumes, or indeed ourselves, before the order came to leave for the South-western Front in the east of the Ukraine. It took us a week to get there, through Baku, up the Caspian Sea and into Rostov. In Rostov we had to give a concert for the SMERSH before they would endorse our documents for our final destination, the little town of Kamensk, in the Donbass Coalfields, where Staff HQ were quartered. (Kamensk was later made famous by Alexander Fadeev's book *The Young Guards*, about a group of youngsters who organize a sabotage unit to create havoc and destruction among the Fascist invaders. Fadeev became President of the Writers' Union and after the Stalin Disclosures committed suicide.)

Only after we had given a few concerts in Kamensk did we find out that Staff HQ had been moved to Lysichansk, in the heart of the coalfields. So off we went on another hazardous journey. The Donbass is criss-crossed by railway lines, and after three changes we landed up at a station to find a two-coach train going to Lysichansk. The station-master warned us that the line ran parallel to the front, with the Germans entrenched on the other side of a long chain of hills. Whenever they saw steam rising they would open fire. 'So,' said the station-master, 'be prepared for surprises.'

I will not pretend that we weren't scared. To take our minds off our troubles we played cards, our ears cocked for the big bang. In such situations there is nothing like a glass of vodka to steady the nerves. As luck would have it, we hadn't a drop left. It was then that I remembered the lotion Elena used to wipe off her make-up. The ingredients were cognac, an egg, lemon juice and cream. 'What a beautiful cocktail,' I thought. Elena must have read my mind, and though she was sorry to lose her lotion, we drank the cognac. It didn't help.

Suddenly the train stopped, and the driver announced he was going no further. So we had to get out and, together with some officers, we picked our way awkwardly along the sleepers until we came to what had once been a small station. The roof had gone but the benches were still there. We sat down to rest. Almost immediately an officer screamed at us to clear out, as the Germans must have seen us and would start shelling the place. When we asked him where we should go, he told us. It was certainly not to Lysichansk. Off we went again, dragging our cases. A mile further on, Elena and I, who were ahead of the main party, came to a fork in the road. There was no signpost to indicate the direction, right or left. We tossed a coin. It came down tails and we took the road to the right. That coin saved us from walking straight into the hands of the Germans. We learned later that they had taken the road on the left some few hours before. That is why, to this very day, whenever I toss a coin I always call 'tails'.

The South-western Front was probably the worst of all the battle fronts we toured. The deep snow had been transformed into impassable mud by the spring floods. We arrived at a division stationed near the front lines. We had travelled all day in a lorry across the dreary flat steppe, had given our performance and were just sitting down, dead tired, to a well-deserved supper, when an officer approached us and asked us to give another concert straight away. 'It's a special case,' he explained. 'We have just liberated about twenty men. During the enemy advance they were surrounded, but held on against tremendous odds and staved off the attack. For five days they held on, quite literally up to their necks in mud, with nothing to eat but pieces of black bread.' We protested that they really needed a hot bath, supper and a clean bed to sleep in. 'We know that,' the officer replied, 'but they nearly wept when they heard they had come too late for your concert. What do you think?'

As long as I live I shall never forget those men with their gaunt faces and exhausted, sunken eyes, sitting in their torn greatcoats with the mud still clinging to them. How they laughed, how they sang along with us, how they sat full of wonder at our conjurer's tricks, and roared at my comic antics. My heart was ready to burst. When the last chord had been played, one of them climbed on to the stage to thank us. We wanted to stop him, to thank him and his comrades for their bravery. It was these simple lads from the Siberian tundra who had never before even seen a concert who won the war for Russia.

I recall one morning when, during a respite between concerts, we went for a walk to enjoy the bleak but welcome sunshine. As we sat on a mound, watching a neat formation of German bombers fly past, it suddenly dawned on me that the Russians couldn't be relied upon to manage a whelk-stall. The Donbass was a gigantic quagmire in which thousands of tanks were helplessly stuck, but still the High Command was pushing in more and more tanks. These would have to be abandoned when the Germans began their advance. I remembered a tipsy Colonel who once confided in me the reason why the railways were in such a mess. 'The bloody fools gave all the engine-drivers rifles and sent them off to be killed at the front.'

While I was on the South-western Front I came into contact with the man who was destined to become one of the KGB's top hangmen, Beria's deputy, Ryumin. At that time he was Political Commissar for the South-west Front.

Although we artistes were semi-military, we had no official status and were not entitled to army rations. Most of the time we had to depend on being fed by the units where we gave a concert, and often we went hungry. There came a day when we were almost dropping with starvation, so three of us, Solomon Berman, an international concert pianist, our compère, Iosif Vyazner, and myself, decided to approach the Political Commissar. It was two days before we were ushered into his office. He had a list of our names. It was obvious that Solomon and Iosif were both Jewish and I suppose that he thought my name sounded Jewish as well. When we explained our problem and asked him to help, Ryumin's initially bland manner changed. His voice rose to a shriek as he pounded the table. Red-faced, he stumped up and down, shaking his fist in our faces, the very image of a Jew-baiting Gestapo bully.

'You lousy bunch of scroungers have come to deprive our glorious Army of food,' he roared. I tried to ease the tension with a little light comedy. I quoted an old Russian saying: 'Do you know what happened when the gypsy stopped feeding his horse? It died!' He simply frothed at the mouth and accused me of insulting the Soviet Union by comparing it to a gypsy. He said he'd have us arrested and shoved into the *Shtrafnoe* Battalion, the Penal Battalion for criminals and deserters. We were scared stiff but stuck to our guns. Solomon declared coolly: 'You still have to feed us.'

Ryumin shrieked. 'Von otsyuda!' ('Out with you!') and at that moment his adjutant appeared and announced a member of the Front Supreme Military Council, General Korneichuk, who walked in behind him.

Korneichuk, apart from being a wartime general, was a writer and dramatist, and so influential that he was called 'the Prince of the Ukraine'. Elena and I had been very good friends with him before the war. When he saw me, he bawled: 'Villi! What the hell are you doing here? Where's Elena?' And he hugged and thumped me on the back. Seeing Ryumin's flushed face, he asked what the trouble was. Quick-witted Solomon explained that a mistake had been made, someone had forgotten to put us on the Provisions List and Comrade Ryumin was very angry about it and was about to rectify the blunder.

'Put them on officers' provisions,' Korneichuk commanded.

'Those are my orders. They are doing a fine job.' I didn't know where to look. I never saw Ryumin again and I didn't shed a tear when I heard he had been executed along with Beria.

About the middle of April, as a massive German attack was expected at any moment, we were ordered to return to Tbilisi. No trains were going to Rostov, so we decided to take pot luck and hop on to the first train that came along. The engine struggled through the floods from the overflowing Donets. There were times when we had to climb on to the wooden seats while the water rushed into the carriages carrying mud and slime with it. After changing three trains, we took a fourth which, much to our delight, carried the sign-board, 'Stalino-Moscow'. Maybe we could break through and get home. Our joy was short-lived. We arrived the next day on the outskirts of Voronezh, about 250 miles from Moscow, and heard the order 'all out'. It seemed the Germans had captured the line further north.

The station Commandant sent us to a deserted school nearby where we could sleep the night. Next morning we debated whether to take our cases with us to the army canteen, a couple of miles down the line. The 'ayes' had it. It was a rule with us never to part with our costumes. While breakfasting in the canteen, we heard the sound of air-raid sirens coming from the town, followed by the familiar whine of falling bombs. We did not hurry over breakfast, and only when the radio announced 'all clear' did we start back along the line to the school. Imagine our horror when we saw a giant crater where the building had stood only an hour ago. It had received a direct hit. As we stood looking at the pit our singer suddenly gave a horrified shriek. 'My stockings! My stockings!' she wailed. 'I left them hanging to dry by the stove!'

Our only chance of breaking through to the Caucasus now was to go south along the main line by way of Rostov. We found a goods train and had no option but to climb aboard. The radio was already announcing that the Germans had entered Voronejh. Hundreds of other citizens had the same idea and the trucks were packed. However, there were many who did not evacuate and the market was full of peasants, bartering their wares. They refused to take Soviet currency—they spat if you offered it to them—but were prepared to exchange food for almost anything. I got a dozen eggs and a pound of butter for a pair of old socks and trousers.

'We are not communists or Jews,' they scoffed, 'so we have nothing to fear from the Germans.' They were mistaken. The peasants of the Voronezh region were either murdered by the Nazis or transported to Germany as forced labour.

For two days and nights we travelled, without sleep, and with only black bread, spread with the butter I had bartered, to eat. When at last we got to Kamensk, it was announced that the train could go no further; Rostov was in German hands. A call from the station to the Major-Director of the Army Club brought him quickly with a lorry. He was jubilant. 'A regiment is off to the Front, so we'll give them a farewell concert,' he cried. He was an enthusiast. The sight of ten scarecrows, dead tired, dirty and starving did not dampen his ardour.

'A hot shower, a hot meal and an hour's rest in a . . .'
'. . . a hot bed!' we finished the sentence for him.

His name was Bukhgalter which means book-keeper. He regarded life as a huge joke. While I was in his office, the telephone rang incessantly as officers from many regiments competed to get tickets for our concert.

'Can I speak to the Army Club Director?'
'Book-keeper speaking,' Bukhgalter would say.
'I don't want the book-keeper, I want the Director.'
'This is the book-keeper speaking . . . '
'I tell you I don't want . . .'

And so on, until they gave up. Then Major-Director Book-keeper would roar with laughter.

True to his word, Bukhgalter arranged for us to have a hot shower and a hot meal, and ten beds awaited us in a big room behind the stage. Every artiste left the stage to tremendous applause and it would be difficult to say which of us was the most popular. When our singer rendered the familiar folk songs or 'Katya, Katyusha', the soldiers' song that replaced the Party song about Stalin, the packed hall joined in with her lustily. These peasants in soldier uniform gazed unbelievingly at our conjurer's tricks and roared with laughter at the discomfiture of some sergeant when Evgeny Shukevich extracted playing cards, gold coins and ladies' underwear out of his pockets. But, with all due modesty, Elena and I stole the show. We had converted our 'picture gallery' number to make it suitable for any impromptu stage, whether it was a barn, a dug-out or a proper theatre. Elena's beautiful dancing, my comic antics and the final tap dance always brought the house down.

Where we got the strength to perform I do not know, we had been itinerants for so long—undernourished and exhausted. But somehow the moment one steps on to the stage some source of hidden energy takes over and the show goes on. No sooner did an act take its last bow than the artistes collapsed straight into bed, in make-up and costumes, and were fast asleep in a second.

Elena and I were the final act and when the audience demanded encores again and again, we gathered the last of our energy and gave them what they wanted. In two hours they were leaving for the Front. It might be the last time many of them would laugh. On that occasion, after the final curtain fell at last, Iosif, Elena and I were making a bee-line for bed when a girl soldier came up to us. She was tall, blonde, and even in her ugly uniform, smart. I remember a large brown birthmark on her right cheek but even that didn't spoil her good looks. She introduced herself.

'My name is Anna Smirnova and I am eighteen. I am a machine-gunner and am off to the Front tonight. After seeing your show, I have decided I want to be an artiste. It must be such an interesting life, travelling everywhere and enjoying yourselves.'

Over a cup of tea we tried to temper Annyushka's illusions with a little reality, and advised her not to think of becoming an artiste. Years later, Elena and I happened to be on tour in a town called Lipetsk. On a free evening we went to the local theatre to see *Othello*. Desdemona was, of course, a blonde, and there was something familiar about her which aroused our curiosity. It was only when she turned her right cheek and we saw the brown mole that we remembered Annyushka. The name Smirnova did not appear on the programme, but after the performance we went backstage. It was Annyushka all right. She had changed her name when she got married. She hugged and kissed us and confessed, 'You see, I didn't heed your warning. You were right, though. It's not an easy life but I wouldn't change it for anything.'

Annyushka was one of many thousands of girls who fought alongside the men in the Soviet Army, and fought with matchless courage. A soldier once told me the following story.

A General was walking along the trenches and seeing a group of soldiers huddling round a campfire, greeted them with a hearty: 'Hullo, comrades soldiers!'

The soldiers snapped to attention. 'My goodness, but it's so cold,' said the General. 'Enough to freeze your balls off, eh!'

'Not for us, Comrade General,' one of the soldiers replied.

'Why? Are you something special?' said the General.

'Yes, Comrade General,' the soldiers chorused, 'We are women!'

We were wondering whether we would ever get back to our main base in Tbilisi when the joyful news came that the Germans had been driven out of Rostov, fifty miles away. By hitching rides on lorries we reached the city in a few hours. It was amazing how the Germans had managed to transform Rostov. Everywhere, even in the Russian baths, signs and notices were in German, the markets were full of German goods and the vendors were doing a roaring trade in razor blades, contraceptives and pornographic post-cards.

We were quartered in a private flat. Our landlady was a buxom, loquacious Ukrainian. Elena asked her how the Germans had behaved during occupation and she replied confidentially that it was not so much the Nazis she had feared as her fellow-countrymen. Neighbour had betrayed neighbour to the Gestapo as cheerfully as they had formerly done to the KGB. Only a week later the Germans were back in Rostov, but by that time we were on our way to Tbilisi.

We had to change trains in Baku but the cashier wouldn't sell us tickets until we brought a *spravka*, a certificate from the sanitary inspection station declaring that our clothes had been cleaned of any vermin. When we got to the place we learned our clothes would be in the oven for an hour, and as the train left in forty-five minutes, we thought we were finished. We described our predicament to the Azerbaijanian receptionist. It cost us ten roubles each for the *spravka*, and our clothes never saw that oven. The ticket clerk at the station knew this and asked us how much we had paid. He was very upset and said he could have done it for five roubles. But seeing we 'understood life', he sold us each tickets for the Wagon-Lits at five roubles above the fare.

For three months we had slept in barns, cowsheds and dugouts, and at the very end of our journey for one night we were in luxury. White sheets, mahogany compartments, hot tea with lemon! On the subject of tea our compère, Iosif, had a separate mind-reading act with his wife, Lidia, a cantankerous, quarrelsome woman. Before leaving for this tour she fell ill and, to our delight, couldn't go with us. She entrusted Iosif with a thermos flask (more valuable to her than her diamond rings). Her parting words were 'Take care of that flask or don't come back!'

All through our journeys on lorries, over potholed roads, through the Donets floods, Iosif held that flask as if it were a newborn baby. The smooth running of the Wagon-Lits lulled his vigilance, and just as our train came slowly into Tbilisi station, the driver jammed on his brakes. The small handbag in which Iosif kept the flask flew out of his hands and it broke into a thousand pieces. We were all very upset. The first person to enter our coach was Major Vergassov of the Red Army House asking for us, Elena, Iosif and me. It seems the rumour had been spread that we had been killed. 'Thank God!' he cried sincerely as he hugged us. 'Lidia will be overjoyed!' A group of artistes and friends cheered as we appeared. Thinking that his wife too would be glad to see him alive, Iosif opened his arms to embrace her. Before he could do so she fended him off, demanding to know where the thermos flask was. Iosif held up the handbag and when she heard the dreadful rattle, she let out a shriek and, turning on her heel, quit the station.

In Tbilisi, the Georgians were still busy fiddling while Rome burned. The Soviet Army was trying to drink the town dry, with no great success, while blackmarketeers had bought up from the hospital workers all the drugs and medicines needed by the wounded.

After the hardships of our nerve-racking tour, we were in a state of exhaustion and so, when the Manager of the Armenian State Jazz Orchestra offered to include Elena and me in a tour with them through Central Asia into Iran and back through Armenia, we agreed. It would be good to leave the battle-front for a while.

I hate nationalism in any form (including Scottish) and the Armenians are extreme chauvinists. The Jazz Revue was made up exclusively of Armenians and our act hardly fitted into their programme of folk dance and music. The audiences too were invariably Armenian, and when their pet Rafael Beibutov sang 'Arshin Malalan', they would fall on their knees and make the sign of the Cross in ecstasy. We never received more than polite applause.

When we arrived in Baku, to board the ship to take us across the Caspian Sea, we were astounded to see thousands of refugees trying to find their way to Central Asia. The ship was already overloaded, but our problem was solved when our Manager arranged a free concert for the Supreme Command of the Caspian Flotilla. Then we were transported across the Caspian to Krasnovodsk on a torpedo boat.

Krasnovodsk presented a terrible spectacle. In peacetime, the population of this tiny town was about 3,000, and the only source of fresh water was a tanker that came from Baku once a day. Hundreds of thousands of evacuees were living in makeshift tents on the pavements and along the shore with little to shelter them from the broiling sun. Black marketeers were selling water, firewood and even the space on the pavement nearest to the pier where the water ship unloaded its cargo. To get near the large water tank was almost impossible and even dangerous, as disease was rife. I noticed that the hose lay for a few minutes on the pier before being drawn back on to the ship and I thought there might be a few drops of water left inside it. How I lifted that heavy hose I don't know, but I did, and was rewarded with a stream of water for my kettle. My Boy Scout training came in handy and I lit a fire by rubbing sticks together. And so we had tea in the desert.

We travelled around Central Asia, performing in all the main cities. Everywhere the picture was the same—well-known scientists, actors and writers could be seen in the markets, selling what little was left of their possessions. Food was unobtainable on ration cards, but abundant in the peasant markets—at a price. Typhoid fever was taking a terrible toll. We had a fright when I went down with a raging temperature and the doctors couldn't diagnose the trouble. They ordered me into hospital, where my chances of recovery were small. Elena nearly went out of her mind until by chance she found a specialist in tropical diseases. She had to sell one of her few dresses to pay his fee. He looked me over and diagnosed a non-infectious scrub typhus, contracted from an insect bite. He gave me some concoction of his own, and a week later I was back on the stage again.

Although this was meant to be a rest-cure, by this time we had had enough of Central Asia and the Armenians, and considered it better to dodge bombs at the front than risk death from flea bites. The Armenian musicians and their Manager were showing unreserved animosity towards us and refused to pay us our money. We were living by selling flints for petrol lighters, a stock of which I had bought in Tbilisi. This was my first experience of black marketeering. We tried to get a train to Moscow, but as the capital was closed we were refused tickets. So we decided to return to Tbilisi. Realizing that the Armenians had no intention of paying us our back salaries, I resorted to blackmail. 'If,' I threatened, 'I don't get our money within an hour, I am going to the militia to report you for illegally receiving bread cards in every town where we performed.' Within ten minutes I had all our money in my pocket.

On the journey back, we met two Polish officers who had just been released from the camps to join the Polish Army, commanded by General Anders, in Iran. They prophesied the speedy destruction of the Soviet regime. All the way to Ashkhabad, they tried to persuade us to go to Teheran with them. 'The moment Stalingrad falls,' they said, 'the Germans will overrun the country like cockroaches and you will be trapped in the Caucasus. There's no control at Ashkhabad and we'll fix things with the Polish High Command. The Anders Army is going to join up with the British and you'll be needed. Save yourselves before it's too late!'

The proposal sounded both logical and enticing. We had seen how easily the Germans had advanced through the Ukraine and we had no illusions about the 'loyalty' of the people in the Caucasus. But somehow the repugnant feeling that we would be rats deserting a sinking ship was uppermost, and we wished them goodbye and good luck. But no sooner had we arrived in Tbilisi than we were included in a troupe going off to the Southern Caucasian Front, along the Black Sea coast. The Germans had occupied the whole of the North Caucasus but, as Stalingrad was still holding, had been forced to slow down their advance.

Travelling along the coast was a hazardous affair. The only road from Sukhumi to Taupse, the last town before the Front line, was continuously strafed by the low-flying Foker-Wolf. The only building still intact, by some miracle, was the Oil Workers' Club. It was here that we experienced the horror of being buried alive. As most of our performances were to be given at the Club we decided to stay there rather than in a dugout. We found a room, and with our pianist, Boris, settled down for the first night. Boris declared his right to sleep on the piano. I hauled a big wardrobe over and laid it flat on the floor face down. Then Elena and I climbed on to its back, fully dressed, and lay down covered by our coats. We were so tired that we hardly heard the whistling and crashing of the bombs. All of a sudden, we were awakened by a terrific crash and felt ourselves falling. We stopped, with a jarring thud. Elena was lying on top of me. My God, I thought, it must have been a direct hit and we're lying buried in the basement.

'Elena, are you alive?' I whispered, quite terrified.

'I think so, but I'm not quite sure,' she replied.

'Can you move your arms and legs?'

'Yes.' I felt her stretching her legs.

'What has happened?' she asked.

'I think we're buried. Let's see if we can get out of here. You move first so that I can slip out from under you.'

I felt Elena's knees digging into my stomach, and gasped. Then she was gone, and I was left lying on my back. A moment's silence, and then I was shocked to hear Elena shrieking with laughter. I struggled to my feet, fearing that the ordeal had deranged her, and emerged, blinking, into the room. The building appeared to be completely intact. Boris was grumbling about being woken up by two idiots. After a nearby explosion the back of the wardrobe had collapsed. Instead of being buried alive in the basement, we had fallen into the bottom of the wardrobe.

We had only been in Taupse a month when once more we were ordered back to Tbilisi. From Tbilisi we were sent to the Northern Group at Mozdok, a hundred miles from the Grozny Oilfields. There was a strange atmosphere along the Mozdok Front. The Germans seemed to be marking time indecisively, and the Soviet troops had been ordered to stand to the last man and not let the enemy through to the oilfields. Why had the Germans stopped? They were only ten miles from Ordjonikidze, the Ossetian capital, where we were enjoying the luxury of living in a hotel. Like the Georgians, the Ossetians had no great love for the Soviet regime and were under the false impression that the Germans would be the lesser of the two evils, so much so that they eagerly awaited the arrival of the Germans' advance guard.

We were sitting in our hotel room one night in December 1942, when we heard noises and shouting. 'This is it,' I thought, as we dashed out, expecting to be confronted by SS troops. Instead we saw an excited crowd in the foyer straining to hear a loud-speaker.

'Soviet troops have begun a massive counter-attack at Stalingrad and 300,000 Fascists have been surrounded and are being destroyed. The rest of the German Army is retreating in disorder.'

We laughed and wept, danced, and hugged complete strangers. Was it possible? Had the Brown Scourge been halted? Might we live in peace once more? We dashed out into the streets, expecting to see joyful crowds, but they were deserted and all the houses were in darkness. The Ossetians had closed their doors and shutters to demonstrate their sullen resentment.

As the Germans retreated, needlessly burning everything on their way and leaving a trail of devastation, we joined in the chase. We entered the Kislovodsk Spa on the morning after the Germans had abandoned it. I shall never forget the sight of hundreds of dead bodies heaped in a large pit. It was hard to believe such inhumanity. These people, mostly Jews, had been herded into a goods train which was then shunted into the nearby glass-works at Mineralny

Vody where they were mown down by machine-guns. Among the dead were the parents of our colleague Edik Balaban. However, there was nothing we could do but keep going. Before we knew where we were, we were back in Rostov. Feeling that Stalingrad would go down in history, we cajoled our Political Officer into getting us permission to go there. Performing on the way, we got within ten miles of the city. There we were stopped. Hitler had ordered his army to break the Soviet counter-attack and was sending in new troops, tanks and planes to save the day. A gigantic battle was in progress and there was no time for concerts. All hopes of an end to this wearisome existence were dashed as we heard the news.

How many soldiers laid down their lives for Stalingrad will probably never be known. I spoke to a German prisoner who told me: 'It was like a side-show at the fair. We mowed them down and up they would come again, more and more and more. Some of our men went mad.'

Back in Tbilisi, we found that the Georgians had changed their tune and the People's Commissariat of Culture awarded us Honoured Diplomas for our services in representing the Georgian Republic at the front! Then we were off again, back to the south, where the situation was static despite the presence of a certain Political Commissar called Leonid Brezhnev who, according to his autobiography, played a crucial role in winning the war. Although we were there, on and off, for a whole year and knew most of the commanding officers personally, we never heard of Commissar Brezhnev, but could this be attributable to his extreme modesty, perhaps?

Gradually, the Caucasian Front moved up into the Kuban and reached the southern banks of the Kerch Straits over which we had escaped not so long ago. A number of attempts were made to force the Straits and we were sad to hear that Major Vergassov had been killed during one of these. In newly liberated Krasnodar we saw about twenty men publicly hanged in the City Square, among them a Russian whom the Germans had appointed Burgomeister. The square was packed with thousands of the citizens, some of whom perched perilously on the ruined walls to get a better view. When I commented on this large turnout to the old doorkeeper at the cinema where we were performing he said, 'That's nothing, son, you should have seen the mobs when the Germans hanged the communists.'

For our services the Front Command rewarded us with a week's holiday at a plush sanatorium in Sochi. But it was impossible to accustom ourselves to lie sunbathing on the beach. We bombarded Moscow with requests to allow us to go home. At last permission came through and we trundled off happily to Tbilisi. We wanted to buy all the things like vodka and brandy that we knew we would miss in Moscow. But we had no money. There was no alternative. We would have to sell some of our own things. Elena's sister, Vera, had brought with her a trunkful of clothes, all sorts of black underwear and stockings that nobody wore any more. Now a fellow artiste proposed that I come along with him to the *baraholka* market and try my luck. At first, I refused to go. Half of Tbilisi knew me as a star. I wasn't going to be seen selling ladies' underwear. 'Do you think you are any better than Nemirovich-Danchenko [the famous Director and co-founder of the Moscow Art Theatre]? I saw him last Sunday on the *baraholka* selling a pair of old trousers.' He mentioned a few more names of famous actors who were regular vendors. 'There's a war on, you know,' he concluded.

I have never felt stage fright in my life, but the nearer I got to the *baraholka* the heavier my legs got. My friend opened his case, hung all sorts of ladies' knickers and shifts on his arms and shouted in the true Petticoat Lane manner. The *kikelki* (peasant women) fingered them but didn't buy anything. His things were all in the traditional pink, so I guessed they would not even look at my black stockings and underwear. Fighting down my embarrassment, I furtively took a pair of black stockings out of my case. I held them in my hand as if they weren't mine and nonchalantly looked up at the sky. Before I knew what had happened, some of the *kikelki* women had grabbed my stockings and were pulling at them quarrelling as to who had seen them first. They demanded to know how much I wanted for them. I hadn't even thought about that, but before I could answer one of the women said 100 roubles. My friend had told me to double any offer, so I said 200. She countermanded with 150 and reached under her skirt for her purse. '180,' I replied. She looked at me with disgust, spat, counted out 175 roubles and strutted off triumphantly. I was surrounded by a milling mob of peasant women and within a few minutes I had sold everything in black and had 2,500 roubles in my pocket.

We arrived in Moscow late at night, during a black-out, and as there was a curfew, we had to wait until the next morning to go home. Moscow was half-empty, and in the grey November light the people looked pinched and poorly fed. Rationed food was difficult to get, though there was plenty to be found in the peasant markets at fantastically inflated prices. A kilo of butter cost 800 roubles, or a litre of vodka. The average wage of 800 roubles a month didn't stretch far. So everybody tried to moonlight. But to moonlight they had to be freed from their regular work, so all sorts of tricks were invented. Soon after my return I heard a man with flushed cheeks shouting, 'I have a temperature to sell. Who wants to buy a temperature?' I happened to mention this to a friend later who gave me the likely explanation. Although everybody in Russia is registered at a local clinic, doctors and receptionists rarely remember faces, especially during a war. So you take a genuinely sick man along to your clinic and give your name to the registrar, who sends your file upstairs to the doctor. Here is the trick. The sick man goes into the consulting room and has his temperature taken. He is told to go home to bed and is given a medical certificate exempting him from work for a week. You then give him fifty roubles, and spend the week earning a thousand.

We were excited to hear that we had been included in a group going to perform in besieged Leningrad. The group was made up mostly of Leningrad artistes trying to get home. It took us three days to travel from Moscow, a journey which normally takes only six hours. It was December 1943 and the siege of Leningrad was nearing its end. For 900 days and 900 nights the people of Leningrad had withstood the siege defiantly. Many had died on their feet from starvation or bombing, but everyone refused to give in. What amazed us in particular was the scrupulous cleanliness of the city. No sooner was a building bombed than it was shored up with plywood and the rubble cleared away, and life went on. For example, on the night Shostakovich's Seventh Symphony was played for the first time in the Philharmonic Hall by an orchestra of musicians virtually brought from the Front lines, tickets could not be bought for love nor money. All the theatres were packed. It was an impresario's paradise. Shop assistants were making fortunes by under-weighing the meagre rations or exchanging loaves of bread for valuable art objects.

We arrived at the Moscow Oktyabr Station at the far end of the Nevsky Prospekt, and were met by some sailors who bundled our cases on to a lorry. It was ten o'clock in the morning when normally the Nevsky would be bustling and alive. But as we drove along we counted only nineteen pedestrians hurrying along, looking anxiously at the sky. They were walking on the left-hand side of the street. On the right-hand side, the walls were painted with the warning: 'Do not walk on this side of the street during the shelling.'

We had brought a few little parcels of food for our friends' relatives. One woman, a well-known scientist, survived the blockade by working as a charwoman in a hospital. And the first thing she asked us was whether there was any truth behind the rumour that Peter Uleinikov, the famous actor whom she adored, had been knocked down by a car in Sverdlovsk and killed. She was thrilled to hear that he had survived.

Another parcel was for a friend's aunt, an elderly lady who was partially paralyzed and lived alone. 'Oh, I get on all right,' she said, 'people are so kind to me and help as much as they can. Very kind . . . all except one man. I'm sure you remember my big tom cat, Misha. Well, one day I was sitting here with him on my lap when the plumber came to mend something and made a great fuss of him. Then, quick as lightning, he lifted Misha up and walked off with him. Of course I was sorry for the poor old man, he must have been desperately hungry or he would never have done such a thing. But I was even more sorry to lose Misha.'

The last packet was for a singer's parents. She hadn't heard from them and all she knew was that her father, retired earlier, had returned to his lathe in the Putilov Plant. No trams or buses were running, so Elena and I had to trudge through the snow all the way to their house. I didn't press the bell as I knew by now that there was no electricity in the daytime, but thumped on the door. We had become accustomed to the silence of empty Leningrad houses. All of a sudden we heard a sound which sent shivers of fear up our spines. The silence was shattered by the yapping of little dogs. It was unbelievable! In most houses everything, cats and dogs, had been eaten during the siege. When the door opened, two very small terriers leaped out barking joyously. Our friend's mother explained, 'My Fedor got extra rations for working on the night shift so we shared it with them. Thank the Lord, they don't need much.'

In the middle of January 1944 the radio announced that the siege of Leningrad was over. It seemed to take the Leningraders a long time to assimilate the fact. There would certainly have been a speedier demonstration of their joy if the bread queues had disappeared along with the Germans. As the Germans retreated we followed with the Red Army. It was heart-rending to see the charred ruins of the once exquisite Peterhof Palace, and Tsarskoe

Selo. The walls stood black and crumbled. The Germans, robbed of victory, were taking their revenge by blowing up all that was sacred and dear to Russia. At Narva, on the Bay of Finland, they made one last stand, desperate that the Russians should not enter the Baltic Republics.

It was not until about the middle of March that we saw any public manifestation of joy at the Russian victories. We were returning from Kronstadt Fort, after performing for a week. It was a lovely sunny morning, the air crisp and cold. Spring was on its way at last. As our bus passed the giant Putilov Plant, and trundled through the Narvsky Gates, we sensed an unusual liveliness on the streets which only a week ago had been empty. As we came to the Oktyabr Railway Station we gasped in wonder. The Nevsky Prospekt was crammed with people, not hurrying to and fro, but standing in groups. They had crawled out of their freezing warrens and were blinking in the warm sunshine. They were wandering along the street, peering into each other's faces, searching for friends and relatives. Now and then we heard sudden shouts, 'My God, is it really you?' Then there would be hugs and weeping and laughing.

I had seen individual heroes in the war, but never a whole city of heroes. They had withstood cold, starvation, fire and blitz, and now emerged on to the Nevsky on that sunny spring morning to rejoice at being alive, and to grieve for those they would never see again.

We were among the first passengers to board the famous 'Red Arrow' express making its first trip along the newly liberated line to Moscow. The coaches were spotlessly clean and the mahogany shining like mirrors. The crew welcomed us in their well-worn but still smart uniforms, as if to say, 'We are sorry for any inconvenience. There has been a slight delay, but everything is in proper order now.'

Moscow looked drab and dreary, and it was snowing heavily when we arrived. On top of all this, as a result of our starvation diet in Leningrad, my old stomach trouble returned. The professor to whom I was recommended prescribed chicken and white bread. Elena asked him if he could also prescribe an address where such lost luxuries might be bought, but he failed to see the joke. We paid his fee with a bar of soap. This was far more valuable than money in Moscow.

Further south, the Soviet Army's advance across the Ukraine was slower and even more bloody. The Germans had suffered a psychological and military débâcle at Stalingrad, but their formidable war machine was by no means destroyed. We were sent south to the Ukrainian border, where the most gigantic tank and air battle in the history of warfare, the battle of the Kursky Bulge, was being fought. We had glimpses of this unique confrontation in which human beings seemed to play little part. There were just thousands of metal monsters, German and Soviet, crawling among each other, attacking, colliding and overturning.

It was here that we met our good friend, ex-General Alexei S., whom we had not seen since the day he warned us in Kharkov that the war would come. He was commanding a tank division with the rank of Colonel. He personally led his tanks into battle, in spite of the fact that, as the commanding officer, he was forbidden to do so. I asked Alexei how he could possibly distinguish friend from foe in this kaleidoscopic armada of tanks. He replied with one word: 'Instinct.'

Events now began to gain momentum. The long-awaited invasion of Europe by the Allies had taken place, the Soviet Army had crossed the borders of Russia and was chasing the Germans back to Berlin. We celebrated the New Year with friends in Moscow. Then, in the middle of January 1945, Warsaw was liberated, and we flew off to Poland and Hungary to perform for the troops. I shall never forget Maidanek Concentration Camp, built by the Germans near Lublin, where the Soviet troops had been quartered. We saw a giant heap of shoes, torn off the condemned. It was particularly terrible to see the thousands of children's shoes. We had the eerie experience of having to sleep on the floors of one of the barracks in this camp of death. I lay awake all night, certain that I could hear the groans and wails of the millions of innocent people who had lain on that same floor.

Warsaw created an indelible impression. There was no Warsaw, just a waste of ruins and rubble. I suggested to some Polish patriots that it was beyond the power of man to clear away the destruction, that it would be more logical to build a new city on another site. But they were unanimous in their determination that Warsaw was destroyed but not dead and that she would come to life and breathe again on this very spot. And she did. I saw Warsaw thirty years later and was once more spellbound, but this time by such concrete evidence of man's creative ability.

We arrived back in Moscow in time for the May Day celebrations of 1945, and a gruelling programme of performances. On the night of the 8th we went to bed dog-tired. We were just sliding blissfully into sleep when we were awakened by someone bawling in the street:

'The war's over! The war's over!'

Immediately, lights went on in all the windows and people came tumbling out of their houses, asking if it was true.

'Yes, yes, the Germans capitulated at one minute past twelve— it's all over, it's all over!'

Nobody said, 'We have won!' It seemed to be enough that it was over. Complete strangers hugged and kissed each other. A man in our communal flat, whom I suspected had written an anonymous letter to the KGB about me, now slapped me on the back and dragged me into his room for a glass of vodka.

Nobody went to work that day, and for once no charges were made against them—the courts were all shut anyway. The evening of the 9th, VE Day, saw all Moscow gathered on Red Square and the neighbouring Manejhnaya Square where the American Embassy was then housed. Soldiers, sailors and officers were tossed into the air to the cheering of the multitude. I lost sight of Elena and nearly wept with joy when I saw her head bobbing up and down a few yards away. We'd had enough of the jollifications. Having survived the bombs, the shells and the air-raids, and having narrowly escaped the German army, the last thing we wanted was to meet our death under the stampeding feet of our jubilant fellow citizens. So we struggled all the way up Gertzen Street and made our way home to celebrate quietly together. We were just putting our feet up when the phone rang, and we were informed that a group of Russian artistes were to take part in a grand concert on the square in front of the Berlin Reichstag, and Elena and I must be ready to leave in forty-eight hours.

The giant square, with the ruined Reichstag in the background, was packed with soldiers of every nation. Despite my considerable stage experience, never before had I heard such tumultuous ovations. 'Encore' was shouted in every language. The greatest Russian folk singer, Lidia Ruslanova, sang herself hoarse. (Three years later she was thrown into prison with her husband, a General.) In the middle of our act I sang a comic version of the song 'Some of These Days' to give Elena time to change her costume. The roar that greeted me when I finished suggested that British and

American troops were in the majority. No sooner did Elena and I step down from the impromptu stage than we were surrounded by Tommies and Yanks wanting to know who I was and how I came to be in a group of Soviet performers. If we had drunk all the whisky we were offered, we would have been carried off on stretchers.

For nearly a year after that we travelled all over Germany, performing for the forces and the population. The Soviets were anxious to win the defeated Germans' trust, and indeed the Soviet troops got on well with them, especially the men. Although the Russians had suffered perhaps more than any other nation, with ruined cities and 25,000,000 dead, it seemed that they felt little animosity towards the Germans. One instance of this touched me. Berlin was in total ruins, with the streets blocked by rubble, and finding one's way about was almost impossible, so the Soviet Command placed soldiers at key points to direct traffic. Elena and I noticed that one of these men was acting strangely. He was at a crossroads which must have been a busy intersection before the war. Now it was a maze of broken bricks. With great self-importance the soldier waved his flag to allow the occasional car or lorry to pass. As soon as it was out of sight, he ran furtively into a ruined building. There he covered a large stone with a newspaper, took a loaf of black bread out of his rucksack and cut it into small pieces. Then he opened a tin of corned beef. We suddenly became aware of scores of children's heads popping up from behind the ruins. The soldier took no notice of the children and earnestly continued to lay his impromptu table. When he had finished he looked proudly at it for a few moments, then turned to the children and uttered probably the only words he knew in German: 'Komm, komm, Kinder!' The children rushed across the street and within a few minutes they had devoured the lot, keeping up a chatter with the soldier which he obviously didn't understand. When the ragged group scooted off to play we approached him to find out who he was. His tragic story made his behaviour all the more astonishing. He came from a village in the Kalinin Region, which had been burned to the ground by the Germans. His wife and two children had been mowed down by machine-guns.

'But,' I protested, 'you must hate everything German after that. How can you be so kind to German kids when their fathers might have murdered your children?'

He stopped rolling a cigarette and looked up at me.

'I hated the Germans when we were fighting . . . now they are defeated, what's the sense in hating them any more? As for the kids, well, it wasn't their fault, was it? They're only small and have suffered enough as it is. They need a little kindness now.'

TEN

Radio Moscow

Returning to normal life in Moscow proved no easy matter. It was understandable that people expected a change for the better now that the threat of the enemy had been removed. Yet the food problem was still as acute as ever. The Russian people also assumed that, since the Western countries were now their allies, there would be an easing of relations and the Soviet Union would be brought out of its pre-war isolation. Many doors were flung open to foreigners, especially Embassy staff. It was a familiar sight to see writers, actors and other intellectuals dining and enjoying animated conversation with foreigners in restaurants. Frequently British and French as well as Germans were welcomed into the homes of Russians who paid the penalty. I do not care to remember how many of our friends and colleagues went to the camps for this unforgivable 'betrayal'.

Elena and I politely declined invitations to parties where I could meet my fellow countrymen. We had not forgotten the pre-war purges. Even when we were officially included in a concert at the American Embassy we categorically refused to go. I do not know whether this saved us—the KGB were experts at inventing 'crimes'—and after Stalin's death I did discover that we had been put on their lists. But thousands upon thousands of returning troops were not so careful, and the more loquacious ones found themselves in the camps. That was the beginning of the 1946–7 purges in which the vast majority of the condemned were ordinary, innocent people who had been POWs, or who allowed their tongues to wag in the wrong company. Many of our colleagues travelled the same road and were only released after the death of Stalin. Yet no amount of repression could stop people from talking about the better life beyond the Soviet borders, so a campaign was invented, called 'Anti-Cosmopolitanism', the struggle against the infiltration of Western ideas into Soviet culture. A new slogan became the watchword of the day: 'National in form, socialist in content'.

Stalin himself began the new movement with a condemnation of Muradelli's opera (which should have been banned anyway as it was extremely bad). Then Shostakovich was brought up in front of a Composers' Union Commission, and was forced to declare that 'he would never do it again', though it was not clear what he was supposed to have done. Prokofiev refused to face the Commission and he died unrepentant on the same day as Stalin. The brilliant humorist, Mikhail Zoschenko, was pilloried and insulted daily in the media.

The most incredible campaign was started to stamp out expressions, names and words which had been derived from foreign (and especially Western) languages. As football came from Britain, naturally, all football terms were English words transposed directly into Russian. All sports-writers were ordered to call a football 'match' a 'tournament'. The referee became a 'judge', the goal-keeper was transformed into a 'defender of the gate'. All sorts of Western foodstuffs came under attack. Ketchup was given the long-winded name of 'Georgian Tomato Sauce'. The French roll, or *frantsuskaya bulka*, became a 'city roll'. One lady asked for a city roll, to which the shop assistant replied, 'Ain't got no such thing.' 'But there they are, heaps of them on the shelf there,' the customer screamed back, pointing her finger at the rolls with scarcely hidden indignation. 'Oh, a French roll! Why didn't you say so in the first place?'

Circus and variety artistes suffered particularly from the new campaign, which seemed hell-bent on eliminating all theatricality. It has always been a tradition for such performers to give themselves high-sounding names like the 'Flying Ronaldoes' or 'The Mighty Hercules'. When the order came that all artistes must in future be announced by the names in their passports, the results were absurd. 'The Bronze Giant', a weight-lifter with rippling muscles, was announced as Ivan Kurochkin, which literally means 'Ivan the Chicken'. The girl with the exquisite figure from the Flying Ronaldoes turned out to be called Masha Krivobokova, which means 'Masha the Lop-sided'.

Another difficulty arose with costumes. The Party banned cowboy clothes and spangled dresses and decreed that artistes should appear only in traditional Russian costumes. This posed a particular problem for conjurers. Tails and white tie were not only traditional but also essential for concealing rabbits, handkerchiefs, etc. One conjurer we knew solved the problem in a remarkable way. He appeared with his face and hands painted black, dressed in a turban and a floppy white gown. He struck a heroic pose, and began to recite what we guessed to be Othello's monologue, the one where he confronts Desdemona with the handkerchief (his Armenian accent was so fierce, it was difficult to tell). We nearly fell off our seats when, after ten minutes of murdering Shakespeare, he shrieked, 'Platok! Platok!' ('The handkerchief, the handkerchief!') and then very skilfully began to pull a couple of dozen coloured hankies out of his fingers. From then on his magic act proceeded as usual.

I came in for particularly fierce criticism since I was the only genuine foreigner in the State Variety Agency. The man from the Ministry declared that there was too much of Charlie Chaplin in my performance. I thanked him for the finest compliment any comic could receive and was immediately denounced by the whole Commission. 'Chaplin is an opportunist! He panders to the fashion of the moment! He raises problems and gives no solutions. He does not show the revolutionary way to the people!'

All our sketches were banned and we were ordered to invent new ones reflecting the Party lines. In a whimsical mood, I suggested I should wear a kilt and play the bagpipes on the grounds that I was a Scotsman. This ridiculous proposal was taken seriously, and only abandoned when it was realized that a kilt is a kind of skirt. We rehearsed a rowdy Georgian folk act involving a comic porter from the Tbilisi bazaars dancing with a classical ballerina, and it turned out to be a fine number. But the censors said no. It would be blasphemy to have an *anglichanin* playing a Georgian. The Georgians would be offended. Stalin was a Georgian.

In despair, I did a foolish thing. I wrote hastily to Andrei Zhdanov, Stalin's right-hand man, asking him to tell the censors to take into consideration the fact that I was not a Russian. I had no idea that Zhdanov was the initiator of the 'Anti-Cosmopolitanism' campaign. The letter was sent back to our Directors with one word on it, 'Investigate'. We were brought in front of the Board, reprimanded for our obstinacy, and told to conform. 'The Party requests, the Party demands . . .' and so on. When I reminded them that we were not members of the Party, the Managing Director roared: 'And you can thank your lucky stars you're not, or I'd have had the hide off your backs a long time ago!'

Elena and I had not performed for over a year when suddenly and unexpectedly we were told that we had been included in a two-night programme at the Hall of Columns. Needless to say, we were overjoyed. After a year of gloom and despondency perhaps somebody had, at last, come to appreciate the stupidity of this discrimination against me. We performed on a Saturday evening and pulled out all the stops. It was a thrill to be back on the stage again, and hearing the ovation was balm to our hearts. We didn't know that a specially picked Commission was watching from different seats in the auditorium. The next morning a telephone call informed us that this Commission had ordered us to be taken out of the show. 'Unacceptable for Soviet audiences,' was its verdict. We were completely stunned. The audience had made us give an encore. It seemed that the world was falling in around our ears. The climax came when our cat, Mishka, jumped on to my lap and began to stroke my face with his paw, a thing he had never done before. And that broke the dam. I am not ashamed to say that I wept, as did Elena. To think that people could be so cruel and only a little cat could sense our grief and try to comfort us!

From then on we rehearsed new acts but they were systematically turned down. Our salaries were cut by half and to keep us alive, Elena learned to make ladies' hats. But she could barely earn enough to keep us going, and besides, hat-making was 'private enterprise'. We even had to bribe our neighbours to prevent them from informing on us.

When I got a phone call from the Mosfilm Studios inviting me along for an audition in a new film by the eminent film director, Alexander Dovzhenko, we were overjoyed. Maybe this would be the breakthrough that we felt we deserved so much.

I had heard that Dovzhenko was an ardent Ukrainian nationalist, and that although he lived in Moscow among Russians, he spoke only in his native language. It was my good fortune to have picked up a smattering of Ukrainian during the war. I was desperate to get the part, so when I was ushered into the Great Man's sanctum, I greeted him blithely with 'Zdorovenkie bylie', an expression which, I learnt later, was a standard greeting among Ukrainian market traders. Dovzhenko looked at me in surprise. The Englishman was greeting him like a Kiev costermonger! After the preliminary questioning was over I related how I had stood in a queue all night in London to see his famous epic film *Earth*. (I had seen the film but had stood in the queue about as long as it takes a dozen people to buy their tickets.)

'All night long?' was Dovzhenko's astonished reaction.

'Yes, and in the pouring rain,' I lied. But I did get the part.

Working under the direction of Dovzhenko is an experience many actors will never forget. He stimulated me to heights of acting I had not known I was capable of, but he always left me with the impression it was I who had discovered them. He was a wizard. I had never worked with such a tactful director before.

I played the part of an eccentric American farmer and I had to sing. The story was a banal one, what Soviet actors call a 'Long live . . . Hurrah!' story, but Dovzhenko proved that in the hands of a really talented director, any rubbish can be turned into a master-piece. What amazed me was his intuition. He had never been to America, yet he knew how Americans spoke, and even taught Russian actors how to walk like Americans.

We hadn't quite finished the film when an order came from the Kremlin that Stalin wanted to see it, even though it was not ready. Stalin watched it through to the end then announced the cryptic, insulting sentence, 'Throw it in the rubbish bin.' This was not Dovzhenko's only film to suffer Stalin's censorship. His other masterpiece, *Michurin*, created an uproar at the first showing in Moscow. It was an angry film, ending with a close-up of a red flag flying in the breeze. But this was no tame acknowledgement of the triumph of communism: the flag, instead of fluttering gently, lashed and ripped as though in a hurricane, expressing wrath in its every fold. The film was recut by Dovzhenko's wife, the actress Solntseva, and a masterpiece was transformed into a mediocrity.

Then Dovzhenko, one of a galaxy of great directors, suffered another coronary—and I was back where I started.

At last we came up with an act that was acceptable. It was a Spanish number which the authorities thought was intended to satirize Franco and his Fascists. It was apparently 'National in form, socialist in content'. We were given engagements touring in the most impossible places, one-night stands in Siberia and the Urals. It was a desperately tiring and dispiriting life: there was a general sense of apathy towards the theatre and concert halls in the first post-war years. Theatrical managers were at their wits' end to find a new way of enticing the public. One manager got the bright idea for a combined variety and circus programme with a trained bear act as the main attraction.

Our first monthly stand started in a place called Stalinogorsk, later renamed Novaya Moskovskaya. This town was in the centre of the Tula Coalfields and was our headquarters. From there we travelled to play in the clubs of the mining villages round about. The bear trainer was an eighty-year-old Russian, Timofei Eclair. He had an old and tried method of filling halls. If he heard that tickets were selling poorly in a nearby town, he and a few of us men would climb on to an open lorry along with the bears, the dangerous ones in cages and the tamer ones chained to the sides. When we arrived in the main street, the driver would slow down and Eclair would give the two bears chained to the sides a tremendous kick. They, naturally, roared their displeasure. Immediately, the street was transformed into something like a May Day demonstration. The more Eclair kicked the two hapless Mishas, the louder they roared and the bigger the crowd grew. By the time the lorry reached the theatre, a queue about a mile long was waiting to buy tickets and the cash register rang merrily. Although we were delighted, the bears were not so happy.

A popular Russian joke vividly describes our life in show business in the years of 'Anti-Cosmopolitanism' when the witch-hunters were after us. One winter, when the temperature was thirty degrees below zero, a little sparrow fell to the ground and lay there, freezing to death. Its life was ebbing away when a cow passed by and deposited a large cow-pat on it. The warmth of the cow-pat revived the sparrow, and in its joy it poked its head out of the pat and chirped merrily. Immediately a hungry cat pounced on the sparrow and gobbled it up. The moral, which has become a byword among the Soviet people, is this: 'When you are up to your eyes in shit, don't stick your head out and chirp.'

But no matter how hard Elena and I tried not to chirp until the 'Anti-Cosmopolitanism' campaign died its natural death, the Party officials never lost sight of us. They resorted to the pettiest tricks to force us off the stage. Compères deliberately mispronounced our names. Curtains were lowered before the audience had time to applaud and were only raised when we had left the stage. In one sketch, which I have already described, we had a large picture frame, complete with curtain, which I opened a number of times to reveal Elena standing motionless, each time in a different costume. I lost count of the number of times that frame collapsed in the middle of our act because someone had removed the pins that held it together.

We entered the 1950s in a despondent mood. The Revue had fizzled out and we were back to ordinary concert work, here today and gone tomorrow. We were invited to return to the State Circus, but when I heard talented comics and clowns reciting bad couplets about American imperialism or about Marshal Tito ('Here comes that bandit Tito, the servile stooge of Wall Street-o'), I refused. When we were offered an act in which I was to be Winston Churchill (this was after his 'cold war speech' at Fulton and the coining of the 'Iron Curtain' phrase) and Elena, the brave Soviet partisan, was to pour bags of flour over me, we thanked the Circus Director and said we would think about it. We didn't. It was not that I was loath to portray Churchill, it was that we had never used traditional buffoonery and slapstick. We did not need to make audiences laugh with custard pies or buckets of water, those banal distractions without which many bad comics and directors cannot put an act together.

There is a Russian saying: 'If I had known where I was going to fall, I would have laid a mattress there.' If I had known that Stalin would be dead within two years, I would not have taken the decision that eventually led to my quitting the stage for ever.

We had returned from a month's tour of the Donbass Coalfields, in the summer of 1951, dead tired, frustrated, and with coal dust clogging every pore. A phone call from Radio Moscow invited me in for a talk with the Chief of the English Service. I was told that the External Services were to be increased tenfold and that a 'Soviet–British Friendship Month' was planned for radio listeners. They needed a compère for the daily half-hour programmes. I had been singing and playing on radio for years so I agreed readily.

The Friendship Month was a success, and the fan-mail especially praised the 'pleasant Scottish voice' of the compère. The result was that the Director-General, Vinogradov, invited me to join the English Service. The job sounded enticing: a high salary, a six-hour day, an annual six-week holiday and many other privileges not normally enjoyed by Russian announcers. And I would be free in the evenings for concert work. This clinched it; I signed a contract for one year in the hope that things in show business would change for the better and I could return to my beloved stage.

A year passed and nothing changed, so I signed up for another year. I did manage to carry on with concert work, but with great difficulty. Concert agents gradually ceased to include us in their programmes, and to add to my agony, Elena rehearsed some *pas de deux* with a Bolshoi dancer and began to perform without me.

One day I went to see her at the open-air theatre in the Bauman Park. For the first time I saw her from the viewpoint of a member of an audience and I realized how beautiful, elegant and graceful her dancing was. I escaped into a dark spot in the Park and broke down. Never in my life had I hated anyone as I did Stalin, for depriving me of the greatest joy I knew: being on the stage and making people laugh. Elena, too, found little satisfaction in classical dancing. She and her partner were well received, but their success could not be compared with what she had formerly enjoyed. Gradually, she too lost heart and, after an operation, gave up the stage for ever.

Since I had come to Russia I had been hungry many times, had been out of work, and had been deceived by managers and fellow artistes. But I had never lost heart because I knew a breakthrough must come if I worked hard. And when I met Elena it *had* come. It was she, with her amazing patience and tact, as well as the professional training she had received in the Bolshoi Ballet School, who taught me discipline, taught me to love hard work, and to love and respect the stage I walked on. But now I had lost both my profession and my partner.

It was all so unfair. We were both in the prime of life, at the age when vitality is enhanced by experience. We were popular stars, recognized not only by the public but by the most exacting critics of all, our own colleagues. There had been so much we wanted to do, so many ideas for new acts, so many new images to create—and now everything was destroyed. We had been forced off the stage by stony-faced officials who had never known the satisfaction of seeing an inspiration come to life.

After a time I calmed down and reconciled myself to my fate. There is nothing particularly creative or inspiring about reading the news, but one thing I did enjoy in my new work was the respect that had always been denied me as an artiste.

The Radio Moscow External Services had become a separate organization to fight the Cold War; the broadcasts were designed to extol the Soviet way of life. Most of the announcers and translators were nationals of the countries to which the programmes were beamed. The English Language Services were staffed by Britons and Americans, who tended not to mix with the Russian staff. My stage training and former popularity helped me to achieve a closer friendship with the Russian staff, who were mostly observers and editors, graduates of the International Institute for the Diplomatic Service. It gave me pleasure to help them perfect their English and to teach them to read their own material for the microphone. One of my best 'pupils' was Oleg Troyanovsky, now Chief Ambassador to the United Nations. Unwittingly, I became a 'bright boy'. My belief that it was better for a Russian observer to read his own commentary, even if his accent was not perfect, was welcomed by the authorities, and soon I was asked to train graduates of the Foreign Languages Institute. Altogether, I produced six announcers, all of them Russian. Not only did I teach them how to read English correctly, but I also passed on a lexicon of colloquialisms which they could never have learned in any Soviet Institute.

But for the first time in my life I felt the constant presence at my work of the Party and the KGB, in contrast to the Circus and Variety Organizations where Party members were rare phenomena. The Radio Moscow staff were virtually all Party members and several of them, the ones without any obvious jobs, were KGB. One such was the Chief of the Indonesian Service. One morning he demanded to know what piece the Music Editor had prepared for the first morning broadcast. He was told it was Debussy's *Nocturnes*.

'Who is Debussy?' he asked imperiously.

'The eminent French composer,' came the surprised reply.

'French? Cut! No French music! The Indonesians have been oppressed long enough by the colonialists without having to listen to their music.'

'But, Comrade Chief, it wasn't the French who colonized Indonesia, it was the Dutch!'

'French, Dutch! They are all the same—lackeys of Imperialism and oppressors of the down-trodden peoples!'

This stupidity came from a man who later was promoted to the post of Director of the Moscow Institute of Eastern Studies where he continued to inflict his dogma upon young students.

There were two things I had to learn on joining the staff of Radio Moscow. The first was not to tell 'underground' jokes. They had delighted my theatrical friends but were received with stony faces in Radio House. The second was to trust no one, just as one was trusted by no one. My new colleagues reminded me of a joke which I could not of course tell. A young communist is sitting in front of a triple mirror, gazing at the three reflections. After long meditation, he announces quietly: 'One of us is an informer.'

Working in radio during the Stalin years was a nerve-racking experience. The slightest mistake was reported, and the offending announcer would be summoned by the Party Committee, the Chief Editors and the Staff Department (in other words the KGB). As the External Services now covered over sixty countries, anyone with the slightest knowledge of a foreign language was employed, sometimes with hilarious results. I remember directing an outside broadcast of the May Day celebrations, during which I had to switch off a Russian colleague who innocently declared: 'And here come the little children to give a display for our beloved leaders. The girls are holding their hoops and the boys are playing with their balls.'

To save myself from going mad, I turned to writing sports articles under the pen-name of Bill Kaye. These became popular, and I received fanmail from all over the world. The Russian triumphs at the 1952 Helsinki Olympic Games, and a racy style, put me on the road to success. My running commentaries of the duels between those great runners, Chris Chataway and Vladimir Kuts, could not help but sound exciting. Vladimir's tactic of scooting away in the 5,000- and 10,000-metres races as if he was running in a 100-metres dash was simply devastating to the other runners. After one such heart-breaking defeat, Chataway confided, 'That chap is going to kill me one day!' In fact, Christopher is still alive and well, while Kuts is very much dead from high blood pressure at the early age of forty-eight.

In 1954 I travelled round the country with the Wolverhampton Wanderers and West Bromwich Albion, the first professional teams ever to visit the Soviet Union. A group of Wolves supporters came with the team, and among them was a charming eighty-three-year-old called Lady Mansfield. My chief asked me to interview the group, during the interval, and record their impressions of the Soviet Union. The only volunteer was Lady Mansfield. When I asked her: 'What do you think of Moscow?' She replied: 'So lovely. It *has* changed since I was here last.' When asked the exact date, Lady Mansfield frowned in her efforts to remember. 'Let me see . . . oh, yes! . . . it was in 1898. I was invited to spend the summer holidays with Princess Volkonskaya, you know, one of the Tsar's nieces!' I told the operator to destroy the tape.

I had to destroy many tapes. I found the atmosphere of Radio House stifling and I readily accepted any chance to go on an outside reporting job. But here again I was confronted with the same frustrating demand I had met earlier in show business—that not a single word could be uttered without an approved script. I tried to convince the Radio bosses that the informality of an interview was lost whenever the interviewee had to read the prepared text beforehand, but I had no success. It was only after one farcical assignment that I managed to persuade the authorities to allow me to interview without a script.

I arrived at the Burevestnik Shoe Factory in Moscow on the eve of 8 March, Women's Day, together with an editor and a recording van. This factory had been chosen precisely because the majority of the workers were women. After I had recorded my description of the safety measures, working conditions and the pre- and post-natal privileges, we came to the high point of the visit, an interview with the best woman worker. Microphone in hand, I approached the woman standing at her machine, and with my charming reporter's smile greeted her, 'Zdravstuete, Maria Ivanovna, I am a reporter from Radio Moscow and I would like to congratulate you on Women's Day and . . .' Without even turning her head, she told me peremptorily to piss off.

The impact of her words didn't get through to me immediately, and I carried on, blithely asking her to tell our listeners about herself, her work and how well the women were looked after. She stopped her machine and told me. Every sentence was punctuated with unprintable expressions. The gist of her diatribe was that Radio Moscow and the administration of the Burevestnik Factory could go and stuff themselves. After the last volley, I thanked the woman politely for the interesting talk and made myself scarce. The Foreman explained that the woman had been promised a room of her own on Women's Day, but 'that Director's whore' (I quote the man's words) had jumped the queue and got the room.

The 'interview' with the woman worker was recorded by the sound operator much to my satisfaction. I played the tape for my chiefs to prove to them how much more interesting an interview can be without a script. My point had been made and from then on I was given permission to interview impromptu. 'Only,' said one of the chiefs, 'without any lurid language.'

The Russians love to boast of the immense size of their buildings, projects and plans. Whether or not there is any real need for the electrical energy produced by the Bratsk Hydro Power Station on the Angara River (among the sparsely populated and lowly industrialized region of Siberia) is a moot point. One thing the Soviet public does know from the daily reminders of the media is that Bratsk is five times the size of the Cooley Station, the largest in America. Yevtushenko joined the stream of writers to Bratsk and returned with a long poem eulogizing the grandiose construction. The Kremlin liked it, lovers of poetry did not.

Stalin suffered from the skyscraper disease, and visitors to Moscow can still see about half a dozen of these eye-sores sticking up in various parts of the city. The Moscow State University is the most prominent of these as it stands at the top of the Lenin Hills overlooking Moscow. It was begun during Stalin's lifetime but was only officially opened shortly after his death, in 1953. The immensity of the main building brought tears of emotion to the eyes of proud patriots. The media could not find sufficient words to describe it and barely stopped short of naming it the Eighth Wonder of the World. Architects were invited from all over the world to be present at the opening ceremony.

I was given the job of accompanying three British architects around the University before the opening. I took them and their 'guide' up to the University in my new car, a Russian-made Pobeda, that still smelled of fresh paint. The car seemed to interest them more than the forthcoming visit: how much did it cost, was it expensive to run, what were the servicing facilities? The architects and their 'guide' listened attentively when I manipulated the price, 16,000 roubles, between the exchange rate and the difference in the price of a packet of cigarettes in Britain and Russia (an old trick) to make the price of the car sound reasonable.

When we emerged on to the far end of the large square facing the University, I could see looks of bewilderment on the Englishmen's faces and I took this as a good sign. After interviewing the first two, I discovered I was wrong. They were not at all impressed by the hugeness and splendour of the main building—on the contrary, they were appalled by the uselessness of the many towers and turrets. The architecture itself, in their opinion, was a mixture of every style, Gothic, Rococo, Byzantine, all except Russian, and this dismayed them.

I drove back along a different route, and as we descended from the Lenin Hills on to the embankment, I heard gasps of wonder coming from the architects. They were pointing to the Novodevichy Monastery on the other side of the Moskva River. 'Beautiful! Magnificent! Exquisite!' they cried in unison. 'Can we stop? We want to take some pictures.'

The 'guide' looked around apprehensively for forbidden military installations and grudgingly consented, on condition that the large railway bridge to the right should not be in the picture.

'What, that monstrosity?' said one of the British architects, 'I wouldn't photograph that even if you paid me to.'

They insisted that I record their impressions of the monastery, but luckily for me the recording van had gone. My chiefs would hardly have thanked me for an exultant description of a religious shrine built in Tsarist times.

Russians love an argument and can expound, at great length, an opinion on any subject, no matter how superficial their knowledge may be. The only instance when they become inarticulate is at the appearance of a microphone. To the Soviet public, the innocent mike, the photo and the ciné camera are the professional weapons of foreign spies and provocateurs. I have often been escorted to militia stations, and my tapes played and replayed in search of some incriminating interview.

I remember the occasion on which I was commissioned to rove around the shops to record customers' opinions on reductions in State prices. I was standing inside a store called *Podarki* ('Gifts') waiting for my editor to get the Manager's permission to work inside his shop. The sound operators were searching for a suitable plug to which to connect the equipment in the recording van. As I was idling away the time, looking at one or two 'gifts' in plastic bags—useless, mismatched things that nobody would want—I heard a voice.

'Yes, young man, it does look ridiculous, doesn't it?' I turned round to see an old man well into his eighties.

'Now, I ask you, young man, why do I have to buy that ugly silk shirt just because I need the warm leather gloves that go with it? Heh? Or why can't I get these foreign shoes unless I buy that terrible reproduction of Repin's *In the Forest* that hangs in all the public lavatories?'

I began to murmur assent but was interrupted by the garrulous old man.

'What would your sweetheart say if you gave her a birthday present of that lovely underwear along with the bottle of liqueur that makes you sick by just looking at it? And the prices! Just look at

them. Fantastic! No, young man, I lived before the Revolution and
I can tell you, yes, the shopkeepers then used to cheat the customers
and that's the truth. But the way these—' the old man pointed
upwards suggestively '—have learned to cheat the public would
have made the old *kuptsi*, you know, the old merchants, go green
with envy.'

At that moment, the sound operator quietly slipped the microphone into my hand.

'And let me tell you another thing, young man . . .'

The old man stopped abruptly and gazed at the microphone
apprehensively. In a quavering voice, he asked, 'Is that a microphone, young man?'

I replied that it was and that I was a correspondent of Radio
Moscow, but before I could explain to him that the mike was not
switched on and that I had not recorded his opinions of Soviet
trading organizations, the old man cried out in horror, 'Bozhe moi!
Bozhe moi!' and scooted out of the shop at a speed hardly to be
expected in one of such an advanced age.

ELEVEN

Coming Home

Stalin died.

It was so sudden and unexpected that the rumour quickly spread that he had been assassinated. How was it possible that a man of his constitution, enjoying the finest medical attention, could die from a simple stroke 'brought on by high blood pressure'? After the Stalin Disclosures, another wonderful rumour spread that Khrushchev and his friends had confronted Stalin, read him an indictment of all his misdeeds and demanded his resignation. The 'mutiny' was so daring and unforeseen that Stalin staggered, fell and never rose again!

The impact of Stalin's death on the majority of the population was extraordinary. They looked like children who had lost their father. They had been so thoroughly brainwashed during the twenty-nine years of Stalin's reign that they actually looked to a future without him with blank terror. I was amazed to hear a big, strong man cry in a choking voice, 'We have lost our Great Father! We are orphans!' As far as I was concerned, the news was like a gift from God. We all forgot that Beria, the Head of the KGB, was still in action.

Stalin lay in state in the Hall of Columns in the Trade Union House at the corner of Pushkin Street and Okhotny Ryad. The Soviet leaders kept a vigil by the coffin, wearing the funereal expressions expected at such solemn occasions and, as later events showed, wondering how to get rid of Beria and ascend the empty throne. The silence of the beautiful Hall was broken only by the shuffling feet and stifled sobs of the endless stream of people as they passed by the body lying in the open coffin.

But out in the streets, there was chaos, pandemonium and horror.

Every road and square near the Hall was packed to suffocation-point with people, old and young, struggling and fighting to get a glimpse of a man whom most of them had never seen alive. It was a cruel irony that even as he lay on his funeral bier Stalin continued to cause death and destruction. Hundreds lost their lives on those streets; elderly women and children were trampled underfoot. I saw a tramcar overturned at Nikitsky Vorota. I don't know how many lay dead underneath. It was impossible to get anywhere near the scene. On the other side of the square we could hear agonizing shrieks and cries for help.

Any thought of walking to Pushkin Square along the boulevard from Nikitsky Vorota, as I usually did on my way to Radio House, was absolutely out of the question. Instead of the usual ten minutes, it took me over an hour, picking my way through side streets outside the 'A' Circle, hurrying through courtyards and clambering over walls. From the top of Radio House one could look down Pushkin Street to the Hall of Columns at the other end. This was about as near as I ever got to Stalin's bier. We saw hundreds of people clambering over the roofs of nearby buildings to jump the queue. But the snow and ice had not yet melted, and many of them slipped to their death in the streets below.

Two days later, I found myself squeezed into a tiny room at the top of the GUM Department Store on Red Square, describing the solemn funeral procession in a suitably hushed voice. As I listened to the eulogies to the genius of the Great Father, I remembered how I had once entered a cage, behind the circus, where a lion lay dead, electrocuted after having eaten its trainer. Although we knew that the man-eater was well and truly dead, we kept as near to the door as we could.

When Muscovites want to describe someone 'in the know' they always say, 'He's got his ear to the Kremlin Walls.' Only days after Stalin's death, the listeners at the Kremlin Walls began to circulate rumours of strange commotions inside the ancient palace. There seemed to be a certain amount of disagreement as to who was best fitted to become the next leader. The betting was on Beria. His trump card was the KGB. It was a pleasant surprise, therefore, when we woke up one morning to find an announcement in *Pravda* that Beria had been arrested. Marshal Georgy Zhukov, hero of the Great War of Liberation against Fascism, accompanied by a suite of top officers, among whom was our friend Alexei S. (who told us the whole story), entered Beria's mansion on Kachalov Street and ordered him to surrender his portfolio and, more to the point, his revolver. Beria made a grab for the telephone to alert the KGB, but the wire had been cut. In any case, the KGB barracks and officers' quarters had been surrounded by tanks.

At the time of Beria's fall, relations between Russia and China were still very cordial. The Chinese had presented the Muscovites with a giant carpet that was displayed in Gorky Park. It depicted a touching meeting between Mao Tse-tung and Stalin, surrounded by all their disciples. In the forefront, as usual, was Beria. When Beria was 'slammed against the wall' the Chinese flew in and, in one night, rewove the portrait of Beria, transforming him into an anonymous Chinaman!

However, the demise of Beria did not end the commotions in the Kremlin. On the contrary, the 'ears' reported that the rumpus had become louder. A 'collective leadership' was announced. Nobody believed it would last. The Russians love to have a Tsar, no matter what colour he is, Red or White. The new Prime Minister, Malenkov, a stout, moon-faced man with wavy hair, hardly commanded the people's confidence. For one thing he continued to wear the Stalinesque para-military tunic. The other leaders had realized the popular antipathy to this style and had quickly changed to lounge suits, collars and ties, and velour hats. When the inevitable showdown came, Malenkov was accused of 'seeking cheap popularity'.

And when the showdown did come it was Khrushchev versus Molotov and Malenkov, with the Soviet population as stoical and fundamentally uninterested spectators. The Molotov–Malenkov faction never stood a chance. Khrushchev had elected a woman, Ekaterina Furtseva, to the Politburo, and she displayed her gratitude by organizing an 'Up With Nikita' campaign. On the eve of the Extraordinary Session of the Central Committee, Furtseva phoned or telegraphed every Committee member, calling on them to 'foil the nefarious plans of the Molotov gang to seize power and rehabilitate the Stalin regime'. Molotov and his associates were expelled from the Politburo, from the Central Committee and even from the Party.

Once the new leadership had been settled, there were several weeks of frantic change as the Party toadies scrambled to demonstrate their allegiance. They tumbled over one another to rename all the places called after the old bosses, who were now considered 'International Agents of Imperialism'. The town of Molotov regained its old name, Perm. The Moscow Metro, named after Kaganovich, was quickly renamed after Lenin. It was an expensive affair—name plates on streets had to be replaced, headings on stationery had to be obliterated and hundreds of thousands of portraits destroyed. But this was a drop in the ocean compared to the scramble after Khrushchev denounced Stalin in 1956. Statues of the Great Teacher in their thousands were smashed, millions of books with his teachings were burned. The Party bosses wanted to change the name of Stalingrad which, as the turning-point in the Red Army's fortunes on the Eastern Front, had assumed great historical significance. The local citizens asked for the old name of Tsarytsin to be restored, but the authorities refused because they thought the name had something to do with the Tsars. They didn't know that Tsarytsin is a Tartar word meaning 'sandy place'. But then there never was a Tartar on the Politburo.

The moral is that people in public life should never have anything named after them in their lifetime. Soviet history has shown that with the exception of Lenin, those who did never prospered. If we are to believe a popular joke, even Lenin had his doubts about what he had done. The story goes that he and one of his disciples, Felix Dzerzhinsky, return from the dead to present-day Moscow. Lenin has a good look around at what is happening in the communist society to the creation of which he devoted his life. After seeing the leadership, he disappears. Dzerzhinsky orders the KGB to find him, but without success. At last a phone call comes: 'Comrade Dzerzhinsky, this is Lenin speaking from Geneva.'

'Where are you? What have you been doing? We have been searching high and low for you,' answers Dzerzhinsky.

'What have I been doing? Plotting a revolution, of course. We have to begin all over again!'

The first car I bought in 1952 was a mini-car called the *moskvich* which had only just begun to come off the conveyor line of the new plant in Moscow built from the confiscated German Opel plant after the war. It was a sturdy little machine and to this day you can still see thousands of them chugging along the roads of Russia. A comic incident associated with the buying of this car gives another glimpse into the Kremlin's disregard of the wishes of the people. Devaluation occurred five times after the war and every time it was done without any warning. I had been saving up to buy this car and had put my money in what was supposed to be the 'safest place', the State Savings Bank (there are of course no private banks in the USSR). I woke up one morning to discover our 2,000 roubles savings had miraculously dwindled to 200. All money in circulation had been reduced to one-tenth its value.

After losing our money in this way, Elena and I discussed how to raise the 9,000 roubles—about £700—to buy the car on which I had set my heart. Elena decided to sacrifice a heavy bronze statuette of a nude, a beautiful French sculpture. I placed this on a sleigh and dragged it to a nearby Commission shop. I was delighted to hear that it was worth 1,000 roubles, minus the 7 per cent commission. My joy was shortlived. Nobody wanted to buy a nude figure. One woman declared it would be a disgrace to have such a shameful thing in the house! Only after a present of a packet of Gillette razor blades did the shop Manager agree to keep it hidden away in the shop and to show it only to connoisseurs. But after three months it was still unsold under the counter and we were on the verge of taking it home, when luck came our way. Another strong rumour had been spread about a new devaluation of the rouble. On the day that we went along to the Commission shop to retrieve our valuable nude the jubilant Manager waved to us over the heads of the crowds and pointed to a bearded peasant who was already shoving our statue into a sack. With a grunt of satisfaction, the man hoisted it on to his back and staggered off. 'I hid the 1,000 rouble ticket and sold the figure to that oaf for 1,500! I get 50 per cent of the extra money. O.K.?' said the Manager. We were not overjoyed as we were sure our share would dwindle by a tenth tomorrow. But no! It was only a rumour, and we were 1,250 roubles the richer! By this time people had got the hang of these devaluations, and whenever there was a rumour spread of an impending reduction, everybody rushed to use their savings before they became worthless.

For all his faults, Khrushchev did do something to ease the lot of the Russian people. At his initiative millions of political prisoners were released from the camps. At last we learned the fate of our many unfortunate friends and colleagues, those who had managed to survive and those who had gone to unknown graves. One after the other, the survivors, many of them famous, began to return. That splendid actress and singer, Ruth Kamenska, came back from exile in the Kazakhstan desert. The great folk singer and idol of the people, Lidia Ruslanova, was released from prison after five years. She rang us on the first morning after her arrival and spent the whole day with us. The news spread like wildfire and soon our room was packed with fellow artistes. We were her guests at her first concert in the Tchaikovsky Hall. When she appeared on stage, dressed in her familiar Russian national costume, the audience rose to its feet and gave her an ovation lasting fifteen minutes. 'It's a protest,' someone whispered. I thought grimly that not one person in the Hall would have raised a finger to save Lidia from the horrible experience she had suffered. After the concert, it was pandemonium backstage, with everyone kissing and hugging her. But when I told her that I would be waiting outside in my car to take her home, she burst into tears. The organizers had forgotten to order a car for her.

Not all the political prisoners were released immediately. When my stepfather arrived in Moscow in 1956, as head of a Party delegation, he told me he had been instructed to talk to no one at top level until he saw Len Wincott. Len was one of the organizers of the Spithead mutiny in 1928 and had been sentenced to life imprisonment. He was exchanged by the Soviet Government before the war and came to live in Leningrad, where he worked at the International Seamen's Club. He managed to survive the siege but was arrested at the end of the war and banished to the coalmines beyond the Arctic Circle. 'I should have signed the "confession" that I was the leader of an international spy organization, on the first day after my arrest,' he told me. 'I had to sign it anyway a year later, after they had systematically beaten hell out of me.'

When Father refused to meet Khrushchev until he saw Len, he was informed that Len had been located and would be released. Len was lucky. Afterwards he told me he had given up hope of ever leaving the coalmines. There were hundreds of thousands of prisoners and the one plane a day could only take about a dozen at a time. Suddenly he was awakened in the night by a bang on the door of his basement room and told to pack his belongings as a special plane had arrived to take him and his wife to Moscow. Many more unfortunates waited years for their freedom. They did not have a leading foreign communist to intercede for them.

The first of Khrushchev's new measures to affect us personally was the order to allow Soviet citizens to visit relatives living abroad. Armed with an official invitation signed by my stepfather, I marched into the OVIR Passport Office in May 1957. I expected to receive our passports immediately and to spend the summer holidays with my long-lost family. I should have known better. It took us a whole year of filling in forms, standing in front of commissions and answering idiotic questions before we received our *kharakteristika*, a document declaring me to be 'of unblemished character and exemplary behaviour; morally stable, and politically reliable'.

We arrived at Heathrow Airport in a daze. Over a quarter of a century had passed since I had last seen London. The Immigration Officers examined our passports with suspicion and surprise. We were the first private citizens from the Soviet Union they had ever dealt with. The first thing that struck us as we travelled towards London in the car was the bright street lighting. After the poorly lit Moscow streets London seemed to be ablaze.

I had my first shock when I met my brothers and sisters. My youngest sister, Jean, who was only six when I left and used to climb on my knees, was now a married woman of thirty-two, and my brother Jerry who once had long hair down to his shoulders, was almost bald!

My sister Millie, who had delighted my colleagues of the Jazz Revue in Moscow with her singing, was now known as Billie 'Kilts' Campbell, and had become a star, singing with the top dance orchestras, Jack Hylton, Billy Cotton and others. I was overjoyed at the way my family took to Elena. They behaved as if they had known her all their lives. Like all big families, we always made fun of one another. Elena, now, came in for her share. Despite the difficulties of finding clothes in Moscow, she was always elegantly and fashionably dressed: my niece, Susan, looked at her in wonder and cried, 'My goodness, I thought all Russian women were fat!'

New friends appeared and were all charmed with Elena and her English which had become quite good. Elena in turn fell in love with them and with England. Everyone vied with one another to make our visit pleasant. Whenever they could, they drove us around the sights and into the countryside. 'I want to see the Royal Ballet,' said Elena, and the next day a gift of two tickets came by post from a friend. We saw *Giselle* danced by a ballerina whom we had never heard of, Margot Fonteyn. The production could hardly be compared with those of the Bolshoi or Kirov Theatres, but Elena was amazed at Margot Fonteyn's beautiful dancing. 'It seems there are gifted ballerinas outside Russia,' she commented.

Most of all, we were overwhelmed by people's politeness and courtesy. No bus conductors or shop assistants snarled at us. When we bumped into people in the streets they apologized! The shops were chock-a-block with the most fantastic displays of food and clothing . . . and there were no queues! We listened to criticism of the system, the Government, the Cabinet, the Prime Minister, and no one closed the door or put a pillow over the telephone.

By the end of our three months' stay, the thought of returning to Russia had become unbearable. To add to our problems, the ex-Prime Minister of Hungary, Nagy, had just been executed, and even British communists were shocked. My mother declared she would not let us go back. She would find us a flat, Elena could teach ballet and I could write for the *Daily Worker*. It all seemed so simple. But what about Vera, Elena's elderly sister? She was half-blind by now and had had to give up her job as cashier at the Obrastsov Puppet Theatre. She would be evicted from our flat immediately, and would have to live on the semi-starvation pension of forty-five roubles a month (£8 a week). And so we had to go back. It was nineteen years before we were able to achieve our dream of quitting the Soviet Union.

In 1963 came the downfall of Nikita Khrushchev.

It was not enough for Nikita that the collective farm system was itself a failure; he had to go one better and try to farm the barren lands of Kazakhstan. Like all communist dictators, Nikita thought he knew it all; if he had taken the trouble of asking the peasants why they had never taken their ploughs to Kazakhstan they would have told him that though there was occasionally a decent rainfall, most years there was drought. In the first year there was freak rain and a bumper wheat harvest. Nikita's orders went out to the breadbaskets of Russia to stop growing wheat and to sow maize instead. The next year brought drought back to Kazakhstan, and a miserly harvest. The Soviet people were left without bread. By this time Nikita's colleagues were beginning to realize that the Stalin Disclosures had been a disastrous mistake. Without Stalin's brutal methods, no communist regime could survive. Headed by Leonid Brezhnev they all gathered at Moscow Airport to wave Nikita goodbye as he left for a holiday in his luxurious new villa at Pitsunda, on the Black Sea coast. A few days later, they called an Extraordinary Session of the Central Committee, and gave their leader the boot.

By coincidence Elena and I were spending a holiday that year only a few miles from Pitsunda, at a picturesque holiday resort called Gagra, on the shores of a lovely bay. To play tennis in the early morning, Elena and I had to get into a queue, and we usually arrived at the courts in the dark at six o'clock. When we arrived one morning, we saw a small group of players grouped round a portable radio listening to the BBC World Service. As we approached I heard Khrushchev's name a number of times. When I asked what he had been up to now, everybody mumbled and moved away. On the way back to the private house where we rented a room, we were surprised to see groups of Georgians singing and dancing. In their shouts I could only discern the words in Georgian, 'Ara, Nikita' meaning 'No Nikita now!' Although I knew that Georgians hated Khrushchev after the Stalin Disclosures, I thought their vehemence was strange. Then our landlady's daughter who worked as a cashier at the nearby airport gave us an eye-witness account of the fall of Nikita Khrushchev.

He too had heard about the Extraordinary Session of the Central Committee on BBC radio and immediately tried to dash back to Moscow. But it seemed that all the available Government cars at the villa had broken down! Somehow he managed to travel the forty-odd miles to the airport at Sochi-adler. An order had come from the Kremlin not to sell Khrushchev a ticket, or to let him force his way on to a plane. Khrushchev stamped up and down, cursing and swearing, and eventually, tired out, slumped into an armchair, until the radio announced the closing of the Central Committee session. Then he climbed wearily into an ordinary passenger plane, and arrived in Moscow to find he had 'voluntarily announced' his retirement and was handing over the reins of government to his faithful comrade Leonid Brezhnev.

The new masters of Russia did not 'slam Nikita against a wall', but they did leave this energetic man with nothing to do. On one of my visits to the Lenin Experimental Farm, to record a radio programme, I was surprised not to see the usual notices of board meetings. I was told that Khrushchev, who lived in a dacha not far away, used to arrive every morning at five o'clock to badger the staff with his ideas on what to grow and how. So the times and places of Board meetings were changed daily, and kept secret.

I had last set foot on the stage in 1952; twelve years had passed, and by this time I had forgotten the pain I suffered at the forced parting. Although I was encouraged many times to return to my old profession, I refused categorically. I had become a broadcaster and a journalist. The respect I was accorded in this new field helped me to forget show business. The recollection of the supercilious officials and their insulting attitudes towards all artistes, from the highest to the lowest, was sufficient to make me think twice. I had also ventured into the literary world, and a number of my short stories had been published in influential Soviet journals. 'If they won't let me make people laugh on the stage,' I decided, 'then I'll do it in print.'

My successful stories were inspired by the comic episodes I had seen during my visits to England and by the keen desire of the Russians to learn what was going on beyond the Iron Curtain. My long life among them made me see things through their eyes rather than as a former British citizen. One of my stories, published that year in the Leningrad literary journal *Neva*, was inspired by an item in the London *Evening News* about a man being fined for keeping a canary in a cage smaller than the regulations permit, while he himself lives in a tiny ten-foot attic room. He smashes the cage and finds £100 that has been hidden by his aunt who left him the bird in her will. He pays the fine which saves him from prison, buys the canary a bigger cage and moves into a bigger room.

The story was well received and my fanmail increased. I was not surprised when I heard a faintly familiar voice on the telephone asking for Comrade William Campbell.

'Speaking,' I answered.

'This is Arkady Raikin, the actor. Probably you have heard of me?'

I nearly laughed out loud. Who hadn't heard of Arkady Raikin, our good friend from show business times, the most popular comedian in Russia? He and his Leningrad Miniature Theatre had become famous for the satirical plays and sketches so loved by the ordinary people and so hated by the Party and State officials who were the bait for Raikin's comic disclosures. I wondered why Arkady was being so official with me until I remembered that he knew me only by my stage name, Villi Karlin. So I decided to pull his leg a bit.

'Arkady Raikin? Never heard of you.' I replied. 'I did know an artiste of the same name when I played in the Leningrad Summer Theatre in 1939. We quarrelled on the first night and then made it up. We drank a *bruderschaft* and swore to eternal friendship. Now he's become too big for his boots and doesn't recognize me.'

'Villi!' Raikin shouted. 'You sonofabitch. I've been searching for you. I've read all these stories by William Campbell and didn't know you were one and the same person. Villi, I need your help. I have got a long-standing invitation from BBC television in London but haven't been able to accept it as there is no one who can help choose my sketches and translate them for me. Now that I've found you, I can go one better and ask you to be my partner on the BBC.'

I agreed to help but refused to go to London as his partner. 'I have left the stage for good and don't want to set foot on it again,' I declared finally, despite Raikin's protests. Of course, it didn't work out that way. Raikin did not know English and had to 'parrot' some of his lines. The rehearsals became long and laborious and, much against my will, I realized I would have to go. So I became his translator–partner. We carried on a dialogue where Raikin spoke Russian and I repeated him in English, giving the impression of two people carrying on a conversation.

I redirected many of the sketches to make them look more familiar to British audiences. I also had to rewrite and add to the script. One sketch went over tremendously well. I announced that we would show how things could look the other way round. The wife invites her girl-friends to a game of poker. The poor husband (Raikin) complete in apron runs around in a state of fluster as he serves them vodka and sandwiches. When he begs them not to drop cigarette ash on the carpet his wife orders him to shut up and get back into his kitchen. The highlight comes when the tipsy women break into the song usually sung by Russian drunks; I had them singing, 'Show me the way to go home, I'm tired and I want to go to bed.'

Raikin and I, along with the usual 'guide' or the Man from the Ministry (as everybody at the BBC called him), left Moscow at the end of January 1964, in thirty degrees of frost. We had to change planes in Paris, and the first thing I did was to indulge in a forbidden pleasure—I bought a British newspaper. And there on the front page were the headlines 'Arkady Raikin—Khrushchev's Favourite Comic Arrives Today' and underneath was a photograph with the caption 'Raikin with his Scots friend and partner, Bill Campbell'. We both laughed heartily. It would have been better to say that Khrushchev tolerated Raikin. He certainly could not be a favourite of his or of any other Soviet official.

I disembarked first from the plane at Heathrow Airport and my immediate reaction was to leap back on to it again. This was not the result of any aversion to my former homeland, but because a large crowd was running helter-skelter towards me. Reporters and photographers bawled questions and it was only when I found myself sitting beside Raikin that I recovered from my bewilderment. We were perched on a small platform in a hall at Heathrow Airport surrounded by reporters, television cameras and photographers. The stupidity of some of the questions they put to us only served to convince me how little these people knew about Russia.

'Do bears walk freely on the streets of Moscow?'

'What kind of jokes does Khrushchev like best?'

'How many times has Raikin been married?' They all looked incredulous when Raikin raised one finger.

'Have you got television in Russia?' (This of the country that sent the first man into outer space.)

We were met at the Prince of Wales Hotel in Kensington by a new crowd of reporters who left after an hour and only when I said we had not eaten since breakfast on the plane. Unfortunately, the Soviet Embassy officials dispersed along with them and forgot to give us some English money. We were penniless and very hungry. But our Soviet artistes' precautions, born of extensive touring in the Soviet Union, came to our rescue. Suitcases were opened and our supper of caviare, roast chicken and cognac was a feast for millionaires.

Raikin had never been in a Western country before, so he suggested we go for a walk to see 'what nefarious games these capitalists get up to'. Our 'guide' protested, on the pretext that it was late and already dark. But Raikin insisted, so off we went. We got as far as the Albert Hall when Arkady asked me if it was far to Piccadilly Circus.

'No, no!' cried the Man from the Ministry. 'You mustn't go there. Piccadilly Circus is dangerous.'

'What's so dangerous about Piccadilly Circus?' Raikin wanted to know.

'You might encounter all manner of dangers,' answered our 'guide'. 'Don't forget we are in an imperialist country. We could be accosted by ... well ... Russian defectors and ... and ... prostitutes!'

'As far as the Russian defectors are concerned,' Raikin said calmly, 'we are not afraid of them. As for the prostitutes, they'd better be afraid of us. We've got no money.'

Our Man from the Ministry was not the only one with fears of possible provocations. Even now, the Soviet Consulate in London gives Russian visitors a fearful list of what the wicked British people can do to them. Before leaving with Raikin, I was called to the Party Central Committee where I was given a pep talk by a top official who reminded me that I had been given the responsibility of seeing to it that the 'wicked' (his actual word) BBC did not distort the script or put false meanings into our sketches. He even wanted me to make an announcement at the end of the programme that the toadies, bribe-takers and swindlers portrayed by Raikin were a tiny minority among the splendid Party and State executives working for the good of the people.

When I got to know the BBC producer, Joe McGrath, better, I confided in him and asked him to advise me on what best to do to get round this ridiculous stipulation. He looked at me unbelievingly.

'But that's crazy,' he urged. 'This is a comedy show and my job is to make people understand what Russians laugh at. Raikin is a great comedian, but to tell you the truth, I can't find anything exceptionally critical about his sketches. Have you seen how our comedians take the mickey out of our top politicians? Any artiste impersonating the Prime Minister is bound to get a custard pie slammed in his face.'

I wondered what would have happened to Raikin if he had even suggested the idea of pouring a bowl of porridge over Khrushchev's head.

The rest of the troupe arrived and we started rehearsals in, of all places, a church hall. The actors stared in wonder at the sight of clergymen in dog collars. The atmosphere of goodwill and friendliness couldn't have been better. Joe McGrath was correct when he said that his job was to make a success of the show, and the rest of the BBC group helped the Soviet artistes towards this goal. According to press cuttings we received in Moscow later, our programme, which opened the new BBC 2 channel, was given an excellent press, and Arkady Raikin was acclaimed as one of the world's best comedians. No mention was made of the absence of apple pies and pails of water.

The entire stay of the Leningrad Miniature Theatre and People's Artiste of the USSR, Arkady Raikin, was a pleasant one, and we never met with the provocations so feared by the Soviet authorities. Only once did we run up against any harassment, and that came from a Russian. While waiting for our mini-bus outside the hotel, we were accosted by a man in his fifties who demanded in a loud voice that we return the gold mines stolen from him in 1917. Judging from his appearance he couldn't have been more than five or ten years old at the time of the Revolution. Nevertheless, we humoured him and told him to write an application. We said we would see to it that it was delivered to the proper quarters. We did not see him again, neither did we receive any application.

Much to my surprise, the media seemed to be as interested in me as in Raikin. How had I managed to live through the purges and not been shot at dawn? Was I not scared when Stalin presented me with the Government decoration, the medal 'For Distinguished Labour'? I tried to tell them it was President Kalinin, not Stalin, who gave me the medal, but they weren't listening. That was not the only time my story was misconstrued. I was asked when and why I had gone to Russia. In 1932, I replied, adding that I was escaping from unemployment and that all I had with me was a racing cycle, a ukulele and one suit. The next day I read how I had escaped from Britain on a bicycle and ridden all the way to Moscow. Apparently I had played the ukulele to survive during my journey and sold all my clothes except one suit.

How was it that the Red Army allowed me, a foreigner, to travel around all the fronts during the war without suspecting I was a spy? I explained that I was already a Soviet citizen, that I was a popular comic and that history had never known of a clown being a spy. The fighting troops couldn't have cared less if I had been an Eskimo so long as I made them laugh. And then, I told the reporter jokingly, my Russian was so fluent that I must have fooled them into thinking I was Russian. Imagine my dismay when I read the headlines: 'Bill Campbell Fooled the Red Army!' and a rambling account of how I had played the part of an Eskimo comic speaking fluent Russian and that clowns cannot be spies because they make people laugh.

I can laugh at all this today but then I did not find it funny. I had to return to the Soviet Union and I was terrified of the way in which all these fantastic stories would be interpreted by the Central Committee. So when I was told to put on my best suit for an interview alone on television, I cursed the day I had ever agreed to come on this trip. When I was introduced to the delightful young woman who was to interview me, my suspicions were aroused even more. How many times had I seen the lovely girls sent by the KGB to entrance their innocent victims and to make them say or do things they wouldn't say or do in a torture chamber? All right, I thought, if that is what you are up to, I refuse to be caught out and I'll show you a thing or two. Despite her beguiling looks, I wasn't in the least bit frightened when she asked me whether Raikin was the only comedian in Russia to criticize the many negative features of Soviet life in his satires (as a matter of fact, he was and is to this day, but I couldn't tell her that).

'Satire,' I said glibly, 'has existed in Russia for a thousand years ever since the days of the *skomarokhes* [that was an old trick: you pronounce some strange foreign word and lose time in explaining what it means]. *Skomarokhi* were tumblers and jesters who travelled the country, doing one-night stands. They would find out the faults and vices of the local gentry and, in the performance, would make fun of them by name. They would disappear into the night before the police could catch up with them.'

My interviewer wanted to know about the lack of political expression in the Soviet Union. I was saved by her challenge: 'For instance, you cannot stand up on a soap box and criticize your Prime Minister and Government as we do in this country, can you?'

'Oh, yes, we can,' I replied. 'There is nothing to prevent me from standing on a soap box in the middle of Red Square and criticizing *your* Prime Minister and Government as much as I want.'

I heard the sound of stifled giggles coming from the crew and stage-hands and can remember feeling very pleased with myself. From then on I answered all the questions with stories of life in the circus and show business. After it was all over, I felt sorry for my charming interviewer, thinking she would get into trouble for allowing me to avoid the pointed questions. When I told her, she looked at me in surprise and laughed.

'Oh, no. It was splendid and I enjoyed every minute of it. It was exactly what I wanted and what I expected. It was great fun.' And when I saw the recording, it was shown in full and with no cuts. So I had not been so smart after all.

During the two weeks we rehearsed in London, we were invited to many houses where people wanted to meet us and ask about life in Russia. It was all very interesting, but there was one thing that spoiled my pleasure. I missed Elena. We had been together for nearly thirty years and even in the first five years when we were just partners, we were never separated for more than a day. How she would have delighted in meeting these interesting people and visiting their homes! I told Raikin I would never again go anywhere without her. Unfortunately, he had no say in the matter.

We returned to London a year later and our relationship with the

BBC and our new producer, Ernest Maxin, remained harmonious, although Raikin was no longer heralded as Khrushchev's favourite comic. By now, Nikita had retired 'voluntarily' to his country house, and as the Russians said, 'Yemu nye do smekha' ('He found nothing to laugh at'). His protégé Brezhnev had double-crossed him and taken power.

In 1967 we rehearsed a new programme for a third visit to BBC television, to be followed by a tour of the United States on a contract concluded with the eminent impresario, Sol Yurok. Raikin and the actors arrived in Moscow two weeks before we were due to leave, in order to put the finishing touches to the programme and to receive their passports. Suspecting nothing, Raikin appeared at the Ministry of Culture in a cheerful mood. This soon evaporated when he was told that nobody knew anything about contracts with the BBC or Sol Yurok. No matter how Raikin assured them that he had seen the contracts with his own eyes, he was met with the same innocent replies in every room. Finally, Raikin gained audience with the Minister herself, Ekaterina Furtseva. She expressed amazement at the incompetence of her subordinates and promised to have the Ministry turned upside-down to find the missing contracts. After Furtseva was dismissed from her post, Raikin discovered the true story. The Minister herself had issued the order forbidding Raikin to travel to Britain and the United States. The contracts were hidden in her personal safe. It was the fiftieth anniversary of the Revolution, and the Central Committee did not want any criticism of the Soviet regime, even the mildest, to be heard in the West. Despite many invitations, Raikin is no longer allowed to tour any country beyond the Iron Curtain.

A year or two earlier I had written a short story based on an incident that had happened in my boyhood in the slums of Glasgow. A friend, the writer Arkady Vasiliev, read it and suggested I should enlarge on it to give an insight into what he called 'the colourful events of Red Clydeside in the early twenties'. He maintained that a book of this kind would give me the right to membership of the Writers' Union. I was already a member of the Journalists' Union, but the greater privileges offered to its members by the Writers' Union were very enticing. Membership was equivalent to being an accredited State employee with the advantage of being freelance and not having to clock in and out of an office every day. After two years of hard work, I handed the manuscript of the novel to the journal *Neva*, and that was when my troubles started.

The title of the novel was *Our Sally Ann*, and it was around this girl and our childhood friendship that I portrayed the life and the people of Glasgow. The troublesome events of those years obviously had to take their place as I saw them in reality. From what I heard the elders saying around me, there was never any threat of revolution. The frustrated unemployed were only demonstrating their legitimate demands for work and a decent living. They were not intent on overthrowing the Government by armed force. If it had not been for the mutiny-scared police, there would never have been a Bloody Friday.

However, Soviet communist historians had their own ideas on the subject and, for them, Clydeside had been revolutionary, no arguing about it. Their concept of the events was derived from the controversial John McLean, the Glasgow school-teacher. McLean described himself as the Lenin of the Clydeside. He was so prized by the Russian communists that they made him an Honorary Member of the Bolshevik Party's Central Committee, and even now there is a John McLean Street in Leningrad.

My novel was printed in the *Neva*'s fiftieth anniversary November issue, but only after I produced evidence to support my version written by two of the leaders of Clydeside, William Gallagher and J. R. Campbell. Nevertheless, I had to agree to the words 'No threat of a revolution' being struck out. All further attempts to interest the State Publishing House in my book were unsuccessful. I was accepted as candidate to membership of the Writers' Union, but only with the help of Arkady Vasiliev, who was, at the time, the First Secretary of the Party Committee of the Writers' Union.

Vasiliev was typical of the many middle-grade influential Party functionaries I knew in Russia. He was born in the textile town of Ivanovo into a family of mill-workers. He liked to boast that his education consisted of three years at a theological seminary and for that reason he was considered a specialist on religious rites and customs. He had a sharp mind, an extraordinary memory and a practical business acumen which would have served him well under any regime. I first met him in 1947. He was a stout man of medium height, with a benevolent, hail-fellow-well-met manner, not unlike the person he detested most of all, Nikita Khrushchev. In his youth, he was drafted into the Navy and so excelled as a young communist that he was transferred into the Cheka, as the KGB was then called.

He became a top officer and remained so, unofficially, throughout the rest of his long career in literature. He had started writing seriously after a few articles in the local Ivanovo newspaper and, as a result, was transferred to Moscow where he became an 'editor' on the Central Communist Party paper, *Pravda*. He wrote a number of books about Frunze, his fellow townsman from Ivanovo. Frunze gained fame as a professional revolutionary and later became the legendary Commander-in-Chief of the Red Army. This helped Vasiliev to become a member of the Writers' Union. Later, he was elected to the post of First Secretary of the Party Committee (the KGB needs its agents everywhere) and so came to the zenith of his career. He never concealed his KGB affiliations from his writer colleagues, but it was only after his death that I learned he had remained a full General.

Like many of his kind, Vasiliev began to acquire the pretensions of the Soviet privileged class. When his daughter, Izolda, a Moscow University student, announced her intention of marrying a fellow student, Volodya, it came like a bombshell. Volodya was a poor student whose father was an ordinary factory worker, and this was considered to be a mésalliance. Despite Vasiliev's protests the marriage took place and he had to continue contributing 100 roubles a month for their upkeep. Volodya and I became very friendly. He was a good-natured chap with a keen sense of humour. His opinions of the regime were hardly complimentary and he could tell an anti-Soviet joke as well as anyone. Whenever we met at family celebrations we would always adjourn to some quiet corner and, after a few drinks, he would complain to me about the treatment he got from the elder Vasilievs as a poor relation. I helped him to sell articles to Radio Moscow.

When Volodya graduated I lost touch with him. I heard he had won his Master's degree in economics and had been elected to the post of First Secretary of the University Party Committee. It was then that I began to hear the notorious name of Vladimir Yagodkin, after he had been appointed Chairman of the all-Soviet Commission supervising students' theatrical groups. This was at the beginning of Brezhnev's rule, when he was playing the role of a liberal democrat, and the students were allowed to play witty satires that achieved great popularity. Later they were to become too outspoken and Yagodkin was ordered to clamp down on their activities, which he did with great vengeance and brutality. He rose up the ladder to the post of Ideological Secretary of the Moscow

Party Committee, which gave him unbridled control of the capital's art and literature. He won notoriety in the West as the man who ordered the bulldozers to crush the large exhibition of paintings by nonconformist artists held in a field on the outskirts of Moscow. This exploit was so much to the liking of the Kremlin that he was appointed to the Central Committee and was promised the post of Ideological Secretary of the Soviet Communist Party after the next Party Congress. This wonderful future never arrived. Volodya fell into disfavour for attempting to undermine a rival. He was transferred to the post of Deputy Minister of Education and he is now taking his revenge on Russian school children.

I broke off all relations with Arkady Vasiliev after the Sinyavsky and Daniel affair. These two writers were arrested and tried for publishing their books in the capitalist West. The Kremlin used its favourite ploy of disguising its leading role in such repressions by appointing a writer as Public Prosecutor. Many of the leading writers declined the unenviable honour. So I was shocked when Vasiliev rang me and nonchalantly told me he had accepted the appointment. I spent the whole evening trying to persuade him that it was wrong to help send his fellow writers to prison merely because their opinions did not coincide with that of the Party. I could have saved my breath. Vasiliev was shortly up for re-election as Party Secretary and he intended to demonstrate his allegiance, not so much to the communist ideology, as to the Party hierarchy.

I went to the extent of inviting him to dinner to meet Sam Russell, a leading British communist who had come to Russia for a holiday, and who is now the Foreign Editor of the *Morning Star*. I wanted Vasiliev to hear the opinion of the majority of the Western parties on this affair. And Sam Russell was quite emphatic: these repressions did great harm, not only to the Soviet Union, but to the entire communist world; they could expel Sinyavsky and Daniel from the Writers' Union if their crime fitted the sentence, but by no means must they be sent to prison—this was not democratic. Vasiliev listened with apparent interest, but I could see by the look in his eyes that he could not care less for democracy and the world communist movement.

His speech at the trial would have given Stalin pleasure. Sinyavsky and Daniele were sentenced to seven years' imprisonment. The Kremlin was delighted and Arkady Vasiliev was re-elected Party Secretary of the Soviet Writers' Union. Vasiliev got sadistic delight out of the anonymous letters and phone calls cursing him for his involvement in this despicable trial. Whenever a writer avoided him, his round face became wreathed in smiles. He knew he had the power of the Party behind him and that was all he wanted. I saw no more of him until he lay in his coffin in the hall of the Central Writers' House. His 'poor relation' Vladimir organized a pomp-and-ceremony funeral and Vasiliev was buried in the cherished Novodevichy Monastery, the last resting place for VIP's.

The final sting in the tail was that his grave lay next to Nikita Khrushchev's, the man whom Vasiliev hated most of all for defiling the image of Stalin. The controversial golden-black bust of Khrushchev looked down on us as Vasiliev's coffin was lowered into his grave. I heard someone whisper behind me, 'Those two are going to have something to argue about.' As the Russians say, 'Vce ravnie v grobu i v banie' ('All men are equal in the grave and in the steam baths').

After the Sinyavsky–Daniele 'trial' it became evident that the Stalinist laws of the jungle were being resurrected and the meaning of the words 'traitor' and 'treachery' again given a wider interpretation. Up to now, treachery could mean anything from blowing up a factory to telling even the mildest of jokes. A colleague at Radio Moscow was discharged for repeating a popular play on the name of the legendary Battleship Potemkin. In Russian this sounds like 'Bronenosets Potyomkin'. In describing Leonid Brezhnev's large bushy eyebrows it becomes transcribed to 'Brovenosets v Potyom-kakh' ('the eyebrows wandering in the darkness').

A traitor of the Soviet Homeland is condemned and shot or sent to prison. A British spy who betrays his homeland is welcomed by the Kremlin as a hero of the Revolution and given every privilege and amenity. My acquaintance with one such traitor whose name has become a household one in the West came about by chance.

Elena and I were invited to a party by a friend whom for obvious reasons I shall call Tom. This was in the early sixties and the country had yet to recover from the shock of the Stalin Disclosures. Tom told us he had invited a close friend, an Englishman, who worked as a consultant in the Ministry of Foreign Affairs. He had just completed treatment for alcoholism, so Tom asked us to be careful, and also not to talk about Stalin. Apparently this man had taken to heavy drinking after the downfall of his idol. Many a time Tom had been wakened in the middle of the night after a phone call from the militia who had found this helplessly drunk *anglichanin* lying in a ditch or on the earthen floor of some *zabegalavka* (lean-to huts where vodka is sold in glasses).

We were introduced to Mark and Natasha Frazer, as they called themselves. Mark Frazer was a tall, lanky man, who looked more like a university don, in his well-worn tweed jacket and baggy flannel trousers, than a diplomat. It was not that long since our holiday to England, so most of the conversation was centred around our visit. When Elena described, enthusiastically, how she had fallen in love with England and the people, I thought I saw a wistful look appear in Frazer's eyes. He seemed so eager to know more about his homeland that I could not help asking him why he didn't go to England on holiday himself. I had obviously touched on a taboo area. Tom changed the subject immediately before I could get a reply. But from then on we met often, mostly at parties. Only once did we go to Mark's flat in the large apartment house next to the Kutusov Bridge opposite the Kiev Railway Terminal. His wife, Natasha, was not there and we learned later that she had left him. The children had remained with their father. We were still very careful to avoid mentioning their reasons for leaving England.

Then an incident occurred at which the whole truth came out. We had gathered on the pier of the Moskva River opposite Frazer's house, and were waiting for the river steamer to take us on a trip into the countryside. There were eight or nine of us including Mark. We were all in high spirits when quite suddenly our joking was interrupted and Frazer bent down hurriedly in our midst, asking us in a low voice to surround him. 'There is a man up there on the granite steps trying to take a picture of me. I am sure he is a foreign correspondent.'

We looked round and there was a man with a camera pointing the telescopic lens at us. Tom called out to a militiaman on duty at the pier, and after a whispered conversation the man hurried up the stairs to interrogate the photographer who was already climbing into his car. The number plate was white with the letter 'K' on it, which proved Frazer was correct. The man was a foreign correspondent. But why did Mark think he wanted to take a picture of him? As we strolled through the Serebrany Woods, I managed to catch Tom alone and find out who Mark Frazer was. After some considerable hesitation, Tom confided in me on condition that I never repeat our conversation to anyone.

'Mark Frazer is an assumed name,' he said. 'His real name is Donald Maclean.'

It is difficult to describe my feelings on hearing such unexpected news. I was neither shocked nor outraged. Surprised and curious would be a better description. I looked at this quiet, unassuming man who did not correspond to the image of the spy who had caused such an uproar along with Guy Burgess. Their defection had not been a topic for conversation in Russia. It had never been reported by the Soviet media and was known only to those who listened in to the BBC World Service or to the Voice of America, a risky business in those days as both stations were jammed and forbidden. People were inclined to scoff at the affair and to express the opinion that it was just sour grapes on the part of the British and the CIA who had been led quietly up the garden by 'clever Soviet agents'.

My impression was that Maclean was a very lonely man. His wife, Natasha or Melanie, had dealt a double blow when she left him to live with the other international spy, Kim Philby. She blamed the breakdown of their marriage on Maclean's heavy drinking, and I noticed how determined he was not to touch alcohol. He had cured himself more out of fear than conviction. The first time he came to dinner at our flat, he brought with him a tin of orange juice. When I made a joke about this 'gift', he explained that it was not so much a gift as a necessity: so few houses in Russia keep juice, he explained, and as he could not drink anything else, he had to bring his own.

Another reason for his loneliness seemed to be his position in a 'No Man's Land' in which neither the Soviets nor of course the British and other Westerners would associate with him openly. I remember one particular incident which made me feel sorry for Maclean. The morning after a hectic New Year Party, I got a phone call from Peter Tempest, the correspondent of the *Morning Star*, who told me that John Gollan, the General Secretary of the British Communist Party, was coming to dinner at his house. Tempest wanted Elena and me to come along. We didn't relish the idea. Gollan was a dry, boring Scotsman who couldn't quite define his attitude towards the new Soviet leadership after Stalin. I didn't feel like explaining to him what the Soviet people thought about it either; it was always a difficult task as the Russians themselves were not quite sure what was going on. It was only when Johnnie Gollan himself came on the phone that we had to accept the invitation.

We were sitting in the front room at about eleven o'clock when the doorbell rang. Peter went to open the door and for quite a while we heard the sound of muffled voices coming from the hall. Finally, Tempest returned, followed by Maclean. I was in the middle of some story which Gollan had insisted he wanted to know about. When Maclean appeared in the room, I felt that Gollan lost all interest in what I was saying. He answered Maclean's greeting with a cursory nod of the head. Maclean told us he had been to the Vakhtangov Theatre on the Arbat (just round the corner) and according to Russian custom, *na ogonyek*, seeing a light in the window had decided to drop in, the usual thing to do in Moscow. A couple of minutes passed in silence. It was broken abruptly when Gollan rose, saying he had to go as he was expecting an important phone call.

The incident came to the ears of some foreign correspondent who elaborated on the meeting of Gollan with Maclean. I could well understand Gollan's predicament, but I was amazed to read his version of the events. Maclean, he said, had barged into Tempest's flat blind-drunk and had become so abusive that he, Gollan, had no option but to leave. This was a fabrication as unnecessary as it was unfair. Maclean was not drunk. In fact he declined the usual offer of a drink, and he hardly said a word in the few minutes before Gollan jumped up and left. My presence during the incident was noted and when I was questioned by the Party Secretary of Radio Moscow, I told the true facts and said I would like to put things right. The Party official told me to forget it. And I did.

If any star says he finds publicity tiresome and that he would prefer to live on a desert island, don't believe him. They can't live without it. I noticed that Raikin seemed quite vexed when nobody recognized him on the streets of London. His programme was only broadcast after we had gone back to Moscow. I, on the contrary, was recognized from the three television interviews I gave during this time. I found it very pleasant—and beneficial.

Elena and I were able to get permission to go to London again for the Christmas holidays in 1966. The money we were allowed was not sufficient to enable us to take a proper share in the festivities, so I decided to risk the stringent British Customs and packed about a dozen bottles of vodka and cognac, boxes of cigarettes and cigars into our cases. As the Russians say, risk is noble. But whenever a porter carried our suitcases, I was careful to walk behind him with outstretched hands for fear he let them drop.

We travelled across Europe by train. Two elderly passengers, who had never been abroad before, could not tear themselves away from the carriage windows as we passed through Poland. They went into raptures despite the drabness and threadbare look of this socialist country. They squealed with delight when we passed into East Germany and East Berlin. But as we passed through the notorious Wall, and the bright lights of West Berlin nearly blinded us, they fell silent and looked apprehensively at the only other passenger in the carriage, obviously some minor clerk at the Soviet Trade Mission in London. This was capitalism, and as Soviet citizens they were careful not to praise it.

In conversation, I remarked on the strict British Customs regulations about alcohol and cigarettes. All three, including the clerk, who was also going to England for the first time, looked upset, and I guessed that they had more than their allowance as well. We crossed the North Sea in a Force 12 storm and when we set foot on the quay in Harwich, it even seemed pleasant to see the immigration officers. I handed our passports to one of them. He didn't smile when I joked about never being so glad to set foot on English soil. He looked at my passport and then at me with what seemed to be suspicion.

'I have seen you somewhere before,' he said distrustfully.

'I wasn't here when the train was robbed,' I replied, blithely.

'Never mind that,' he said severely and gazed into my passport. 'Wait a minute. Are you *the* William Campbell?'

I confessed I went by that name.

'I saw your TV programme. My goodness, didn't the missus and I laugh. By the way, who was that tall bloke you kept talking to? (He meant Raikin.) Well, Mr Campbell, have you come to make a new programme?'

He didn't even look at our passports as he stamped them. While handing them back, he turned to the Customs officer nearby and called, 'Jim, look who's here.' Jim looked at me and a light of recognition appeared in his eyes.

'Hullo, Mr Campbell. Welcome back. Is Raikin with you?'

As the porter placed my suitcases in front of him, I thought, 'Here it comes. He won't be so boisterous when he opens those cases.'

He asked a lot of questions and I answered them as I waited for the axe to drop. At last, he dropped his hand on to the cases.

'Are these yours, Mr Campbell? Well, I am not going to ask you how much vodka you've got, am I? Won't spoil your holiday, will we? OK, Bert, take these cases away.' And with a flourish he marked them with green chalk. I was most effusive wishing him a Merry Christmas and a Happy New Year. As I walked away I noticed the two elderly passengers and the clerk were having difficulty in understanding Jim's questions. I returned and asked if I could help.

'Oh,' said Jim. 'Are these gentlemen with you, Mr Campbell? OK. Off you go.' And with the same flourish he marked their cases, too. The two old men were grateful, but from the way the clerk looked at me, I am sure he suspected me of being a British agent.

This was our third visit to London and I had planned it so that Elena could spend the holiday with our relatives and friends during the Christmas and New Year festivities. Our first mournful task was to lay a bunch of flowers at the Golders Green Crematorium to my mother, who had died the year before. We had been refused permission to attend the funeral by OVIR, the Soviet Passport Office. None of the family lived in London any more, and Father was now alone. So Elena, instead of sampling an English-cooked turkey, had to roll up her sleeves and prepare it the Russian way. And I must say, my brothers and sisters and their children, who came from all over England, declared that Elena was not only a lovely woman and a splendid ballerina but a fine cook as well.

As soon as we had arrived at my parents' home, Father told me that he'd had a phone call from the Scottish BBC asking him for my Moscow address. They were delighted to hear I was coming to London on holiday. A few days later, the producer, Gordon Smith, told me he wanted to come to Moscow and make a documentary film of my life in Russia. I told him to contact Enver Mamedov, the Deputy Director-General of Soviet Television and Radio, with whom I had become very friendly, ever since he was made Chief of the Anglo-American Department. This was not the first time I had been invited by a foreign television company to make a film, and as on all previous occasions I knew full well that nothing would come of it. The Central Committee took so long processing the application that foreigners usually gave up waiting.

A year later, in January 1968, I received a letter from Gordon Smith to say that he was tired of waiting for permission. He had applied for visas for himself and his secretary and was leaving in two weeks' time. Alarmed at this news, I rushed to Mamedov with the letter. He read it quite calmly, saying he had not received any request from the Scottish BBC but thought it was a good idea.

'Let them come,' he said. 'We'll see what can be done about it. After all, they are coming at their own risk and expense, so why worry? They can't blame us if nothing comes of it.'

Gordon Smith arrived with his efficient secretary at the end of February. He was a big, bluff Scotsman with a forceful personality. Apart from being a good producer, he was a splendid photographer in his own right. I had written the script as agreed, only I insisted that the film should not be about me but about Moscow as seen through my eyes. Mamedov had appointed an editor, a manager, a camera crew and sound engineer. We had all we needed—except permission to film. A few days were spent on my script, splitting it into film sequences. But the permission was still unforthcoming. Then I suggested we travel around Moscow in my car to look at the prospective shots from all angles. Gordon was delighted. That took two days. Still no permission. All my attempts to find out when we would get it were met with the usual inexplicable word *zavtra* which the dictionary translates as 'tomorrow' but which can mean any time from now to Doomsday. Gordon was beginning to raise his voice in protest, so I arranged for a meeting with a friend of mine, Mikhail Alexandrov, the Chief of the Television Exchange Department. But friendship didn't help. He prevaricated as much as the others. He informed us that the delay was due to the BBC who had not returned the signed contract. Gordon rang Edinburgh and was told that they hadn't seen any contract.

Two days later, Gordon gave up and declared he was leaving for home the next day. I was in a panic. There was no one left to talk to. Mamedov had gone to Vladivostok and Alexandrov had gone into hiding. I knew the delay was the fault of the Party Central Committee, but I couldn't find out who was personally responsible. I was wandering through the foyer of Radio House, head bent with anger and despair, when I heard a voice addressing me.

'What's the matter, Comrade Campbell? You look as if your last day has come.'

I looked up and saw Sergei Lapin, the Director-General of the all-Soviet Television and Radio. Although he was a notorious despot, he had always been very kind to me and had helped me a great deal in my first steps in journalism. I told him I was in such trouble that I was considering a watery end in the Moskva River.

'I don't advise you to do that just now, as the ice hasn't broken yet and you'll find it very cold. Come along to my office and tell me all about it.'

This was an unbelievable stroke of luck. I had thought of approaching Lapin, but it was about as difficult to pass his secretary as it is for a sinner to get through the Pearly Gates. After I had recounted my pathetic story, Lapin asked me to show him the script. Luckily I had a copy with me and it didn't take him long to read it.

'There's nothing the matter with this script,' he said, finally. 'I see you don't bang the viewer over the head with propaganda but do the same thing by showing him the beauties of Moscow and the inner life of the people. Only don't go too deep into that. I would suggest you sing the song 'Ya idu, shagaiu po Moskve' ('I stride merrily over Moscow'). (This song was popular at the time until the composer applied for permission to leave for Israel; then it was banned.) 'Anyway,' Lapin continued, 'here is my signature on the script. Go ahead and tell the producer to start filming. I take full responsibility.'

I never enjoyed myself so much as I did making that film. I had no intention of putting over any propaganda as Lapin thought, I simply wanted to show the Moscow and the people I loved so much. Shots were taken of Elena and me swimming in the giant open-air pool, a favourite leisure spot, at the Kropotkin Vorota. One of the largest and most beautiful cathedrals in Moscow, the Temple of Christ the Saviour, once stood on this site until it was destroyed to make way for the massive Palace of the Soviets with a giant statue of Lenin standing on the top. But the project never went further than the blueprints. Instead, this huge heated swimming pool took its place. After the opening, there were cases of drowning which the old people declared was the Almighty's revenge for the destruction of the cathedral.

Gordon couldn't be torn away from the sight of hundreds of Muscovites revelling in the heated water in contrast to the immense heaps of snow lying on the banks of the pool. The crew was packing the equipment when a shout of anguish from Gordon stopped them. A lovely young girl had climbed out of the water on to the heaps of snow and was rolling about, laughing merrily. This was quite a feat as it was about 15 degrees below zero. Gordon was distraught at the loss of such a magnificent shot. Without a word, I approached the girl and asked her if she could repeat it for the camera.

'A hundred times if you like!' she replied with a shrug of her exquisite shoulders.

We went to Serebrany or Silver Woods, called thus because of the white birch trees so typical of Russia. We took shots of the *morzhie*, the winter swimmers. Gordon knew of individuals going for a dip in a cold river or lake in the winter, but he couldn't believe his eyes when he saw groups of men and women coming every hour according to schedule and diving into the large pool hacked out of the ice-bound river. I recalled the story told of Churchill when he first came to Moscow in the winter during the Second World War. When he saw the long queues for ice-cream, with the thermometer showing 25 degrees below zero, he was heard to exclaim, 'This people cannot lose the war. They are amazing, they are invincible.'

I went walking with my big brown poodle, Malysh, in the streets, and the camera recorded how the working people of my neighbourhood greeted him and not me. 'Zdravstvui, Malysh, kak dela!' they would shout, laughing heartily when my aristocratic beast stalked past them disdainfully. Malysh was highly respected by these former peasants who usually considered all animals useless if you couldn't milk them. Malysh's strong point was the clipped hair that Elena used to give to the old grannies in the neighbourhood. They knitted mittens and socks from it and these, thanks to some obscure medicinal quality, relieved the pain of their rheumatism and sciatica. The camera filmed an old woman making the Sign of the Cross over Malysh's head thanking him for his hair. I was taking Gordon to places in Moscow to see people that no foreign tourist would ever know.

We finished the film by playing a sketch with Arkady Raikin where he made fun of my love for Moscow and Muscovites. Gordon was delighted and said he had never made such a splendid documentary.

'I shall hold it until late autumn when everybody will be back from their holidays, and then it will be assured of a greater rating. This film is going to be a success,' said BBC producer Gordon Smith as he returned to London on 15 March 1968.

On 20 August 1968, Soviet troops invaded Czechoslovakia and mowed down a valiant people fighting for freedom from Soviet communist domination. The whole free world was angry and disgusted and Gordon's hopes were thwarted. My film was put on the shelf and has never been seen since.

1970, the centenary of Lenin's birth, was a year of awards. I was told to present myself in the Director-General's office at ten o'clock on 28 April just before the May Day celebrations. As I always conducted the live commentary on the military and civil parade on Red Square, I expected to hear the usual instructions. I was surprised to see a gathering of all the Chiefs of Departments as well as the Party and Trade Union Secretaries. The Director-General invited me to the top of the table and began a long eulogy of my achievements in 'cementing the friendship of the great Soviet and British peoples', and of my work on the radio and in other fields. This was true, as I had always tried to promote this sort of *entente*. Then the Director-General said it gave him great pleasure to present me with the cherished Honoured Radio Worker Medal. The number on it was 522. Considering the thousands of people working in television and for the radio, this number looks impressive. When the company applauded, I wondered what they would have said if they had known that this Honoured Worker had nearly defected only six months previously. In May, only four weeks later, I was among some forty colleagues in the Assembly Hall of Radio House when I was presented with the Lenin Centenary Medal 'For Valiant Labour'. It was all I could do to keep a straight face when the representative from the Central Committee announced me as 'Viliam C'mbell'. It reminded me of my old mates in the Leningrad aircraft factory where I worked thirty-eight years before.

From 1973 two delightful experiences stand out. I was delighted to receive yet another award. The Soviet News Agency, Novosti, to which I had been contributing sports reviews for the last fifteen years, announced me as among the authors of 'The Best Material of the Year'. My reviews had become popular and were now translated into sixteen languages, including Swahili. Undoubtedly their success was due to the tremendous impact on the international arena of Soviet athletes whose 'amateur' status could very well be a subject for controversy, but whose achievements were really impressive and a pleasure to write about. One had only to mention the name of that charming gymnast, Olga Korbut, to be assured of an audience—especially when, after winning three gold medals at the Munich Olympics in 1972, she missed gaining the absolute title by the margin of one point. She became the world's darling when millions of televiewers saw her in tears of frustration after the contest.

The second delight came on the day I bought my new car, a Zhiguli or Lada. To the reader who can walk down to the High Street any day and buy a new car, this may sound curious. But it is not like that in the Soviet Union. With the aid of my Soviet Journalists Union Card and an influential friend in the Ministry, I had managed to jump the three-year queue for cars. Even then, four months passed after I had paid cash, 6,000 roubles (£5,000) in advance. (I might mention that the same Lada sells for half that amount outside the Soviet Union.) Finally, on a cold and drizzly morning in October, I received the necessary documents in the only shop in Moscow selling cars, and was directed to a railway depot on the city's outskirts. When we arrived, a queue had already formed and Elena and I were twenty-fifth. We had to wait for the cars to be unloaded from open trucks. At about six in the evening, now wet and miserable, we saw a white estate machine being trundled out. Fortunately nobody wanted a white car. Without a word, Elena climbed in and declared, 'It's mine.'

As we could not afford our usual holiday on the Black Sea coast we decided to go to Estonia, a good two days' drive away. Armed with recommendations for hotel accommodation, we left Moscow in a snowstorm. There are no motorways and even the best roads are second-rate. The Moscow–Leningrad highway, for instance, has a dual-carriageway that ends about twenty-five miles from the capital and then becomes a narrow road with only room enough for single traffic. We branched off at Novgorod, eighty miles from Leningrad, and toured along country lanes until we reached Estonia. Here the roads were better, wider and well-kept.

I knew there was no love for the Russian people in this Baltic Republic, but had not realized the hostility was so extreme. When I lost my way in the old narrow streets of Tallin, the capital, I asked for help in Russian. I was either brushed off rudely without an answer or sent in the wrong direction. I corrected my mistake by approaching a small group of youngsters and addressing them in English, articulating every syllable clearly, 'Does anyone speak English?' The response was immediate, polite and helpful, and although their English was faulty it was sufficient for us to find our way to the Intourist Hotel.

Here again my native language came to our aid and Elena and I were provided with a double bedroom and bath, a luxury of which we were desperately in need. We spent a fortnight in Tallin, roaming around the old streets, castles and monasteries. Nevertheless, the Estonians' animosity towards the Russian people became frustrating. We could well understand it; they had suffered terribly from Stalin. So in the end we packed up and drove back to Moscow.

Although in many respects our lives had never been so easy and happy, Elena and I never lost sight of our dream to live in England. 1974 saw us back on holiday in London, but any thought of defecting was mere fancy. Inflation had set in and the £400 we were allowed to exchange would not have lasted us long. Britain was in a turmoil with industrial relations at their worst; there was a three-day working week, an energy crisis, and the price of the traditional pint of beer had gone up—in short, once again I heard the British complaining that 'the country was going to the dogs'. I had heard that one before, but this time it seemed people were not crying wolf. That would not have deterred us, but my parents, who had been the only ones upon whom we could have depended, were dead. We had nowhere to live and very little chance of getting a place. Most important of all, Vera, Elena's elderly sister who lived with us in Moscow, was now a complete invalid and partly blind. To desert her now would have been a crime. So we resolved to wait for better days and went back to Moscow.

When Vera died in 1976, we decided that the time had come for us to quit the Soviet Union for ever. Very discreetly, we began to make preparations. Although we trusted our friends completely, we gave no hint of our intentions, fearing that a slip of the tongue might ruin our plans. We received an official invitation to Britain from my sister, and armed with this document, appeared at the OVIR Passport Office to begin the degrading rigmarole of begging permission to spend a holiday with our own family. We sold a few of our valuable possessions, but only a very few, as we could not risk anyone noticing their absence. The sale of a large mirror, in a silver frame, that hung in the hallway nearly gave the game away. I bought a cheaper one that looked quite like the old one but I reckoned without the vanity of women, who always check their make-up on entering and leaving. The very first visitor after the sale looked at the replacement and exclaimed, 'What on earth have you done with your lovely mirror?' And from then on, every single female visitor wanted to know the same thing!

Apart from this, everything seemed to be going well, until a major problem arose. What were we going to do with our two cats, Feelka and Teemka? The problem was solved by a young teacher at the Anglo-American School. She sent snapshots of the cats to her mother in New York, who immediately rang back saying that she had fallen in love with the two handsome Siberians. But how were we to smuggle them out to New York? Our friend could not come to our flat in her car, as it had diplomatic number plates. Eventually she told us that she had made arrangements with the Pan American agent to fly the cats to New York, on Sunday 17 July.

We rose at five-thirty in the morning. I had to drive to a certain courtyard where June's car would be parked. There I was to lift the boot, place the cats in their basket inside and then drive off. Before I set out Elena took Feelka and Teemka into the kitchen, to give them tranquillizing pills. I was surprised to hear an unusual noise coming from the street below. I looked out, and to my horror saw that the pavements were crowded with people. Only then did I remember that it was polling day. How was I going to shove a cat-basket into a diplomatic car without anyone noticing? By a stroke of luck, the courtyard where June's car was waiting was empty and I completed the operation quickly. So now Feelka and Teemka live on Park Avenue and their new owner, Colette, feeds them on their favourite cod, which was always a headache to buy in Moscow. Colette sends us photographs now and then, and I must say that they seem to be flourishing under capitalism.

Meanwhile a postcard from OVIR ordered us to appear at the office with 300 roubles each, the price of our passports, allowing us to stay in Britain for forty-five days. We sighed with relief. The KGB had not woken up to the fact that, with the death of Vera, they had no 'hostage' for our good behaviour. We made our final preparations, sold our car, and paid our rent up to the end of the year, again to avoid suspicion. Our friends gathered to see us off, little knowing that they would probably never see us again. Elena and I were afraid to look at each other. I knew Elena was on the verge of tears.

The 'Red Arrow' express carried us to Leningrad for the last time. We had our last experience of *blat*, obtaining a privilege through bribery. Soviet citizens cannot make cabin reservations on passenger ships going abroad, even if they have passports, but a friend had discovered a loophole. For a certain sum of money, and only after I had signed a paper saying that I was a British citizen, we procured a first-class cabin. This final lie made me more panic-stricken. Suppose someone asked to see my 'British' passport? All our plans would be wrecked. The nearer the time came for our departure the more panicky I became.

I shall never forget the ordeal of watching the uniformed KGB officer examine our passports, thumbing through the pages again and again. Would he never stop? I wanted to shout at him, 'Come on, get it over.' I almost jumped out of my skin when he barked at me, 'Where's your wife?'

When I found my voice, I managed to stammer, 'My wife? Oh yes, my wife. She's over there.' I pointed to Elena, standing guard over our cases, a very necessary precaution.

'Well, what is she standing there for? She ought to be here. Call her over at once!'

I dashed over to Elena, almost tripping over other people's cases, and dragged her over to the window. This seemed to put the KGB man on his guard. He compared Elena's face with her photograph half a dozen times, and after what seemed an age, grudgingly handed back our passports with a gesture of silent dismissal. I felt like a drunken man trying to pretend he is sober, as we walked over Russian soil for the last time, towards the ship's gangway, where we faced a final inquisition from the Border Guards. Then we climbed up the gangway towards freedom.

We woke next morning in a state of high excitement, until a Russian voice announcing breakfast over the tannoy brought us back to reality. We were not out of the woods yet. This was still Soviet territory.

During breakfast we gradually forgot our usual reserve in speaking to foreigners, and soon were the centre of attraction, especially Elena. 'To think I am actually talking to a Bolshoi ballerina!' one lady exclaimed. As we emerged from the restaurant I heard a woman's voice behind me asking, 'Excuse me, are you English?' The accent was American, with a tiny, almost unnoticeable lisp. Something stirred in my memory . . . I had heard that voice before. I turned. I felt confused. I tried to cover my embarrassment with a joke.

'Well, if you can call a Scotsman English, then I am English.'

'I don't suppose by any chance you could have lived in Leningrad in 1932 and 1933?' she asked.

As she spoke it all came back to me.

'Helen!' I cried.

Tears came to her eyes and she just nodded her head. We stood there, holding each other in silence, and after a while I remembered the group of tourists, and my Elena, all of whom were watching us in astonishment.

'This is Helen, my first love!' I announced. And taking my wife's hand, I introduced them.

'Helen, this is my wife, Elena, your namesake, and my last love.'

I turned to Elena: 'You remember, I've told you about the lovely girl I knew in Leningrad the first year I came to live in Russia.'

At that moment, one of the tourists broke in: 'It seems you've been lucky in your first and your last love. Both beautiful and both called Elen!'

Everybody laughed and the tension evaporated.

Helen turned to Elena and said, 'I'm sorry for causing such a scene.'

'Not at all,' said Elena. 'I know all about you. Bill's told me so many times about that terrible year. How you must have suffered before you escaped to America!'

'Yes, I did. The only good thing in my life was Bill. When I went to America I tried to forget the horror of Leningrad. But I never forgot Bill. In the few days I've just spent in Leningrad, I looked at all the faces in the streets, hoping I would meet him again. He was my very best friend.'

Another lady, who I learned later was one of those enthusiasts who thought the Soviet Union was a paradise on earth, interrupted Helen.

'You don't mean to tell me you found life in the Soviet Union so unbearable that you had to escape to America? Why, those years of the First Five Year Plan were glorious. The Russian workers throwing down the gauntlet to the capitalist world, drawing in their belts, and proving that they could create the mightiest state in the world!'

I was about to answer that Russian workers were still drawing in their belts, when I remembered that I was still on Soviet territory and that this fervent communist could easily inform on me. I was saved by an insistent English lady who turned to the rest of the group saying, 'Have I got your support in imploring these three interesting people to recount their fascinating lives? I won't be able to sleep a wink until I hear their story.'

The five-day voyage to London was taken up in recounting the story I have written in these pages. It was only when we were alone that I ventured to ask Helen about the American whom she had introduced to me as her husband. I told her laughingly how upset I had been and had considered her to be a deceitful hussy. Helen looked at me in surprise.

'Which American?'

'Don't you remember that time in 1933 when I met you in the foyer of the Hotel Astoria in Leningrad with that elderly American and you told me you were off to the States to get married? I was so sure you were going to marry me. I thought the world would fall in.'

Helen looked at Elena enquiringly.

'Oh, don't mind me, I'm only his wife,' Elena answered with a laugh. 'You are still a beautiful woman and I can understand him being in love with you.'

'Oh, no,' Helen hastened to reply. 'He was not in love at all or I would have married him. Now, Bill, you don't mean to say you didn't understand what I was doing. In the first place John was not elderly, he was only thirty-nine. Secondly, I had no intention of marrying him. He was an engineer at Mother's factory and when he heard of my frustrations and desire to return to the States, he proposed this fictitious "marriage". He announced to the authorities he could only register the marriage in America. He was a splendid man and was kind to me even after we arrived in the States until I found some relatives who took me in. I will always remember him gratefully as he saved me from a living hell in Russia.'

Helen told us how she had eventually married a fine Irishman, and had borne him two children, a boy and a girl. He had died young. She had brought the children up, and given them a college education.

We docked at Tilbury and the time came to say goodbye to Helen, who was going on to Montreal and then to her home town, Detroit. It was now safe to tell her of our intention never to return to the Soviet Union.

'Quite right,' she said. 'I wish you all the luck in the world. It's not going to be easy for you, but you have each other and that is everything. I was alone when I returned to America, but you see I made the grade and have my splendid children. And we are not saying adieu? You are free now and you can come and stay with me whenever you like. Goodbye, and the best of luck to you both.'

And we crossed the threshold of Tilbury and walked into a troubled but free world.

TWELVE

Epilogue

Three years have passed since that day on 11 September 1977, when Elena and I, already in our mid-sixties, began a new life. My own circumstances bore a striking resemblance to that day forty-five years previously when I docked at the Troitsky Bridge in Leningrad with only a pound in my pocket. Once again I had arrived in an unfamiliar country (and my old homeland seemed entirely new), with barely a penny to my name. In one respect I was richer now, because with me was the finest friend I ever had, Elena. She is still the lovely woman whose room I burst into on that wintry New Year morning in 1941, and who listened to me confessing I had fallen in love with her while I stood by the frozen Moskva River opposite the Kremlin.

It is this love that helped us all those years to overcome the hardship and tribulations of the Soviet way of life. Never have I heard a word of complaint or reproach. Earlier in the book I described how Elena danced alone just a few hours after our third partner, Tamara, was arrested. Then I said, 'All that is beautiful and courageous in the Russian people I saw in Elena on that stage.' I continue to love the Russian people and certainly do not regret the interesting life spent with them, however turbulent. They were kind to me from the moment I arrived in Russia, and in many of my hungry moments they would move over to make room for me at a table that was already spread thinly. As one old granny said when I tried to protest, 'Never mind, son, one more mug of water in the pot and you get another plate of soup.'

These three years in my homeland have not been easy ones: when we left Russia we knew what we were doing and I didn't expect to be welcomed as the Prodigal Son. But, as Burns said, 'The plans of mice and men Sometimes gang aglay,' and some of our plans did go wrong unexpectedly. If it had not been for a few friends, old and new, on several occasions we would have been in a very, very difficult state. The first disappointment came when I was informed that under a law passed in 1914, I was no longer a British citizen. Strangely enough, this law was rescinded in 1949, since when no one loses his British citizenship under any circumstances. Bureaucracy remains bureaucracy no matter whether the system is capitalist or communist, and nothing could be done. I am now an alien in my country of birth. Never mind, thank the Lord I am a comic who always sees the funny side. 'British bureaucracy,' I was told, 'is such that if you are entitled to something, you get it, but if you are not entitled to it, you don't get it.' In this respect Soviet bureaucracy has the advantage—a bribe here and a timely influential word there, and you can get round any laws. That's what they are there for.

After five years' residence, I will apply to become a naturalized British citizen. My Scottish ancestors must be turning in their graves—a Campbell, a naturalized citizen! Already Elena and I have been granted permanent residence with no restrictions; we don't need to register our movements with the police, we have travel documents and can go to any country in the world. It was this sort of irritating restriction on foreigners which prompted me to become a Soviet citizen. Every three months I was obliged to apply for a further stay, and I had to register at the militia station in each town, wherever I performed.

Elena loves England and the British people and she gets on with everybody splendidly. She teaches classical ballet at the Urdang Dance Academy in London, where her fine and dedicated pupils call her the best and jolliest teacher in London, who manages to turn the tedious, strenuous exercises into good fun. It has taken time to build up this class: the first few months were spent wandering from one class to another trying to make head or tail of the British methods and only gradually gaining acceptance in this closed ballet world. To our astonishment, we discovered that the Russian school of ballet was taboo. To us it seemed ridiculous and snobbish. Since the beginning of the century when Diaghilev astounded the world with the Ballets Russes, Russian ballerinas and male dancers have dominated the field, and the names of Pavlova, Karsavina and Nijinsky among many others will never be forgotten. Even now, the two defectors to the West, Natalia Makarova and Rudolf Nureyev, are rated super-stars of the ballet outside Russia. But you don't have to be Russian to be a great dancer, there are gifted artistes in every nation. The secret is an old one—hard work and dedication.

Elena's pupils come and go, but no matter where they go in the world, they write to her telling of their successes and mishaps. Recently Desirée wrote from Brazil, telling us that she took part in the International Ballet Contest in Bulgaria and in the middle of her performance, her point shoe broke so that she had to hobble off the stage without even finishing the dance: you could almost see the teardrops on the paper. But in her next joyful letter, we were overjoyed to read that she had been noticed and is going to dance with the famous Stuttgart Ballet.

Six months after we arrived in London, I fell ill and for two months the doctors could not diagnose the trouble. Finally I landed up in the Royal Free Hospital in Hampstead, which proved to be an amazing experience. Even the hospital for Soviet VIPs, popularly known as the *Kremlyovka* (Kremlin), cannot be compared to this one. The ward was about the same size as the one in Leningrad. That had thirty patients crowded into it, but here, there were only four. When I was given the menu to choose my meals, I was afraid I had got into an expensive sanatorium by mistake. I was reassured that the National Health Service was free and available to everybody. I couldn't believe my ears when I heard a new patient remind the nurse (and not in a whisper) that he was kosher. I wondered what would have happened if he had said this as loudly in a Soviet hospital?

Initially even the doctors at the Royal Free were baffled, and my case became something of a whodunit. For a whole month, they searched painstakingly for the trouble, with one test after another. As a last resort, the doctors decided to operate. It all sounded dreadfully ominous and I was scared I had cancer. I remember how Elena and I sat holding hands, too afraid to utter our thoughts out loud. 'What have I done?' I thought. 'I have brought Elena to a new country among strangers and I am going to die leaving her all alone.'

After the operation the next day, when I was coming round, I saw the consultant, my two doctors, the head sister and, I believe, the tea lady, standing round my bed.

'Mr Campbell.' (Everybody is called Mr or Mrs. I like that. None of your Ivan or Masha.) 'Can you hear me?' I nodded my head. 'We have wonderful news for you. We have solved the mystery, Mr Campbell!'

I made an attempt to show my pleasure.

'Mr Campbell, it is only TB!'

They all looked overjoyed at this shattering news.

'Bozhe moi,' I thought (in Russian), 'are they all crazy. Only TB. Why, Chekhov died of TB. Who am I to join him?'

Afterwards, Dr Jenkins (may his tribe increase) calmed my fears.

'TB is easier to cure than the flu. According to the laboratory you must have drunk milk from a sick cow some five or six years ago. Anyway, two pills every morning before breakfast and in a year you'll forget you ever had TB.' And that was that, thanks to the National Health Service and British doctors.

While writing this book, I have managed to write and read many short stories on BBC Radio and also talk to audiences on my years in Russia. The range of questions people ask me reflects the immense ignorance of life over there. 'Has Russia got television?' is one favourite. As I have had the unique opportunity of living first under capitalism in my youth, then for over forty years under communist socialism and finally under capitalism again, there is one question I ought to be particularly well qualified to answer: which is the better system? But I'm not a political economist so can only draw from experience and observation. It is possible this opinion may sound naive, but I do believe it is a suggestion and all the better for being indirect. In the Moscow Tretyakov Picture Galleries there is a famous painting depicting a beautiful woman walking naked among the oppressed peoples: the allegory is similar to the legend of Lady Godiva. The artist very much wanted the image to be perfect but couldn't find a suitable model, so he amalgamated the best features from six different beauties.

Communism and capitalism have both got their advantages and I am convinced that, like the artist and his six models, these could all be combined so that, ousting the bad in both, we might find a political and economic structure that could bring peace and prosperity to everyone. There is a lot to be said for the complete nationalization of the economy, as in the Soviet Union: the profits provide for cheap rents, electricity, fares and low income tax. Unfortunately, in exchange for this, one has to suffer the 'leading role of the Communist Party'. In most cases, only Party members can be promoted to any senior position, so to get on in the world you have to join the Party. As there are always more fools than clever people, and Russia is no exception, the result is chaos, inefficiency and shortages as is well-known throughout the world. And another thing: the Russians have a favourite saying, 'Can you imagine how rich our country is in resources that, despite incompetence and theft, there seems to be no bottom to the barrel?' Despite these drawbacks, the Soviet authorities should be given credit for minimizing very many social evils such as pornography, race hatred and the display of violence (except in war films where the Soviet hero can mow down the enemy just as efficiently and extensively as any Western cowboy). And good taste is in demand; for example Arkady Raikin is one of the world's greatest comedians and satirists, and the force of his humour can be seen the moment when the audience leaves the theatre still wiping away the tears of laughter. But the message comes home as they begin to think of what Arkady was saying. He always hits the bull's-eye. It is clever and meaningful. He could so easily string some Irish jokes together without the slightest connection, as so many of these so-called comics do on television, but if he did then Arkady wouldn't be the great artiste he is. He could pour buckets of water over the bureaucrats or throw custard pies in their faces, but you can have too much of that, also. I sometimes feel that a number of British and American comedy directors would be like shorn Samsons without their comic gadgets.

On the other hand, British comedians are given the advantage of a free rein. Just when we are about to switch off the television, programmes are announced which make us sit up and take notice, programmes which even the best Soviet script-writers would never dare to write. When British comics poke fun at the eccentricities of leading statesmen and politicians, it is all I can do to stop myself from locking the door and putting a pillow over the telephone, a habit born of necessity. To hear the Prime Minister, Margaret Thatcher, being called 'Maggie' sounds almost blasphemous. Can you imagine a Russian artiste calling Brezhnev 'Lonya' from the stage? Or a Soviet Parliament of puppets raising their hands unanimously for some absurd law and then voting again to reverse it with equal enthusiasm. It would be the comic's last performance, and I shudder at the thought.

'How was it I continued to live in the Soviet Union for forty-five years?' When I am asked this I want to answer—why do men climb Everest or risk their lives in deep sea diving? My life in Russia was interesting and exciting. I lived through events that changed the world. I knew and came to love a splendid people. I do not regret one single second of those forty-five years. Given the choice, I would do it all over again.

The nine years I experienced after arriving in Russia before the beginning of the Second World War saw an unbelievable wave of enthusiasm among the Soviet people to build a new life and a better world. Only a complete cynic could have stood on the side-lines and not joined in. When I found my vocation in show business and rose to stardom with my greatest friend, Elena, I was convinced I had found my place in life. The war brought a wave of patriotism. There was only one aim: to do one's bit in destroying the scourge of Nazism. The post-war years brought disappointment and frustration and a witch-hunt that forced me off the stage. But by then all roads to my homeland were closed—I was a Soviet citizen.

There is a popular joke in Russia. 'What would you do if the Government was to raise the ban and allow Soviet citizens to leave freely and to live in any country?' 'I would climb a tree!' 'Climb a tree? Why?' 'To avoid being crushed to death in the stampede!' Actually, there would be no stampede. The Russians have a fanatical love for their homeland and the majority would not leave. So, as they say, *bykruchivaetsya*, they wriggle along, getting round laws, jumping the queues, procuring food and clothes from under the counter. Life in the Soviet Union is not the horror portrayed by the Western media. It is not a paradise, either. People live, love and die still believing that they are better off than those living under capitalism. For much of my life I was no different.

There is another question which seems to worry everyone:

'How is it that when you were so well off by Soviet standards, you gave up everything at an age when people retreat to a comfortable life in retirement, and then ventured into the unknown with no home and not even a chair to sit on?'

Looked at objectively, it does seem crazy. I think the answer can be found in a popular joke and then I will leave it at that.

A communist dog tries to talk another dog out of leaving for the West. He tells of the tribulations of capitalism, of heavy taxation, inflation and strikes. He extols the Soviet way of life. The other dog listens patiently and then says. 'I agree with you entirely . . . but I would like to bark now and again!'

Index